*f*P

FALLOUT

THE TRUE STORY OF THE CIA'S SECRET WAR ON NUCLEAR TRAFFICKING

CATHERINE COLLINS
AND
DOUGLAS FRANTZ

Free Press

New York   London   Toronto   Sydney

Free Press
A Division of Simon & Schuster, Inc.
1230 Avenue of the Americas
New York, NY 10020

First Free Press hardcover edition January 2011

FREE PRESS and colophon are trademarks of Simon & Schuster, Inc.

For information about special discounts for bulk purchases,
please contact Simon & Schuster Special Sales at 1-866-506-1949
or business@simonandschuster.com.

The Simon & Schuster Speakers Bureau can bring authors to your live event.
For more information or to book an event, contact the Simon & Schuster Speakers Bureau
at 1-866-248-3049 or visit our website at www.simonspeakers.com.

Designed by Carla Jayne Jones

Manufactured in the United States of America

1   3   5   7   9   10   8   6   4   2

Library of Congress Cataloging-in-Publication Data

Catherine Collins
Fallout/Catherine Collins and Douglas Frantz.
p. cm.
1. Nuclear weapons. 2. Illegal arms transfers. 3. Nuclear nonproliferation.
I. Frantz, Douglas. II. Title.
U264.F727 2010
382'.4562345119—dc22   2010030246
ISBN 978-1-4391-8306-9
ISBN 978-1-4391-8308-3 (ebook)

To Deborah Berger,
friend and inspiration

Contents

Contents

INTRODUCTION

This book started in the spring of 2009 with a copy of a report published that January by a Swiss parliamentary commission on the nexus between nuclear trafficking and political influence. The clues in that fifty-eight-page report led us down a winding path that exposed the invisible world of counterproliferation and the inner workings of the Central Intelligence Agency. *Fallout* is part spy story and part cautionary tale. It shows how three decades of miscalculation and mistakes by the CIA and American policymakers squandered our security and left us more vulnerable to nuclear terrorism. The evidence collected through interviews on three continents and from dozens of previously unreleased, unclassified documents demonstrates in dramatic detail how those errors contributed to the spread of nuclear weapons technology to some of the most volatile places on earth—Pakistan, Libya, North Korea, and Iran. The failure chronicled here constitutes a danger to the security of the United States and the world. Sadly, it is a failure that could have been prevented.

The Swiss report was no ordinary anodyne government document. It recounted an extraordinary series of events in which senior members of the George W. Bush administration and U.S. intelligence officials intervened at the highest levels of the Swiss government to pressure it to destroy evidence in a criminal investigation of nuclear trafficking. The Americans also used their influence to persuade the Swiss to abandon plans to prosecute six CIA agents for espionage. The demands were applied with rising intensity for nearly four years. Secretary of State Condoleezza Rice weighed in, and so did Attorney General Alberto Gonzales and Federal Bureau of Investigation director Robert Mueller. There was even a tantalizing reference to a role played by former president George H. W. Bush. In the end, the Swiss parliamentary commission concluded that their government bent to U.S. pressure and destroyed evidence that three of its citizens had sold nuclear-related technology to Libya as part of the Abdul Qadeer Khan network. The Swiss government had also agreed not to prosecute the CIA agents though they clearly had violated Swiss law.

Oddly, the report received almost no attention in the American press after it was made public in January 2009. There was some fine reporting done by American and Swiss journalists on other aspects of the Khan network and its aftermath. But no one bothered to put flesh on the bones of what appeared to be a devastating account of political manipulation by the U.S. government on another nation.

We set out to remedy that omission. A. Q. Khan was familiar territory to us. We had already published a book, *The Nuclear Jihadist,* that told the story of how Khan, a rogue Pakistani scientist, had created a nuclear black market that helped build Pakistan's nuclear arsenal. The book described how he had expanded his black market to sell the same technology to Iran, North Korea, and Libya. The first book touched on questionable decisions by the CIA and American policymakers that had allowed Khan to flourish over the years. It described in detail how the Pakistani scientist had been working at a Dutch research laboratory in the middle 1970s when he stole top-secret plans for centrifuges, the spinning machines that enrich uranium for civilian energy-generating plants and for nuclear weapons. From the very beginning, Dutch security police had suspected that Khan was stealing the material, but when they sought support from the CIA for arresting him, they got a strange answer: The CIA told the Dutch to let Khan go, so they could watch as he developed a procurement network for Pakistan. The CIA continued to watch as Khan returned to Pakistan with the stolen plans along with a shopping list of European suppliers who would help him build what became known as "the Islamic bomb." We had even recounted how a CIA case officer nicknamed "Mad Dog" had recruited a Swiss technician as a spy inside Khan's ring. The technician, Urs Tinner, was one of the three people the Swiss wanted to prosecute over the American objections.

As we researched *Fallout*, it became clear that the Swiss report only touched on the political battle and power struggle waged by the U.S. officials against the Swiss government. We filled in the details and context of those events with documents and interviews that took us behind the scenes in capitals around the world. It was clear, too, that in our first book we had only glimpsed the depth to which the CIA and its British counterpart, MI6, had penetrated the Khan network. Urs Tinner was not the only spy inside the Khan network; his father, Friedrich, and brother, Marco, had also gone to work for the CIA. We tracked the meetings they had with the CIA, saw records of the millions in payments made for their information, and talked for hours with Urs himself. We found other traces of how the CIA and MI6 learned what was happening inside the network long before they chose to shut it down—and long after the most damaging secrets had been leaked to traffickers.

As we followed up with old sources and tracked down new ones, a full and riveting picture emerged of a clever espionage operation in which the CIA had inserted sabotaged equipment into the illicit pipelines that were sending material to the nuclear programs of both Iran and Libya. Some of this equipment was altered to break down at critical moments in the uranium enrichment process, presumably setting back the efforts of both countries. But there was worrying evidence that the CIA had been too clever; the Iranians appear to have spotted the flaws and fixed them, giving them crucial new technology. Certainly as we were reporting this book, Iran was making steady progress at its Khan-equipped enrichment facility, producing enough enriched uranium by mid-2010 for two nuclear weapons with some further effort.

One of the questions that baffles the intelligence services of the United States, Britain, and Israel is how far along Iran is in developing a warhead to carry the fissile material it is enriching. Here again, evidence gathered for this book is cause for grave concern. Perhaps the most startling discovery in the months of reporting was the vast amount of material that the Americans pressured the Swiss government to destroy in early 2008, after it was seized from the Tinners. The volume was extraordinary, far beyond anything hinted at in the Swiss parliamentary report or the follow-up articles in the press. At least as staggering was the quality: As central participants in Khan's network, the Tinners had amassed a trove of blueprints and designs for complete uranium enrichment plants along with the centrifuges to stock them. They also possessed designs for two variations of sophisticated nuclear warheads straight from the arsenal of Pakistan, courtesy of Khan. All of this material, and much more, had been converted into digital formats. Instead of dead drops and risky exchanges, this was valuable information that could be passed on with the click of a computer mouse. What we have not determined is just how far those warhead designs and the other sensitive material may have spread. The Tinners also had thirty years' worth of business records related to nuclear trafficking, ranging from business cards and invoices from network suppliers to e-mail exchanges with participants whose names had not yet come to the attention of investigators. The destruction of this cache erased most of the trail and robbed the international community of a road map to a safer world.

Fallout looks at the events over the last thirty years, charting the spread of the world's most lethal technology to adversaries like Iran and North Korea through Khan and his accomplices. The full extent of Khan's assistance to Iran is described here for the first time. There is strong circumstantial evidence that the network sold its nuclear wares to at least one still-unknown customer—a country or a terrorist organization. All of this trafficking in nuclear technology occurred while the CIA and U.S. policymakers in a series of administrations watched and debated when to act. The men and women who made these decisions were not malicious. The majority were dedicated public servants who took enormous risks and deserve our admiration. But too often, they failed to take action to stop Khan and his accomplices because of other policy considerations or because they were addicted to secrets. In the end, when given the chance to eradicate the worst proliferation network in history, they used their power and influence to suborn a legitimate criminal investigation by the Swiss government and damage efforts to understand the full scope of Khan's perfidy and the danger he loosed upon the world.

But this is not a history lesson. We researched and wrote *Fallout* for the same reason we wrote *The Nuclear Jihadist*: There is no more serious threat to our national security than nuclear terrorism, whether it comes from a rogue state or a terrorist organization. What we have uncovered is a real-life espionage tale that begs for a thorough review of the nation's priorities in stopping the spread of nuclear weapons. Too often in the past, U.S. officials have allowed short-term policy objectives to override legitimate concerns about the risk of nuclear attack. The odds of such an attack seem too remote. The prospect of a terrorist group buying or building a bomb seems impossible. Let's hope it is. The problem is, when it comes to nuclear weapons, we can't afford a single mistake.

Early in our research, we finagled a lunch with the CIA case officer known as Mad Dog. He is a man of honor, tenacity, and humor; he wore a baseball cap to the meeting, embroidered with the image of a bulldog and the words "Mad Dog." He steadfastly refused to discuss any aspect of the decade he spent leading the CIA's investigation of Khan or his role in bringing it down. He was scrupulously silent about everything except the weather, running, and how he got his nickname. He brought along a copy of our first book and said we got some things wrong in it, but he would not say what. As he stood to leave, he reached into his wallet and pulled out a slip of paper. "I thought of you when I saw this," he said.

The paper contained this quote from Barbara Kingsolver's fine novel *The Lacuna:*

"The most important part of the story is the piece of it you don't know."

What we have written here may not be the whole story. No doubt pieces are missing. But to the best of our ability we have told the fullest story. We hope it serves as a warning. Only sheer luck has allowed the world to avoid a nuclear catastrophe. We can no longer rely on fortune or on misplaced priorities. The Central Intelligence Agency and the policymakers and political leaders who oversee the U.S. intelligence community must make fighting proliferation their highest priority.

—Catherine Collins and Douglas Frantz

Part I

The Setup

CHAPTER ONE

JENINS, SWITZERLAND

Six people—five men and a woman—approached a whitewashed house in the postcard-pretty village of Jenins in eastern Switzerland. Glancing cautiously up and down the narrow, darkened street, two members of the team walked to the door while the others hung back. They knew that no one was home. The owner was a few miles away, just across the border in Liechtenstein. One of the men pulled out a leather pouch and extracted a slender piece of metal. He slipped the metal into the lock and gently wiggled it deeper into the mechanism. As he twisted the pick, the slight torque turned against the lock's internal pins and, one by one, they fell into place and the lock opened. Less than a minute later, the pick man and four other team members slipped silently into the apartment and drew the curtains. The sixth stayed outside, motionless in the shadows, watching the street.

Inside, the intruders moved with an economy of motion, each carrying out a preassigned task. Their instructions were precise: Search for and copy every document and computer file in the house. One of the intruders sat down at a desk in a spare bedroom being used as an office and powered up the computer. Removing two screws from the back of the computer, he exposed its hard drive. He plugged a small device about the size of a deck of cards into the computer. The device enabled the technician to download the entire contents of the computer quickly. Two other team members were busy opening drawers and rifling through the bookshelves. They photographed every document that appeared to bear any relation to the occupant's business. While the others were doing their jobs, the team leader moved into the other bedroom, where he pulled open dresser drawers, searching beneath the socks and underwear for anything suspicious. It did not take long. He was short, barely five foot eight, so all he could do was run a hand along the top shelf of the closet. That was where he found the first laptop. Pulling it down, he took the laptop to the person sitting at the computer in the other room. "Have a crack at this," he said.

The team leader, who was known by his nickname Mad Dog, took out his cell phone and hit speed dial. It was just after midnight on June 21, 2003. Back in Langley, Virginia, where it was early evening, the call was answered on the first ring. Mad Dog used clipped, careful language to tell the person on the other end that the operation was going according to plan. The team expected to be back on the street within a couple of hours.

The call contributed to a building sense of anticipation four thousand miles away. On the third floor of the Central Intelligence Agency's main building on the campus at Langley, a handful of senior officers from the agency's Counter-Proliferation Division had been waiting for word from Switzerland. One of them picked up the telephone to relay the status of the first phase up the chain of command. The call went to Stephen Kappes, the ambitious ex-marine who was the deputy director of clandestine operations. Kappes had a strong personal interest in the goings-on in the small village in eastern Switzerland that night. He was no doubt pleased with the news.

The break-in was an ultrasensitive, "compartmentalized" operation. Only a handful of agency personnel with a "need to know" were aware that a specially formed CIA team was inside the home of a private citizen in an allied nation. Certainly, the Swiss authorities knew nothing of the operation. Even the CIA station chief in Bern was in the dark so that he would have deniability if events went sour. The B&E squad had been assembled outside Switzerland. There were two pick-and-lock specialists from the agency's secret facility in Springfield, Virginia. In a warehouse-like building there, the CIA trains a cadre of technical officers to bug offices, break into houses, and penetrate computer systems. A third team member was a nuclear weapons expert who actually worked for the national weapons laboratory in Oak Ridge, Tennessee. He had come along to provide an instant analysis of documents that would later be scrutinized far more carefully back at Langley. The team's chief, Mad Dog, was a veteran case officer who had spent his career carrying out delicate and sometimes dangerous assignments overseas. These days, he was posted to the counterproliferation unit at Langley. The four-man crew from the States had been augmented by two agents from the CIA's huge station in Vienna, Austria. One of them was the woman in charge of the counterproliferation section there; the other was a case officer who had been left outside the house to watch.

The team members had arrived in the country via separate flights a few days earlier. They held a final planning session to make sure everyone understood the mission and their individual responsibilities. Then there had been an initial break-in at the target's office to copy information from files and computers there. Entering the office was relatively easy because it was in a fairly isolated industrial area, surrounded by a small parking lot, other businesses, and open fields. There had been little chance of someone stumbling across the operation. Entering an apartment in a tiny village was a riskier enterprise. A neighbor or passerby might catch a glimpse of what was going on and call the police.

Despite what you read in thrillers or see at the movies, break-ins are rare in the world of espionage. This is particularly true for the CIA when it involves an allied country like Switzerland. A few months earlier, two CIA counterterrorism officers had come from Washington to interview an Iraqi defector in Zurich. While they were conducting what they thought was a secret meeting with their asset, someone had slashed the tires of their rented car. They were certain the vandalism was a not-so-subtle warning from their Swiss counterparts: Swiss law prohibited foreign intelligence agents from operating on Swiss soil without prior approval. Frankly, no country likes having the CIA or any foreign intelligence service operating on its soil. Intelligence operations are tolerated only when they are compatible with the interests of the country and remain secret. Simply interviewing an Iraqi defector was a minor infraction, meriting nothing more than a warning. As part of their professed neutrality, the Swiss had a reputation in intelligence circles for being particularly rigorous in enforcing the legal restrictions imposed on foreign intelligence operatives.

The break-in that June night was a much riskier operation. It had the potential for embarrassment that would extend far beyond slashed tires and Swiss borders if the Swiss authorities found out about it or, far worse, if it ever became public. But Kappes and Mad Dog had decided that the potential rewards far outweighed the risks.

THE EVENTS THAT LED THE agents to take that risk can be traced back almost thirty years to the activities of a Pakistani scientist named Abdul Qadeer Khan. Khan had done more to destabilize the world's delicate nuclear balance than anyone in history, emerging as the common thread in today's most dangerous nuclear threats. For nearly three decades, Khan had been the mastermind of a vast clandestine enterprise designed to obtain the technology and equipment to make atomic bombs—first for Pakistan and then later for the highest bidder. After helping Pakistan achieve its goal, a task that earned him the nickname "the father of the Islamic bomb," Khan had provided critical assistance to Iran's nuclear efforts. In addition, he had helped North Korea develop an alternative source of nuclear material in the face of international sanctions, which had crippled its plutonium-based bomb program. And finally, he had sold more than a hundred million dollars' worth of nuclear technology to Libya, including plans for an atomic warhead. The fact that Khan was still operating in the summer of 2003 was rooted in the failure of the Central Intelligence Agency to take decisive action to stop him at several junctures over three decades and the failure of American policymakers to insist that the threat of nuclear annihilation take priority over all other tactical and strategic objectives.

Khan had first appeared on the CIA's radar in the fall of 1975, when he was a young metallurgist working in Amsterdam for Urenco, a consortium of European countries developing the technology to enrich uranium to fuel civilian nuclear plants. With a freshly minted doctorate from a Dutch university, Khan had started working on the project in 1972. He became such a fixture at the research center in Amsterdam and at a nearby enrichment plant that he had the run of both facilities, even though his low security clearance should have prevented him from seeing the most sensitive designs.

In October 1975, the Dutch security service had become suspicious about some of Khan's actions and his contacts outside the Netherlands. Some of the senior officials were certain he had stolen top-secret designs for the centrifuges that Urenco was developing to enrich uranium. The designs were considered secret not only because they had commercial value, but also because the same centrifuges could be used to turn uranium gas into fissile material for a nuclear weapon. The security service went so far as to draw up detailed plans for arresting Khan, but then they were stopped by senior officials in the Dutch government. The officials worried that exposure of a spy within the Dutch arm of Urenco would alarm the other partners in the consortium, Germany and Britain, and damage the budding high-technology business that the Netherlands was trying to develop. Faced with this resistance, the Dutch security service turned for help to the CIA station chief for the Netherlands, assuming that he too would argue for Khan's arrest. They described the situation to him and asked that he persuade Washington to weigh in with the Dutch government.

The move backfired. Instead of insisting on stopping Khan in the name of counterproliferation, the bosses at CIA headquarters recommended that the Dutch move him to a less sensitive position and monitor his activities. At the time, Pakistani prime minister Zulfikar Ali Bhutto had embarked on a nuclear weapons project to match that of rival India and the Americans wanted to see how the Pakistanis were getting along. It was better, they told their Dutch counterparts, to watch Khan to see what kind of procurement network the Pakistanis were building. Then, they argued, everything could be rolled up at once. The CIA's attitude was also shaped by the conviction at the agency and among U.S. nuclear weapons experts that Pakistan was too backward technologically to build a nuclear weapon, and that a metallurgist like Khan had no chance of altering his country's fortunes.

So Khan operated without interruption until December 1975, when he told his coworkers that he and his family were returning to Pakistan for their annual holiday. He promised to return with small gifts for everyone, as he had done in previous years. But when Khan left that time, he took the gifts with him. Over the past year, he had managed to copy the most advanced centrifuge designs from the most secret portions of the Urenco facilities. He also had assembled a list of Urenco suppliers in Europe who could sell Pakistan the technology required to enrich uranium for its nuclear arsenal. It was a major espionage coup that put Pakistan on the road to nuclear parity with India, and a major blunder by the CIA, though it would be years until anyone realized what had happened. In the meantime, the CIA watched and waited while Khan went to work.

Khan was fond of saying that when he returned to Pakistan in late 1975, the country was so backward that it could not build a good bicycle. How then did he hope to master the enrichment of uranium for a nuclear weapon, one of the most complex technological tasks in the world? He would do it by creating an international black market, tapping the same European suppliers who had sold their equipment to Urenco.

One of the names on the Urenco list was that of Friedrich Tinner. In the years Khan was at Urenco, Tinner had been in charge of exports for a German firm called Vakuum Apparat Technik, known as VAT. Khan started buying vacuum valves from VAT through Tinner not long after he began building his government-financed enrichment complex at Kahuta, on the outskirts of the Pakistani capital of Islamabad. Tinner was one of dozens of businessman willing to provide nuclear-related technology to Khan, who had been given a blank check by Bhutto, and was spending money freely to get his plant up and running as soon as possible. Unlike some of the others, however, Tinner worked for a company that had scruples. When U.S. intelligence identified nuclear-related shipments of technology from VAT to Pakistan, Tinner was forced to leave the company and return to his native Switzerland.

There he started his own company, CETEC, in a village called Sax, which was in the high-tech corridor known as Vacuum Valley in eastern Switzerland, only a few miles from the border with Liechtenstein. In the laissez-faire world of Swiss export regulations, Tinner was free to resume his dealings with Khan.

Tinner was a talented mechanical engineer. While at VAT, he had patented several types of valves that were used in the elaborate systems of pipes and pumps that suck the air from machinery to create the vacuum required for optimum performance. These valves had applications in all kinds of sophisticated technologies, but it was their use in uranium enrichment that had made Tinner attractive to Khan. Centrifuges are slender metal cylinders that spin at nearly twice the speed of sound to produce the enriched uranium required to fuel nuclear plants that generate electricity. With slight adjustments, the same machines can produce a higher level of enriched uranium that can be used in nuclear weapons.

Khan's acquisitions eventually expanded to suppliers in Asia, Canada, and the United States. The growing procurement web did not escape the notice of the CIA and other American agencies. Tinner was among many suppliers who were identified as part of the black market that became known as "the Pakistani pipeline." The U.S. government sent legal notifications, called demarches, to the Swiss and other countries, asking them to impose restrictions on people like the Tinners. The responses from Europe were uniformly negative; the Germans and the Swiss, in particular, believed the Americans were simply trying to restrain their development of high-tech businesses. Other countries said their export laws did not cover the types of equipment going to Pakistan.

Khan did not stop with producing fissile material for Pakistan's nuclear arsenal. Beginning in 1987, he reversed the flow of equipment and expertise to create the beginnings of a private global proliferation ring the likes of which the world had never seen. The first customer was Iran. For help, he had turned to some of his original suppliers. The deal with Iran required Khan and his accomplices to provide the centrifuge designs and other equipment required to build a secret enrichment plant. As part of the arrangement, Khan or someone within his network also provided the Iranians with some rudimentary designs for parts of a nuclear weapon.

Word that Khan was engaged in nuclear deals with the Iranians reached the Central Intelligence Agency by 1988. Certainly there was time to intercede by pressuring the Pakistani government to put a stop to the proliferation activities of its senior nuclear scientist. But the CIA and U.S. nuclear weapons experts once again underestimated Khan. Just as the Americans had decided in 1975 to watch as Khan helped Pakistan develop nuclear weapons, this time they decided that his sales to Iran did not pose a real threat. The assessment by the CIA was that Iran was unlikely to develop a nuclear capacity. This would turn out to be a major miscalculation, which would mire the United States and its allies in a dangerous diplomatic game two decades later as they attempted to stop Iran from taking the last steps into the circle of nuclear weapons powers.

The blunders were not all committed by the CIA. In the mid-1970s, the United States had taken some steps to curtail Pakistan's clandestine nuclear efforts. Pressure had been brought to bear on governments whose companies were selling goods to the program, and in April 1979, President Jimmy Carter slapped sanctions on Pakistan. But eight months later, after the Soviet invasion of Afghanistan on Christmas Day, Carter lifted the sanctions in order to secure the cooperation of Pakistan and its intelligence service in supplying American-purchased weapons to the guerrillas in Afghanistan who were fighting the Soviets. It became American policy to ignore the nuclear aspirations of its temporary ally.

A decade later, when the first reports arrived that Khan was helping Iran, the tide was turning against the Soviets in Afghanistan. President Ronald Reagan and his successor, George H. W. Bush, remained unwilling to do anything that might upset the relationship with Pakistan at a critical moment in history.

Unimpeded by the Americans, and encouraged by his own government, Khan continued to expand his black market. In 1990, he offered to sell his nuclear expertise to Iraqi president Saddam Hussein. Saddam was operating his own clandestine nuclear weapons program at the time, and had actually moved fairly close to developing a weapon. But when Khan's offer arrived in October that year, the Iraqi leader had other things on his mind. Troops from the United States and other countries were massing in Saudi Arabia, preparing to try to oust the Iraqis from Kuwait. Fearing that the offer was an American sting, Saddam did not take Khan up on the proposal. But before long at least two other countries would. By the end of the 1990s, Khan had provided North Korea with enrichment technology and he was in the early stages of building a complete atomic bomb factory for the Libyan strongman Moammar Kaddafi.

Friedrich Tinner had continued to work with Khan, and by the time the Libyan project rolled around in 1997, he had been joined in the family business by his two sons, Urs and Marco. The Tinners were established citizens in the small village of Haag. Friedrich was the head of the local school board and an avid ham radio operator, and collected orchids. But there had always been a dark side to the business, and the father and two sons signed up to help Khan fulfill Kaddafi's nuclear ambitions.

OVER THE YEARS, THERE HAD been many internal debates within American intelligence and among other government agencies over the right time to shut down Khan's nuclear bazaar. The CIA and its backers always argued that they needed more information, more evidence, more time. The rationale was that they wanted to know everything about the ring so they could wipe it all out at once. They also needed a foolproof case against Khan, who was a national hero in Pakistan for his role in building the Islamic bomb. By the spring of 2003, however, American and British intelligence had penetrated Khan's network enough so that almost everyone believed it was time to act. They had tracked shipments to Libya. They had secretly dispatched sabotaged nuclear equipment to Libya and to Iran, where a massive underground enrichment plant was nearing completion. And they had developed a family of moles deep inside the network, people who were providing them with real-time information about the status of nuclear weapons work in countries that worried the United States the most—Iran, Libya, and North Korea. The waiting was about to come to an end. But first the CIA had to make sure that it understood everything it could about the reach of the Khan network.

One of the keys to understanding the Khan network was Urs Tinner. In late 1999, Tinner had moved to Dubai and gone to work overseeing Khan's efforts to build centrifuges there for shipment to Libya. The CIA case officer who used the nickname Mad Dog had followed on Tinner's heels, and eventually he had used sweet talk, money, and veiled threats to turn the young Swiss technician into a spy in the heart of the Khan operation.

Newly obtained records, including detailed travel records and material from the files of the Tinners themselves, show that by the end of 2002, spying for the Americans was a Tinner family affair. Some details and dates remain unclear about how the Tinners came to spy for the

CIA. But the new information, and interviews with people who were involved in tracking the network, provide the fullest and most accurate account to date of how the CIA recruited Urs, Marco, and Friedrich Tinner, and the role played by some of Khan's most trusted accomplices in bringing down his network.

The world of espionage is never clear-cut. The players on both sides are often trained liars, steeped in deceit and misdirection. So, at the same time the Tinners were betraying Khan, the CIA was worried that it was being deceived by its spies.

In the summer of 2003, the agency was preparing to shut down Khan's operation. But at CIA headquarters in Virginia, there were concerns about whether the Tinners had been withholding critical information. If the agency shut down the network without knowing as much as possible, there was a real danger that elements would remain in place and open for business. In an attempt to learn as much as possible about the network, and determine how truthful the Tinners were being, Mad Dog had invited all three of the Tinners to a hotel across the border in Vaduz, the picturesque capital of the tiny principality of Liechtenstein, for a final debriefing before the curtain was brought down on Khan's long-running atomic bazaar.

Mad Dog, who was using a cover name of Jim Kinsman, was in Vaduz to supervise the sessions. He was joined by several other CIA officers and a nuclear weapons expert from the national weapons laboratory at Oak Ridge, Tennessee. From June 16 until June 25, the Americans met daily with the Tinners. During the days, the CIA and its experts interrogated the Tinners relentlessly about every aspect of the network and its global operations. At night they adjourned for drinks and dinner, which was all part of the CIA's strategy for creating the sense that they were all playing on the same side.

The Tinners were asked in painstaking detail about shipments made to Iran, Libya, Dubai, and elsewhere. The Tinners admitted providing components and designs to Libya, explaining where the components were manufactured and how they were shipped using false invoices and other deceptions. They provided the names, dates, and places that gave the CIA a view of the overall architecture of the Khan network. But they flatly denied helping Khan on his deals with Iran and North Korea.

When there were doubts about the information the Tinners were providing, the interrogators returned to the beginning, starting a line of questioning all over again. Over the course of nine days, the Tinners listed witting and unwitting suppliers in a dozen countries around the world who had provided sensitive equipment for the network. They identified collaborators in Africa, the Middle East, Europe, and Asia. Over and over, the Americans stressed that they had to understand everything possible about the network before they shut it down. It was vital that they close off every avenue for future proliferation.

The Tinners' help did not come cheap. Over the previous months, Kinsman had paid them a total of about a hundred thousand dollars. But in Vaduz, the final price tag went up dramatically. Kinsman and a second CIA operative, who called himself Sean Mahaffey, signed a contract agreeing to pay the Tinners a million dollars for their help. The contract was on letterhead from a CIA front company called Big Black River Technologies. Its address was nothing more than a mail drop in Washington, D.C. At the end of the debriefings, the money would be wired to a bank account for Marco's company, Traco Holdings, in the British Virgin Islands. But despite the payment and the extensive debriefing, the CIA still did not trust the Tinners.

In any intelligence operation, the people running it must recognize that there are elements that they do not know. The key to a successful outcome is minimizing the risks associated with those unknowns. In the case of Khan's nuclear ring, the CIA officials knew they would have only one shot at closing down the network. If they missed a major customer or a huge shipment of deadly technology—if some major unknown existed—a significant intelligence victory could turn into a career-ending embarrassment and yet another in a series of failed missions that had dogged the CIA over the years. Far worse, the failure to identify and stop another country or even a terrorist organization with access to the means to build an atomic weapon would be a colossal risk to international security. It also would contribute to the potential resurgence of the nuclear proliferation ring the CIA hoped to eliminate.

There had been clues in recent weeks that the Tinners had not been telling their handlers everything. As the clock wound down, it was imperative that the agency find a way to verify what they were hearing—

and determine what, if anything, these particular spies were leaving out. "They needed confirmation that Urs and the others were not double dealing," said a senior intelligence official who was involved in aspects of the Tinner case. "So I think they needed to go in and check what was on Marco's computers to see if it coincided."

Marco Tinner kept most of the family secrets on personal computers stored at his apartment in Jenins, a sleepy little Swiss village of a few hundred people about ten miles away from Vaduz. Kinsman had decided against asking for access to the computers. He feared that crucial information would be erased or transferred elsewhere. So with the Tinners tucked away in a Vaduz hotel in the midst of the debriefings, he informed them that a team of CIA specialists was going to enter Marco's apartment and his office. They would make copies of everything on the computers there. He explained that this was part of the deal for the million dollars. He made it clear that the Tinners could not object. "I would say the Americans forced them to let them see their computers," said a Swiss official involved in the later inquiry. "It was part of the agreement for the payment. Because no one trusted the other side."

Kinsman tried to portray the break-in as protection for the Tinners. From the start, he had told the Tinners that he and his associates could not meet with them on Swiss soil. Doing so would mean that the Tinners and the CIA were violating Swiss espionage law, which prohibited Swiss citizens from working for foreign intelligence agencies and forbade foreign intelligence agents from operating on Swiss soil without written consent. That was why the debriefing was conducted across the border in Liechtenstein and why earlier meetings had always taken place outside Switzerland. And that was why Kinsman said the CIA would copy the records and the computers in the guise of a break-in. The story was created in the event the Swiss authorities learned later that the Tinners had cooperated with the CIA. If they could claim that the CIA had broken into their homes and offices, the Tinners would have a better chance of avoiding prosecution for violating Swiss espionage law. It was a flimsy justification for an unusual action. But the Tinners had to agree to allow the CIA to search their records if they wanted to collect their million dollars.

On June 20, the CIA intrusion team led by Kinsman had broken into Marco's office. They knew that most of what they wanted was kept at Marco's home. The next night, the team broke into the Jenins apartment and spent more than two hours downloading thousands of files from those computers and copying all of his business and personal correspondence and other records. Randomly examining some of the files before leaving, the CIA officer and the nuclear expert from Oak Ridge saw what appeared to be at least partial designs related to a sophisticated nuclear warhead. No one would know for sure until the contents of the computers were examined thoroughly back at Langley. But the discovery caused grave concern on several levels. The Tinners had never mentioned the existence of weapons designs. What else were they hiding? Even more frightening, the designs were completely transferrable because they were digital. Pushing the "send" button could send an e-mail, with the designs attached, anywhere in the world.

Even before the designs were evaluated fully back at Langley, the existence of these highly dangerous digital weapons plans on a computer belonging to someone with a long history of trafficking in nuclear goods should have rung the loudest possible alarm bells. There is no question that these were among the most sensitive nuclear designs imaginable. They were the road map to a bomb. Every computer in that apartment, and every computer, flash drive, and piece of paper from wherever the Tinners lived and worked, should have been confiscated immediately. It was the only way to eliminate the chance that the Swiss spies would send the material into the netherworld of the Internet. And that assumed they had not done so already. The discovery made it clear to Kinsman and his colleagues that the Tinners could not be trusted. Who knew what they might do? There was no justification for leaving those computers, with those designs, in place. But orders were orders. The break-in team had been instructed to make copies and leave the computers and original records behind. When Kinsman and the others locked the apartment door behind them on the way out, the most dangerous nuclear documents ever to have found their way into such an unsecure location were left in the hands of known traffickers who had been lying to the CIA even as they were paid huge sums.

CHAPTER TWO

WASHINGTON AND PARIS

The CIA was created as the successor to the Office of Strategic Services, which had been formed during World War II to coordinate espionage activities among the branches of the United States military. The intention was to provide the president and other leaders with the ability to see beyond the horizon in order to protect their people and interests against attack. The concept for a powerful, centralized civilian agency to coordinate all the intelligence services was embodied in the National Security Act of 1947, which was passed by Congress and signed into law by President Harry S. Truman. Its role was refined the following year by a White House directive that gave the CIA the authority to carry out covert operations "against hostile foreign states or groups or in support of friendly foreign states or groups."

From the outset, the secrecy and deception at the heart of the CIA's mission conflicted with the openness enshrined in American democracy. Soon after the agency's creation, Dean Acheson, who was soon to become secretary of state, wrote, "I had the gravest forebodings about this organization and warned the President that as set up neither he, the National Security Council, nor anyone else would be in a position to know what it was doing or to control it." Truman's successor as president, Dwight D. Eisenhower, shared some of Acheson's concerns, later referring to intelligence operations as "a distasteful but vital necessity." The contradiction is not lost on thoughtful CIA officers. One longtime agency official, whose career included stints working undercover overseas before he retired, explained the inherent tension between a democracy and an effective espionage service. "It is important for U.S. policymakers to know that we have a CIA to do things that are unpalatable, things that we may not be able to achieve through diplomacy or any other way," said the former officer. "We're the agency of last resort."

In the years after its creation, the organizational structure of the CIA evolved into two separate and unequal halves. The less powerful segment, known as the Directorate of Intelligence, is where analysts process the intelligence collected from the field and strive to provide the president and other policymakers with accurate and timely assessments of international developments. The DI, as it is known, is chronically underfunded and underappreciated, existing in the shadows of the intelligence gatherers in the Directorate of Operations, otherwise known as the DO. The DO was set up as home to the various components of the agency that carry out the covert actions commonly associated with the world of espionage. Its officers are responsible for spying on foreign governments and recruiting double agents to collect human intelligence, or "humint." They are sent into the world with false identities and the training to lie and, if necessary, break the laws of foreign countries, in the name of protecting the United States. They are focused on combating the most dangerous security challenges confronting the country, such as threats from foreign governments and terrorist organizations, narcotics trafficking, and the spread of nuclear weapons.

The counterproliferation mandate was relatively low-profile within the CIA until the aftermath of the Persian Gulf War. The discovery that Saddam Hussein had come close to building a nuclear weapon without the knowledge of the United States and its allies sent shudders through the agency and led to the creation in 1994 of the Counter-Proliferation Division within the DO. Experienced operatives from various specialties within the DO were recruited to join the new division, where they would combine espionage tradecraft with scientific understanding of nuclear weapons. The Counter-Proliferation Division differed from most CIA divisions because it was organized around a topic, nuclear proliferation, rather than by geographic boundaries. The fledgling division's low status was reflected in its real estate. Most of the workers were relegated to subterranean office space divided by shoulder-high cubicles. Its mission was regarded with skepticism by the established power centers within the CIA, resulting in what one of its officers described as "savage bureaucratic turf battles." CIA stations around the world often ignored requests for information and cooperation from the nuclear experts.

One of the division's early recruits was a young woman named Valerie Plame. In her 2007 autobiography, *Fair Game*, Plame described her new colleagues as "undeniably brilliant and experienced." One of them was a grandmotherly woman whom Plame first encountered in an elevator wearing a Chanel suit and pushing a baby carriage. Plame looked into the carriage, expecting to see a child, and instead saw two pugs wearing Burberry plaid jackets and collars. Another case officer in the division was a wiry, intense veteran who was nicknamed "Mad Dog." To Plame, the group seemed so quirky that she referred to the division as "the island of misfit toys."

Plame was one of the fortunate few to have an office with a window, and she shared her quarters with the team of case officers who had been assigned the task of tracking and bringing down A. Q. Khan. The leader of the Khan team was Jim Kinsman, the officer known as Mad Dog.*

Kinsman had joined the CIA in 1980 after graduating from law school. He had trained to be a case officer within the DO. Two years later, he received his first overseas posting, to Switzerland. His job was to gather information by recruiting assets among the assortment of Swiss government workers, bankers, and foreign operatives who moved through one of the world's great financial centers. The confluence of business and finance had made Switzerland fertile territory for spies throughout the world. Switzerland was the leading center for bank secrecy and home to untold billions of dollars in illicit fortunes. It was also a country where the high-tech industry was noted for its willingness to sell anything to anyone.

Case officers are known for their ability to think outside the box, for solving problems in the field in creative, unconventional ways, and Kinsman is a prime example. He soon established a reputation as a recruiting wizard and his skills later won him a coveted posting in Paris

----

* The real name of the agent known as Jim Kinsman, aka Mad Dog, is being withheld.

in 1989, a plum assignment that allowed him to indulge two of his passions—wine and running. Kinsman was a passionate runner, clocking six to eight miles a day no matter what the weather and no matter where his peripatetic job took him. He was more whippet than pit bull, all endurance and stamina. In Paris, one of his favorite running courses was through the Bois de Boulogne, the two-thousand acre park on the western edge of the city. The route took him past the Jardin d'Acclimatation, an amusement park with a small zoo, and along a strip of roadway that becomes the city's most prominent red-light district at night. He usually passed a number of large dogs, which the prostitutes used for protection.

Early one morning in the summer of 1989, he passed a particularly large German shepherd and the dog barely raised its head. Then Kinsman felt a searing pain in his right calf and halted mid-stride. The dog had attacked from behind, in complete silence, and sunk its teeth deep into the muscle. He pried open the animal's mouth and staggered a couple of steps. The dog snarled and started to attack again. Kinsman grabbed a stick and brandished it, which was enough to send the dog back to its resting spot.

Kinsman limped home and went to the medical office at the United States Embassy, the imposing building overlooking the gardens of the Champs-Elysées from the northwest corner of the Place de la Concorde. The bite was serious, so the nurse sent him to the Pasteur Institute, the research hospital named for Louis Pasteur, its founder and first director, who had successfully developed the first antirabies serum in 1885. Cautioning Kinsman that the dog might have been rabid, the physician ordered up a painful regimen of injections. Kinsman was impressed; the CIA officer's first thought was whether he could recruit the doctor who treated him at the famous institute. The attitude reflected nothing about the doctor's potential as an asset, but rather the lens through which Kinsman viewed the world.

Later that morning, when he finally arrived at the CIA offices inside the embassy, Kinsman joked about the incident with his colleagues, warning that he was going to bite every official back at Langley who had ever thwarted him. Someone referred to him as "Mad Dog," a nickname so appropriate for the driven and obsessive man that it stuck. The agent embraced the moniker and in later years he occasionally wore a cap with an embroidered bulldog and the words "Mad Dog." In many ways, those two qualities, the drive and the obsession, made Mad Dog an ideal member of the clandestine arm of the Central Intelligence Agency.

When the Counter-Proliferation Division was established in 1994, Kinsman was a natural choice for the team. As a teenager, he had read *Hiroshima*, John Hersey's transformative book about the atomic bomb dropped on the Japanese city during World War II. The image of sixty-six thousand people killed instantly was seared into his memory, and he later told friends he was awestruck by the devastation that a nuclear bomb could deliver. In the back of his mind, there was always the lurking threat of nuclear holocaust. Part of his motivation in joining the CIA had been to keep such devastating weapons out of the hands of the wrong people.

CHAPTER THREE

DUBAI

By the time the CIA set up its first full-time counterproliferation operation, Khan had fulfilled his role in providing the highly enriched uranium required for Pakistan to develop its nuclear arsenal. The scientist had gradually worked himself out of a job at home, so he had turned his sights on selling his expertise to countries that shared his hatred for the United States. He had first reversed the flow of the vast clandestine enterprise he had created on behalf of Pakistan in 1987 in the deal with Iran.

In the final months of its eight-year war with Iraq, Iran had developed an appetite for nuclear weapons. Saddam Hussein had launched a series of attacks with chemical weapons, killing thousands of Iranians and turning the tide of the war in Iraq's favor. When Iran protested to the United Nations that the use of chemical weapons violated international law, it was ignored by the world's superpowers. Iran's religious and military leaders decided that they needed a new deterrent and they began shopping for the makings of a nuclear weapons program.

Iran was not new to nuclear technology. Its first civilian nuclear program was developed under the shah in the 1970s with help from the United States and Germany. The program had been mothballed after the Iranian revolution in 1979 brought the Ayatollah Khomeini to power; Western countries imposed tough sanctions on the sale of nuclear technology and other weapons material to the fundamentalist regime in Tehran. So when the country's leaders decided to restart the program, they were forced to turn to the black market—and they found willing sellers in Khan and his network.

In early 1987, representatives of Iran's Atomic Energy Organization made contact with two of the Europeans who had previously sold nuclear-related technology to Pakistan. The Iranians wanted to acquire centrifuge technology to enrich uranium, and the Europeans ran the proposal past Khan, who had access to centrifuges and other components for an enrichment plant. The deal was appealing to Khan and certain members of the Pakistani leadership, who sought an alliance with Iran as part of a regional strategy to counter the United States and other Western powers. After several weeks of negotiations, Khan agreed to sell two used centrifuges and other components from his plant in Pakistan. The material was shipped to Dubai, the city-state of the Persian Gulf, where it was to be handed over to the Iranians.

Three representatives of Iran's nuclear organization arrived in Dubai in the fall of 1987, where they were greeted by two of Khan's associates, a Sri Lankan expatriate named Mohammed Farooq and his nephew, Buhari Sayed abu Tahir. The Iranians were taken to Farooq's apartment, where they were given the centrifuges and other components that Khan had shipped from Pakistan, a small library of drawings and technical plans for setting up an enrichment plant, and a list of potential suppliers in Europe. As a bonus, the Iranians received a fifteen-page dossier portraying an elaborate process for manufacturing uranium metal, which can be cast into the hemispheres used to form the core of a nuclear weapon. After turning over the material, Farooq accompanied the Iranians to the Dubai branch of the Bank of Credit and Commerce International, where $10 million was transferred to his account. The money was later divided up between Khan, Farooq, Friedrich Tinner, and other members of the network.

A year later, in an effort to expand his network, Khan offered to sell advanced enrichment technology to South Africa, but he was turned down because the South Africans were already producing highly enriched uranium for their covert weapons program. In the 1990s, Khan traveled throughout the Muslim world, trying to sell the same technology to other countries. He made trips to Egypt, Saudi Arabia, Syria, Sudan, and the United Arab Emirates, telling military and political figures in each country that he could help them build nuclear weapons to fend off the Americans and counter the Israelis.

In October 1990, two months after the Iraqi army overran Kuwait, Khan had tried to interest Saddam Hussein in a package of nuclear equipment similar to the one he had sold to Iran three years earlier when Iraq and Iran were locked in a war. In meetings with Iraqi intelligence agents, one of Khan's representatives presented a written offer from the Pakistani scientist. "Pakistan had to spend a period of 10 years and an amount of 300 million U.S. dollars to get it," said the offer for what was labeled "Project A.B.," for "atomic bomb." "Now with the practical experience and the world-wide contacts Pakistan has already developed you can have A.B. in about three years time and by spending about 150 million U.S. dollars." The package included blueprints for a nuclear bomb at a price of $5 million. In addition, the written offer promised to provide all of the components necessary for manufacturing a bomb through Khan's Dubai office, with a 10 percent commission. The offer specified that technical advice would be free and added, "If absolutely necessary 2/3 scientists can be persuaded to resign and join the new assignment."

Saddam had his own secret nuclear weapons program and might have benefited from Khan's assistance but Iraqi intelligence agents wrongly suspected that the offer was a sting set up by the Americans. After considering it for several days, they turned down the proposal.

After some fits and starts, Khan had better luck with Colonel Kaddafi, the Libyan leader who was regarded by the West as one of the world's major sponsors of terrorism. The Pakistani scientist first met with Libyan officials in 1984. Kaddafi had provided suitcases of cash to finance the beginnings of Pakistan's nuclear weapons program, before he had become interested in developing his own atomic arsenal. By 1991, Khan had negotiated an agreement with the Libyans and had begun shipping them centrifuge components and associated equipment through his network to Dubai, where Khan had a small logistics operation up and running to supply the Iranian program. The project came to a halt in 1992 when the United Nations imposed sanctions on Libya after Kaddafi refused to hand over two Libyan intelligence officers implicated in the 1988 bombing of Pan Am Flight 103 over Lockerbie, Scotland.

Khan made the Libyans a new offer in 1997, providing his old contacts in Tripoli with a written proposal to build an entire nuclear weapons production facility. Libya still lacked the technical infrastructure to actually build a weapon of such complexity, so Khan offered a solution: He would provide everything, from a massive centrifuge plant to enrich uranium to the design for the actual nuclear warhead to mount on Kaddafi's missiles. As part of the full-service deal, he promised to train Libyans to run the operation independently. A few weeks later, Khan got word that the Libyan leader was interested. A Libyan nuclear official invited Khan to meet with him on the sidelines of a scientific conference in Istanbul to discuss the project.

In the summer of 1997, Khan was sixty-one years old, still erect and handsome but growing fleshy from the banquet circuit and too much of his favorite food, fried chicken. He was wealthy from siphoning off money from Kahuta and from his nuclear sales to Iran. He was comfortable with the elite from the scientific, business, and political worlds and even entertained thoughts of running for president of Pakistan one day. But when he arrived in Istanbul, Khan also was weary. The internal battles with the Pakistani nuclear establishment had taken a toll on him. Ever since he had succeeded in producing the highly enriched uranium for the country's atomic arsenal, Khan felt as if others in the nuclear program had been trying to push him aside. He was looking for something that would renew his energy and finance a retirement in which he could enjoy fishing and reading poetry, two of his favorite pasttimes. Perhaps he could even finish the twenty-four-room hotel he was building in Timbuktu, the legendarily remote former trading center in the West African country of Mali. He planned to name it the Hotel Hendrina Khan, after his wife.

B. S. A. Tahir, the young Sri Lankan who by then was running parts of Khan's operation in Dubai, had joined him in Istanbul. They went together to a small café on the mega-city's Asian side. Waiting for them were two Libyans. Mohammad Matuq Mohammad was the head of the country's secret nuclear program. Accompanying him was a technician who gave his name only as Karim. Mohammad greeted Khan and Tahir in American English, which he had learned studying physics in the United States in the 1970s. He motioned for Khan to sit down. Tahir was directed to a small table far enough away that he could not hear the conversation. Khan, however, listened carefully as Mohammad described Kaddafi's interest in acquiring everything necessary to build an arsenal of nuclear weapons. Khan was eager to seal the agreement, but the two Libyans said they needed final approval from Kaddafi.

A few weeks later, Khan met with the two Libyans and several other officials in Dubai. The second meeting resulted in an agreement that launched Khan on a nuclear deal that dwarfed what he had provided to Iran and represented a challenge as great as the one he had undertaken two decades earlier in Pakistan. Libya was as technologically backward as Pakistan had been in the mid-1970s. Bringing a nuclear weapon to the country would seal Khan's reputation as a scientific genius and burnish his image throughout the Muslim world. But Khan knew that he could not accomplish this alone. He had succeeded so quickly in Pakistan because he was one of the first to recognize the value of a globalized world, relying on a network of suppliers from many countries. For the Libyan project, he would enlist the same suppliers who had helped build Pakistan's bomb and were providing technology to the Iranians. This time he would have to go beyond his trusted associates to recruit fresh blood. But the fortune to be made was staggering—Khan estimated that Libya would pay hundreds of millions of dollars out of its oil revenues to build Kadddafi's bomb.

The Libyan project taxed Khan's network in another critical way. For the Iranian deal, he had been able to obtain a handful of centrifuges and components from the stocks at Kahuta. Iran had a corps of well-trained scientists and technicians, many of them educated at the best universities in the West. This meant they had the knowledge and facilities to use Khan's models to build their own centrifuges to produce the fissile material for a weapon. But Khan learned quickly that Libya was not Iran. His initial plan was to build a factory to produce centrifuges in Libya, and he sent twenty of the machines to Tripoli near the end of 1997. However, it soon became evident that it would take years and possibly decades before the Libyans could manufacture the machines themselves, so Khan decided to construct the factory in Dubai and train workers there. It seemed like a logical second choice; Khan had been exploiting the notoriously lax customs controls in Dubai for years to ship sensitive technology from Europe to Pakistan and later to Iran.

For assistance and a modicum of cover, he had turned a computer business run by Tahir into a front for the illicit operation. Though only in his middle thirties, Tahir was a veteran of the nuclear underworld. He had worked with an uncle in the 1980s to sell specialized furnaces to Pakistan and South Africa for their clandestine nuclear programs. When Khan first set up his operation in Dubai to begin providing technology to the Iranians, Tahir was a junior partner who later claimed that his main task then was serving tea to the Iranian officials when they visited. In the years that followed, Tahir had built up his computer business in one of Dubai's free-trade zones and eventually grown into the role of logistics manager for Khan's deals with Tehran. Along the way, Tahir had become wealthy from his legitimate business and his work with Khan. He loved driving around Dubai in his red Ferrari, and he lived in one of the city's gleaming new high-rises. As the Libyan deal unfolded, Tahir would become an even more useful partner, arranging for the shipment of literally hundreds of tons of equipment and material through Dubai to Tripoli.

As Khan became immersed in the Libyan project, he struggled with the scale of the new deal, which was far beyond what he had been providing to Iran. Unlike the strategy he employed for Iran, he could not pillage the stockpiles at Kahuta for enough used centrifuges to build an entire enrichment plant. So Khan began mapping an expansion of his black market, relying once again on old friends and adding a new group of suppliers willing to turn a blind eye to nuclear trafficking.

Not long after closing the deal with the Libyans in Dubai, Khan had telephoned Friedrich Tinner and asked if he would be interested in participating in the new project. Tinner agreed to help Khan assemble the equipment necessary for Libya's bomb, and the work began in early 1998. They also approached a veteran of the Iranian smuggling operation, a German engineer named Gotthard Lerch. He lived about three miles from the Tinners in Switzerland and had been involved in nuclear trafficking with them and Khan for many years. In the months that followed, Khan, Tinner, and other trusted members of the network met with the Libyans in Dubai, Casablanca, and other cities where they thought they could operate outside the prying eyes of Western intelligence services.

KHAN HAD GROWN MORE ANTI-WESTERN over the years. He believed the United States and its allies employed a double standard that allowed Israel to possess nuclear weapons but sought to deny them to Muslim countries. Long ago he had become convinced that the Americans in particular had tried to block his efforts to build Pakistan's atomic arsenal. On many occasions he boasted to associates that the Americans, British, and Israelis had failed to stop his efforts on behalf of Pakistan. He was well aware that the CIA and its British equivalent, the Secret Intelligence Service, known as MI6, had been gathering extensive intelligence on his operations virtually from the start, but he had no idea of the depth to which they had penetrated his network.

Even though the Americans and British had not shut down Khan's proliferation ring, they had kept a close eye on its operations. Khan's foreign travels were monitored by both intelligence agencies, and at least one technician was recruited by MI6 inside Khan's enrichment plant at Kahuta. In the early 1980s, MI6 agents had broken into Khan's hotel room on one of his foreign trips and photographed the contents of his suitcase. The photographs were developed and shipped to London, where MI6 technical experts determined that the information included designs for a nuclear warhead tested by the Chinese in 1966.

After the British shared the discovery with the CIA, Vernon Walters, a former CIA deputy director, was sent to Islamabad by then president Reagan to confront the Pakistani leadership with the evidence. Walters spread copies of the warhead designs on a table and watched for a reaction. "What is this thing that looks like anyone could have drawn?" asked Pakistani president Mohammad Zia ul-Haq. Walters explained that he was certain Zia already knew that he was looking at a nuclear warhead. He warned the Pakistani dictator not to proceed with developing a bomb. At the time, however, the Reagan administration was using Pakistan to funnel millions of dollars in weapons to the guerrillas who were battling the Soviets across the border in

Afghanistan. Zia knew that Washington was in no position to make good on its threat.

All they could do was keep Khan under constant surveillance as he traveled the world peddling his nuclear wares. So both MI6 and the CIA were well aware of his new project with the Libyans. And in response, both intelligence agencies increased the resources devoted to penetrating Khan's operation.

Near the end of 1998, Khan and Tinner went to Casablanca for another planning session with the Libyans. Among the Libyans at the meeting was Mohammad Matuq Mohammad, who had first met with Khan in Istanbul. Khan acknowledged that he was having difficulty getting the alternative centrifuge manufacturing workshop up and running in Dubai, but he stressed to Mohammad and his colleagues that everything was on track. He didn't want the Libyans getting cold feet. Unknown to the participants, they were under surveillance by British intelligence. In a hotel lobby, an MI6 agent got close enough to Tinner to drop a tiny electronic eavesdropping device in the pocket of his suit coat. For the next several days, the British were able to overhear almost every detail as the participants planned Kaddafi's nuclear weapons plant. They listened as Khan explained his lack of progress to the Libyans, and they listened when Khan and Tinner privately discussed the difficulties of working in Libya.

Later the eavesdroppers heard the Pakistani scientist tell his Swiss friend that he needed someone with technical knowledge to help out in Dubai, where efforts to get the centrifuge plant up and running were stalled. He asked whether one of Tinner's sons, Urs or Marco, might be interested in the job. Though he was younger, Marco was the more accomplished of the pair, and he was running his own small export-import business. But Tinner said he thought that his older son, Urs, might welcome the change. He explained that Urs was experiencing some difficulties at home. Tinner promised to raise the idea when he got back to Switzerland.

Bugging the planning session between Khan and senior Libyan nuclear officials was an enormous coup for the intelligence agencies tracking the network. The information provided a road map for the project under way in Libya. By the account of one former official and nuclear expert who saw a transcript of the conversation, there was more than enough information to close down the smuggling operation that was supplying expertise and technology to the Libyan nuclear project.

Within days of the Casablanca meeting, a copy of the transcript from British intelligence was sitting on Jim Kinsman's desk in the Counter-Proliferation Division at CIA headquarters. He and his colleagues had been working closely with the Brits for years on Khan and other targets. The transcript was rich in details about the network's plans for Libya. There were names of prospective participants, target dates for completing various stages of the project, and a list of prospective participants who might be turned into spies for a deeper look inside Khan's operation. Among them was Urs Tinner.

The CIA had its own window on Khan's network. A few months earlier, the agency had inserted a man into the Tinner operation through a classic clandestine operation. In 1998, a CIA asset had managed to get a job working directly for Friedrich Tinner at his factory in Switzerland. The CIA asset had at one point worked at the International Atomic Energy Agency in Vienna, and then had set up his own technology export business. At some point along the way, the man was recruited by the CIA and instructed to infiltrate the Tinner operation across the border in Switzerland. He made contact with Friedrich and they conducted a minor amount of business. A few months later, the man said that his business was bankrupt and he asked Tinner for a job.

For several months, the CIA asset fed a steady stream of intelligence back to the Counter-Proliferation Division at CIA headquarters. He tracked shipments to Iran and some of the earliest equipment going to Dubai as part of the Libya project. Somewhere along the line, Tinner grew suspicious that his employee might be connected to American intelligence. Near the end of 1998, Tinner fired him. The suspicions must not have run too deep, however, because the CIA sent the man to Dubai, where he set up another business. One of his first steps was to work his way back into the network, so he got in touch with Marco Tinner to say he was eager for business.

The intelligence provided by the mole inside Tinner's factory and the transcripts from Casablanca of the conversations about Libya's quest for nuclear weapons gave the intelligence community its clearest picture so far of the scope and the danger of Khan's network. The new information added to the simmering debate within the intelligence community over when to stop watching and take decisive action against Khan and his accomplices. Each course—continuing to watch or shutting him down—carried real risks and rewards. Watching allowed the network to spread ever more lethal technology to more rogue countries, but acting without understanding the full scope of the network jeopardized the chances of shutting down the entire operation. Even after the discovery of the Libyan project, the decision was made to watch and wait.

CHAPTER FOUR

DUBAI

The British eavesdropping in Casablanca dovetailed perfectly with the earlier information from the CIA's spy inside Tinner's operation and with other intelligence being gathered about Khan's network. Kinsman and his colleagues knew that Khan had embarked on the Libyan project, and they were developing new avenues into the network. One of them started with a tip that arrived at the CIA at about the same time as the British transcript. Confirming the contents of the transcript, a German intelligence agent told the Americans that the Tinners and other longtime associates of Khan were shipping a lot of sensitive material from Germany and Switzerland to Dubai. Faced with a wealth of intelligence, Kinsman and his superiors decided the time had come to try to recruit someone directly inside Khan's operation—and Urs Tinner fit the bill perfectly.

No one ever paid much attention to Urs Tinner. He was a plain-looking man with no distinguishing features. In late 1999, he had just turned thirty-four and his life seemed to be on a downward spiral. The elder of two sons, he had barely finished high school and he seemed incapable of holding a job for very long. He idolized his father, who nonetheless regarded him as a failure. His Swiss wife had divorced him and refused to give him visiting rights to their two daughters. When he had tried to stay with a high school friend, the friend's wife had forbidden Tinner from even entering the home. His second marriage to a Russian dancer he met in a bar was collapsing, and he owed back taxes and debts from child support and other obligations. At one point he was working three jobs—days at his father's business, evenings as a cook at a restaurant, and nights as a bartender at a nightclub. Still, as he later acknowledged, he was barely scraping by. In an effort to escape his financial troubles in Switzerland, he was looking for work outside the country. When his father described Khan's offer of a job in Dubai, Urs jumped at the chance for a fresh start.

It would turn out to be a good choice, on a couple of levels. Despite his social and financial troubles, Urs was brilliant at making almost anything in a machine shop. He had trained in mechanics at vocational school and during four years in the Swiss army. After going to work for his father, he had taken on various temporary assignments for the company on installations of machinery in Germany, France, and the United States. His hands were scarred from the years of working with metal, transforming it almost magically into intricate components for vacuum valves and other equipment. He would prove to be a valuable addition to Khan's growing operation in Dubai. Urs also would be a brilliant choice from the perspective of the CIA, providing a path deep into the Khan network.

INTELLIGENCE COMES IN MANY FORMS and from many sources. Satellites provide precise photographs of secret installations, and conversations intercepted by the ubiquitous ears of the National Security Agency can prove invaluable. But the gold standard is "humint," the information that comes directly from a person with intimate knowledge of the target. When that person is cooperating and providing information while continuing to play a role in the targeted organization, the results can be a bonanza. But it's a bonanza that often carries risks, too.

The axiom that it takes a thief to catch a thief applies to espionage as well. Spymasters must recruit their spies from the world of traitors, lawbreakers, and con men. In the trade, they are referred to as "dirty assets." John le Carré captured the phenomenon when he described Alec Leamas's response to his girlfriend's complaint that he was getting information from a villain. "What do you think spies are: priests, saints and martyrs? They're a squalid procession of vain fools, traitors too, yes; pansies, sadists and drunkards, people who play cowboys and Indians to brighten their rotten lives. Do you think they sit like monks in London, balancing the rights and wrongs?"

The law requires the CIA to apply a balance. Guidelines were established in 1995 requiring case officers to weigh criminal violations committed by their agents against the positive value of intelligence supplied, or likely to be supplied, by these assets.

Kinsman was a creative case officer and he had learned long ago to work with what he was given. A human source directly inside the Khan network, even a questionable one, could prove invaluable. He began crafting a strategy for going to Dubai and ensnaring Tinner.

When Tinner arrived at the airport in Dubai in 1999 to begin his new career, he was met by B. S. A. Tahir, who introduced himself as Dr. Khan's right-hand man. Tinner and Tahir were about the same age, and there was an immediate tension between them. Tahir was worldlier and infinitely more successful, and he saw the newcomer as a potential rival for Khan's affection and largesse. Tahir's business, SMB Computers, was successful in its own right, but it also served as the primary front company for shipping nuclear technology to Iran and Libya. The start of the Libyan project had increased the amount of equipment arriving in Dubai, which meant that the commissions being collected by Tahir and Khan were growing, too. Tahir was making enough money to drive around town in a Rolls-Royce and live in a fancy apartment in the fast-growing metropolis. Tinner, however, occupied a different sphere and would later describe his job in Dubai as something almost menial, calling himself "a normal engineer, an employee of Tahir."

Tinner adjusted to life in Dubai faster than he expected. He had missed the summer, when temperatures regularly exceeded a hundred degrees. He started out in a shabby apartment, so he spent most his off hours in the glitzy hotel bars, where he watched wealthy Arabs pick up thousand-dollar-a-night hookers. But his new boss and his patron, A. Q. Khan, were generous enough to provide him with money to soon move from a tiny apartment to a small house fifty yards from the Persian Gulf in Ajman, the tiniest of the seven city-states that make up the United

Arab Emirates. There he started every day by hauling his scuba gear to the beach and going for a dive. At night he hung out in the bars that proliferate throughout Dubai, the biggest and showiest of the emirates and a short drive from his house in Ajman.

Khan had long been a distant figure in Tinner's life. In the late 1970s, Khan had sometimes had dinner at the Tinner family's modest home in Haag. Urs had rarely seen the Pakistani since then, but in Dubai he found himself spending considerable time with Khan. Soon after arriving in the Emirates, he had gone to visit Khan in the scientist's luxury apartment in the heart of Dubai. He helped Khan hang some new pictures of birds and flowers. Khan had kept an apartment—and a mistress—in Dubai since the days of the first Iran deal. But he maintained a low profile when he visited, so he was pleased with Tinner's company. For his part, Tinner regarded Khan as a friendly old man, someone who would stop his car by the side of the road to offer a lift to a stranger on foot. Their conversations were a welcome respite from a world in which few people spoke German. "He spoke proper German rather well, and in fact that's why he was the only one with whom I could talk," Tinner said later. "When you are abroad, you can't understand what people say. Suddenly somebody arrived who could speak German and I could talk to him. What is more, we talked a lot."

Amid the pictures of birds and flowers inside Khan's tranquil apartment was an unattractive anomaly. Twelve black cases similar to those carried by airline pilots and lawyers were always lined up against one wall in the living room. These were the bulky cases in which Khan had brought most of the documents to Dubai. He never bothered to buy filing cabinets for the material, probably figuring that he never knew when he might have to leave in a hurry. Emptying filing cabinets would take far more time than carrying briefcases to a getaway car. Each case was secured with a combination lock and each bore a letter of the alphabet, which delineated the various aspects of the Iranian and Libyan nuclear programs. One of the cases, for instance, contained copies of a 1966-era nuclear warhead designed by the Chinese. Another held designs for centrifuges that were far more sophisticated than the ones the network was selling to Libya and Iran. At this point, however, the contents were a mystery to Tinner.

- - - - - -

KHAN HAD IDENTIFIED MOST OF the cast for his Libyan production by early 2000. That spring, he decided to set the most ambitious aspects of the project in motion by summoning the main participants to his apartment in Dubai. Khan was clearly in charge, and everyone referred to him as "Boss." Because the boss was worried about ever letting any of his partners see the whole picture of what was going on, he invited each of his accomplices to meet with him separately. Gotthard Lerch flew down from Germany. He was given the assignment of finding someone to manufacture the elaborate equipment required to process the uranium gas that would fuel the centrifuges in Libya. Friedrich Tinner arrived; he was there to help Urs set up a plant in Dubai to manufacture most of the components for the thousands of centrifuges that would be needed for Libya's enrichment plant. Some of the most delicate pieces would still be made at the Tinner factory in Switzerland. Two Turkish businessmen, Gunes Cire and Selim Alguadis, were instructed to supply the sophisticated electronics. Khan also established a system for handling the money. Libya would be paying exorbitant commissions to the suppliers, payments likely to run into the tens of millions of dollars. Khan said the money would be funneled through a series of bank accounts in Switzerland, Dubai, and Liechtenstein in order to conceal the source and size of the payments.

Dubai prides itself on being what is benignly called "business friendly"; in point of fact, the gleaming new city on the Persian Gulf has a reputation as a modern Casablanca, where anything goes in terms of deals and dealers. But it is also a center of international espionage, a vantage point from which the world's intelligence services monitor shipments going to Iran and other dubious locations. In fact, Khan's expanded operation there had already attracted unwanted attention.

In May 1999, a shipment of specialty aluminum bound for Tahir's office in Dubai was seized on the docks of London by British customs agents. An MI6 agent had tipped customs that the aluminum, which required an export license, was destined for the Khan network. The shipment had been arranged by Abu Bakr Siddiqui, a British-based businessman. A search of his home found records of millions of dollars worth of equipment shipped to Khan and related people over the past decade, much of it through Dubai. They also found a photo of Siddiqui and Khan together.

After spending weeks sorting through the records, customs submitted a formal request to the Ministry of Justice in Dubai in August, asking permission to carry out an investigation. The request listed the names of several entities suspected of being part of Khan's network in Dubai, including Tahir and SMB Computers. After several months the authorities gave permission for the lead British customs investigator, Atif Amin, to pursue his investigation of the Khan ring there.

Amin was a young member of the special counterproliferation team at customs and he was eager to pursue his investigation of the biggest proliferator in history. Before he could leave for Dubai in March 2000, however, he was warned by MI6 to steer clear of one of the companies on his list, Desert Electrical Equipment Factory. No reason was given. When Amin arrived in Dubai, he met with the chief of the MI6 station for the United Arab Emirates. This time he was cautioned to stay away from one of the financial institutions on his list, Habib Bank. The bank had been used by Tahir to send payments to Siddiqui. Again, Amin was not told why.

With the help of a Dubai police lieutenant, Alwari Essam, Amin went ahead with his investigation and the young customs agent turned up evidence that SMB Computers and other companies were involved in the Khan network. When Amin discussed the information with the MI6 chief in Dubai, he had the distinct impression that no one wanted to see his investigation proceed. A few days later, the documents he had found implicating several companies and at least one bank in the network were confiscated by British intelligence. Amin was ordered back to London because the intelligence officials said they had uncovered threats against his life. "These people are dangerous," the MI6 officer in Dubai warned him. "They have assets in the local mafia they use for smuggling. They won't hesitate to kill people."

The threats against Amin were most likely manufactured. The truth was that senior MI6 officials back at Thames House in London wanted him out of the way. The young British customs investigator had stumbled into the ongoing intelligence operation monitoring Khan's network. Desert Electrical Equipment Factory was not just another Khan supplier; it was the company set up by Urs Tinner. And Tinner was not just another supplier, either. He had been recruited by the CIA, in cooperation with the British.

Several months before Amin got on the case, Jim Kinsman had arrived in Dubai, armed with a plan to enlist Urs Tinner. The circumstances surrounding the recruitment of Tinner are murky. Kinsman had to weigh the role he might play in bringing down the Khan network against the dangers of permitting Tinner to continue trafficking in nuclear technology. He would adjust the ledger as he went along, but from the outset the CIA case officer was convinced that overlooking Tinner's criminal activities was worth the opportunity to go after the network.

Tinner later acknowledged that he started working for the CIA in late 1999, but he refused to discuss how he was recruited. One version of the recruitment, provided by a former senior CIA official and confirmed by an outsider, was that Kinsman had used allegations that Tinner had engaged in criminal behavior in France to blackmail him into working for the CIA. A senior Swiss official discounted that story, claiming instead that Tinner was turned into a paid informant after being threatened with the exposure of his role in the Khan network. Either way, there appears to have been an element of blackmail, which is one of the most delicate recruitment methods. In the jargon of the espionage world, it's called a "coerced recruitment," and its fruits are always suspect because the case officer can never be certain of the asset's loyalties.

CIA operatives assigned to the agency's base in Dubai had assembled a picture of Tinner's daily routine. The agents had watched him shuttle between Tahir's office in the Jebel Ali Free Trade Zone and his own nearby office at Desert Electrical, where he was beginning to train workers for the planned centrifuge plant. At the end of each day, Tinner still stopped by the bar at one of the hotels to unwind before the drive to Ajman.

One evening Kinsman waited patiently in a hotel bar until his quarry entered. When Tinner sat down, the CIA officer took the seat next to him. Introducing himself, the American started what seemed at first to be a casual conversation. Eventually, according to one account of the recruitment, Kinsman got to the point, telling his companion that he knew Tinner had potential problems with law enforcement that could land him in jail. The American alluded to vague criminal charges in France. Tinner had no idea what this stranger was talking about but he was too frightened to stop listening. Perhaps, Kinsman suggested, he could use his position with the American government to resolve those legal problems with the French. In exchange, perhaps Tinner would share some information about his work in Dubai with the American. Kinsman did not identify himself as a CIA officer; he left his affiliation vague. The vagueness left Tinner room to avoid confronting the fact that he was betraying Khan and even his father. Only later, after his spy was in too deep to get out, would Kinsman let Tinner know that he had been turned into a CIA asset.

Uncertain of the American's true purpose, Tinner was worried by the approach, but he was not necessarily surprised. He understood that his work for Khan was far outside what anyone would regard as normal business channels. He was aware that his father had long helped Pakistan's nuclear program, and he had heard the elder Tinner's rationalizations that he was not doing anything that was actually illegal. Urs would later maintain that he did not understand that his work in Dubai involved developing a nuclear weapon for Libya, but he knew that he was operating on the dark side of the ledger. His surprise was that the approach had come from an American, not Britain's MI6, the agency that Tinner had expected to hear from. He tried to extricate himself from the uncomfortable situation with Kinsman several times that first night. Each time he stood to leave, Kinsman persisted and persuaded Tinner to sit back down. Finally Tinner said he would think about the offer and accepted an invitation for dinner a few nights later at the same hotel.

At the dinner, the American sweetened his proposal, saying he might be willing to pay for the right information. Several conversations took place at various hotels in the following days, all part of the slow seduction of Urs Tinner. Eventually Tinner agreed to begin providing information on shipments coming into Dubai for the Khan network. In exchange, Kinsman would pay him small sums in cash.

The work of an intelligence service in any democracy requires maintaining a delicate balance between openness and secrecy, a bargain between the public's right to know and its need for protection. The balance is never more delicate than when the security service has to work with criminals to catch people deemed to be a bigger threat. Striking a deal for information with someone involved in illegal activities requires weighing the costs of allowing them to remain in business against the value of the intelligence they are providing. In Kinsman's world, Tinner and his family were less important than bringing down Khan and his entire network. If he needed to absolve Urs of wrongdoing to get the evidence required to shut down the network, so be it.

From their first days at the Farm, the secretive Virginia facility where the CIA trains young recruits, those determined to join the agency's covert arm get careful instruction in how to develop potential sources. They learn about the laws they must follow and the ones they can ignore. The instructors stress that loyalty is essential and that it takes many forms. The first loyalty is to their country and the second is to their colleagues in the agency. But they are also instilled with an obligation to be loyal to the people they recruit. As unappetizing as it can be under some circumstances, loyalty is a two-way street in these sorts of transactions.

Kinsman expected Tinner to provide him with accurate information, though he was savvy enough to know that he would have to corroborate everything possible and that he could never count on being told everything. In exchange for his help, Tinner received absolution from Kinsman and the promise of future protection.

"Once they have signed on with the CIA, they are absolved of all past wrongdoing and the case officer is committed to doing everything he can to protect them," said a veteran CIA officer, explaining the bond formed between case officer and asset. "How could you ever recruit someone else if you didn't protect your recruits? These aren't nuns or choir boys, but you have to absolve them." There is pragmatic honor in this code of loyalty. There is also a danger: The case officer can become hooked on the flow of information, entranced by the inside view, loyal to a fault when it comes to protecting his asset. This is more than an individual threat; it is systemic. Locked in a secretive, tribal world, the case officer runs the risk of losing sight of the larger goal of espionage, which is translating intelligence into timely action. An operational success can still end in a policy failure.

Kinsman recruited his new inside source at an opportune moment in the long history of the Khan network. The Libyan project required a dramatic expansion in business. The CIA would have an inside track on everything that transpired in the coming weeks and months. Or so the case officer hoped.

EVEN WITH TINNER'S ARRIVAL, PLANS to start the factory to build Libya's centrifuges in Dubai were going poorly. Tahir leased several warehouses and they were filling up with equipment—centrifuge prototypes from Pakistan, lathes from Spain, a specialized furnace from Japan, electronics from Turkey, specialty metals from Singapore, valves and pumps from Switzerland and Germany. Some of the equipment was destined for Libya, some for Iran, and some remained in the warehouses for use in the centrifuge factory. The problem was recruiting enough skilled technicians to get the plant up and running. Shipping sensitive technology into and out of Dubai was easy enough. The government's own website bragged that its customs laws were written to enable "traders to transit their shipments . . . without any hassles." But most of the workers from developing countries who made up the city-state's workforce were unskilled laborers and training them was proving difficult for Urs.

Tinner set up the training operation at his warehouse at Desert Electrical. There were two types of students. The largest group was the foreign workers who would be trained to run the initial centrifuge manufacturing plant in Dubai. They were Sri Lankans, Filipinos, Indians, Pakistanis—the floating mass of unskilled workers from developing countries who search for work throughout the Middle East. These workers were taught to use basic machinery to cut pieces of steel, mill the metal, and shape it on lathes; the goal at the start was to create nothing more complicated than a small steel box. Once those simple steps were mastered, the plan was for the workers to move on to the more elaborate work of turning out precision parts for centrifuges. But the workers from Dubai were more accustomed to cleaning offices or sweeping streets, and they proved incapable of accomplishing even the basic jobs. Over several months Tinner was unable to develop even a skeleton crew for a proposed centrifuge manufacturing plant.

The second group of students was smaller and fared better overall. The Libyan government had sent several groups of men with some technical experience to Tinner's workshop. There he taught them the same basic steps so that they could one day supervise the centrifuge production, either in Dubai or at a factory in Libya. The Libyans had more experience than the previous trainees, but Tinner still had difficulty teaching them to master the complexities of precision machine tools, so the project lagged.

Khan had a reputation at his laboratory in Pakistan as a demanding taskmaster. Despite his affection for Tinner, he was growing impatient with the delays. Tinner explained repeatedly that the foreign workers had no aptitude for even the most basic mechanical work. Finally Khan agreed that Dubai might not work as the location of his centrifuge plant. For a short time the focus shifted to Turkey. The education and skill levels of workers there were higher. And the network already had a strong Turkish connection through Cire and Alguadis, the owners of two large Turkish electronics businesses. The Turks agreed to look for a location and the skilled workers required for the plant. But Turkey was a NATO member with a sharp-eyed military and much tougher border controls than Dubai, so the idea was abandoned before it got far.

Whether Tinner fully understood what sort of work he was engaged in remains unclear. He would later claim that he wasn't sure about the final use of the tons of sensitive technology coming into Dubai. He was excluded from the strategy sessions conducted by Khan when he was in Dubai, and explained that Tahir kept him in the dark about the destinations of some of the equipment. Mostly, he said, he concentrated on the narrow task of manufacturing the same sorts of components he had produced for his father over the years.

There is plenty of evidence to cast doubt on the notion that Tinner was fully in the dark, both about his work with Khan and his work with Kinsman. After all, his father had collaborated with Khan since the beginning of his nuclear black market. Another obvious clue that the work was not legitimate was the shroud of secrecy wrapped around almost every aspect of the project. Shipping invoices were routinely falsified and even the most apparently innocuous documents were shredded. Tahir was constantly telling Tinner to avoid drawing attention to their work. For instance, one day Tahir arrived in the office with a stack of documents that he wanted scanned into the computer. Saying he could not entrust the work to a clerk, he told Tinner to help. As he fed documents into the scanner, Tinner noticed that some of the designs were not related to any kind of centrifuge he had seen before. "It's logical that you end up seeing things, documents which you start to read and which are bizarre," he said later. His suspicions were deepened when Tahir transferred the scanned material to a hard drive and ordered Tinner to shred the originals. On many occasions, Tinner said, he found himself working from paper blueprints from which Tahir had carefully trimmed anything that would have identified their origin.

After several weeks of meetings with Kinsman, Tinner must have suspected strongly that he was dealing with someone from the Central Intelligence Agency. Kinsman always paid for their expensive meals, which tended to be eaten in the city's most lavish hotels and restaurants. He routinely paid Tinner small amounts of cash—five hundred dollars here, a thousand dollars there—for passing on information about the shipments to and from Dubai or for handing over names of some of the principal network participants and the companies that were helping get the Libyan project up and running.

Kinsman unfailingly treated his spy with respect. He thanked him for his work and praised his bravery. Tinner was tacitly grateful for the guidance, believing that he was being taken seriously for the first time. In one of their conversations, Tinner mentioned the row of black cases in Khan's apartment to his American friend. The spymaster perked up. This could be important. Kinsman pressed his spy: How many were there? Were they locked? Could he find out what was inside them? Tinner thought for a minute. He said the cases were locked and he wasn't sure how to get into them.

The chance to get into the black cases arrived a few weeks later. Khan was in Dubai and he summoned Tinner to the apartment. The Pakistani used one of the bedrooms as an office, and it contained a copy machine along with a computer and file cabinets. This particular day, Khan asked Tinner to take some documents out of some of the black cases in the living room and copy them for him. It was a menial task, but Tinner was one of the few people Khan could trust to do it. The Pakistani spun the combinations and opened several of the cases, withdrawing stacks of documents for Tinner to copy. Khan said he was leaving for a couple of hours and he hoped that Tinner could finish the task by the time he returned.

Tinner faced a stomach-churning task. He had no idea what would happen if Khan caught him copying documents for himself. Perhaps Tinner would be killed. There were stories that a North Korean spy had been shot to death in Khan's own backyard in Islamabad. The Pakistani scientist also had a nasty temper, which Tinner had seen directed at Tahir on more than one occasion.

As the episode was explained later by someone involved in the investigation of the network, Tinner worked frenetically to copy the documents—making two copies of each page, instead of the one for which Khan had asked. As he worked, he strained to hear over the whir of the copy machine, listening for Khan's return, thankful that the apartment was at the end of a long marble hallway, that the door key made a loud grating noise every time it was turned. Tinner was good with his hands and he worked fast. By the time Khan got back, Tinner had stacked one set of copies on the desk in the room. The other set had been tucked into his own bag.

Later Tinner met with Kinsman and turned over the copies he had made. The documents told a story well beyond the work being done for Libya. Some of them provided new information about Iran's nuclear program. One thick stack contained the complete plans for converting processed uranium ore into uranium hexafluoride, the feedstock for centrifuges. Other papers contained blueprints for centrifuges themselves, floor plans for massive halls for the cascades of centrifuges required to transform uranium into the fissile material used in weapons. Tinner may not have understood everything that he pulled from the cases, but the cache represented an unprecedented window into the extent of the assistance that Khan and his accomplices were providing not only to Libya but also to Iran. Kinsman paid his spy and returned to Washington with his treasure.

Back in the offices of the Counter-Proliferation Division at the CIA, the intelligence was plugged into a massive and growing matrix of suppliers around the world who were contributing to the illicit nuclear network. The flow of intelligence was increasing concerns at the CIA and White House about the progress Iran was making toward a nuclear weapon. President George W. Bush was receiving regular updates on the Iranian program through the daily presidential briefing from senior CIA officials. But no one could tell him how close they were getting. Regardless, even with the arrival of this new intelligence, Iran never got the full attention of the president and his top national security advisers. They were engaged in what they believed was far more pressing business: They were planning for the invasion of Iraq, where they believed Saddam Hussein was working on his own nuclear weapon.

CHAPTER FIVE

DUBAI AND KUALA LUMPUR

The drive from Urs Tinner's small house on the beach to his work-shop in Dubai took about twenty minutes on a normal day. In early 2001, as he was starting his second year working for Khan, he arrived at Desert Electrical and opened the door to find the building empty. Overnight, everything had disappeared. The machine tools he had been using to train workers, the computers that held his business records, the filing cabinets, the office furniture, even the trash baskets, all of it had vanished. Alarmed, Tinner immediately telephoned Tahir at his office a few miles away. The Sri Lankan told Tinner to calm down. He said that he would drive over and explain the situation.

"We decided to sell everything," Tahir said when he arrived in the empty workshop. "We got a good price."

"Where is my private stuff?" asked Tinner, who had kept his personal laptop and some of his papers in his small office there.

"Don't worry," said Tahir. "We will buy it all new."

Tahir said he and Khan had been discussing plans to move the train-ing and production operation to a country with a bigger pool of skilled workers. Plans to shift the operation to Turkey had been abandoned. Tahir mentioned looking for a location in Malaysia; he said the country had an educated workforce and he had political connections that could smooth the way for opening a new factory quickly. Tinner knew that Tahir had married a young woman from a wealthy and politically con-nected Malaysian family in 1998. Khan had mentioned attending the lavish wedding in Kuala Lumpur, the sprawling capital of Malaysia. Tinner suspected she wanted to move closer to her family. Tahir reassured Tinner, telling him wherever they wound up, his job would be safe. The explanation did not justify the sudden nature of the move. Only later did Tinner learn what really happened.

The previous morning, Tahir had gone to his office at SMB Computers. As he unlocked the doors and settled into his desk, he had the sense that things were amiss. Files were out of place; a couple of computers that he was certain had been turned off the night before were on. Someone appeared to have given the premises a thorough search, going through business records, trying to get into computer files.

Tahir's suspicion focused on MI6. The British intelligence service had been monitoring the Khan network in collaboration with its American counterparts for years. He was well aware that the British had arrested Siddiqui two years earlier and he had been expecting an attempt to link him to the aluminum seized in London. The morning he discovered the search, Tahir assembled a team of workers and ordered them to clean out every piece of paper or equipment that could have linked him to the Khan network. Sophisticated technology waiting for shipment to Libya was transported to another warehouse. Papers were run through shredders, and the bags of waste were carried away. He ordered everyone in the office to pull the hard drives out of their computers and turn them over to him. Emptying Tinner's place had been the second phase of the emergency scrub.

Tahir's story to Tinner about the decision to pack up and move had the advantage of being rooted in some practical reasons, too. It had become increasingly clear that Dubai lacked the right workforce to open the centrifuge factory. Tahir had been talking with Khan for several weeks about the possibility of moving the operation to Malaysia. Malaysia was a technically advanced Muslim country with lax export controls. It had the added advantage of being off the radar of Western intelligence services. Khan liked the idea and told Tahir to explore a move. The break-in had the unintended effect of speeding up the timetable.

Tahir and his wife, Nazimah Syed Majid, already owned an upscale chocolate shop in Kuala Lumpur and she was an investor in a company called Scomi Group, which worked mostly with the region's booming oil and gas industries. One of her partners was Kamaluddin Abdullah, the only son of Malaysia's prime minister, Abdullah Badawi. Shortly after explaining the intrusion to Khan, Tahir flew to Kuala Lumpur and quickly reached a deal with Scomi to take over a factory that belonged to one of its subsidiaries. The subsidiary was called Scomi Precision Engineering, and it was known by its acronym as SCOPE. He told his new business partners that the SCOPE factory would be used to produce metal tubing for the petroleum and water-treatment industries.

Within a month, Tinner found himself in a small factory in Shah Alam, a city about fifteen miles west of Kuala Lumpur in a part of the country once famous for its rubber plantations. The tool-and-die factory and its staff of about thirty blue-shirted workers had been producing car parts and industrial tubing for several years. Tinner set about upgrading its capabilities, ordering the specialized lathes and other machinery required to begin manufacturing the centrifuge components. Material began pouring in from around the world: three hundred tons of high-strength aluminum from Bikar Metal Asia in Singapore, one hundred tons of steel alloy from Kobe Steel Company in Japan, and components shipped from the Tinner factory in Switzerland. Khan sent drawings for the factory layout and a video of the centrifuge manufacturing facility within his complex back in Pakistan. Within weeks, the SCOPE factory was transformed from a run-of-the-mill operation into a small replica of Khan's own centrifuge manufacturing facility. Unlike the polyglot workers from Dubai, Tinner found himself instructing experienced men who had worked in the factory when it manufactured products for the oil-and-gas and automotive industries. They adapted quickly to the new equipment, and Tinner was confident they would soon be turning out components for centrifuges.

Jim Kinsman adapted quickly, too. When he first learned that Tahir had packed up and left town after MI6 searched his offices, the CIA case officer was furious. The Americans and the British had been cooperating closely on the Khan chase for years. MI6 had shared its transcript of Khan and Friedrich Tinner in Casablanca. Kinsman had kept his counterparts in London up to date on the information coming from Urs Tinner. That was one of the reasons British intelligence had warned young Atif Amin off looking into Desert Electrical. And even now, senior officers from the two intelligence services were negotiating secretly with Libyan officials to persuade Kaddafi to give up his nuclear ambitions. But some elements of British intelligence had been impatient for action against Khan. On several occasions, there had been debates at senior levels of the two intelligence establishments about when to stop Khan's network. Kinsman was well aware of the growing impatience from the British cousins, and it was possible that someone from MI6 had tried to force the game to its conclusion by entering Tahir's offices. But he did not know for sure what had happened.

Fortunately for the CIA, the sudden decision to move the centrifuge operation to Malaysia was not the end of Tinner's usefulness as a spy. He was still in place, and his early reports indicated that Tahir had found a facility that was finally going to manufacture centrifuge components for Libya. Kinsman would have to take advantage of the new situation, and he thought he knew just how to do so.

FOR MONTHS, THE CIA HAD been working to insert sabotaged equipment into the procurement process that the network was using for Iran and Libya. It was delicate work. If the sabotage was too extensive, it would be discovered; the Iranians or Libyans could then work backward and find the vulnerable spot in their pipeline. But if the sabotage was too subtle, the equipment might work at or near expectations, with the end result of helping a rogue nuclear program rather than hindering it.

A few people within the intelligence community believed that was exactly what the CIA had done in early 2000 in an audacious plan to sabotage Iranian attempts to build a nuclear weapon. The CIA was well aware that the Iranians aspired to join the nuclear elite, and there were concerns about the pace of Tehran's progress in designing a workable atomic warhead. In February of that year, the Counter-Proliferation Division at the CIA had secretly dispatched a Russian scientist to Vienna. The scientist carried blueprints for a critical part of a Russian design for a nuclear weapon, called a TBA 480 high-voltage block. The device was a "firing block" that was critical to triggering the perfect implosion required for a nuclear chain reaction. It was the very kind of engineering accomplishment that contributed to the success of the Russian and Americans nuclear weapons programs, while some other countries struggled. The Russian scientist had been given a startling mission—make contact with the Iranian permanent mission to the International Atomic Energy Agency in Vienna and sell them the design. It was called Operation MERLIN.

Years earlier, the Russian had defected secretly to the United States. His CIA contact explained to the reluctant spy that the agency had received the plans from another Russian defector a year before. This operation was an effort to see how far along the Iranians were in their bomb building and to identify the person at the embassy in Vienna who was involved in gathering intelligence for Iran. The Russian was instructed to portray himself as a disaffected former Soviet weapons expert who needed money. The scientist could not believe that the Americans wanted to give Iran the solution to one of the biggest engineering hurdles in building an atomic weapon. He thought it would offer the Iranians the chance to move much more quickly toward developing a nuclear weapon. Don't worry, the case officer told him, the Iranians already had the design. Still, the Russian was frightened by the prospect of walking around Vienna with plans for a nuclear bomb. After difficulty persuading the Russian to carry out the assignment, the CIA officer did not want to increase his agent's fears by explaining to him that he would be double-crossing the Iranians because U.S. nuclear scientists had altered the design slightly to render any firing blocks built from it unworkable.

The Russian was told not to open the envelope containing the design, but he disobeyed orders shortly after arriving in Vienna. Studying the blueprints, he easily identified several flaws that had been inserted into the plans by American nuclear scientists. Sure, the flaws would render the firing block inoperative, but the Russian suspected they were so obvious that the Iranians would identify and correct them. Again acting on his own, he added a letter warning the Iranians about the flaws and offering to help them figure out how to make it work, provided they were willing to pay for his assistance. The Russian dropped off the package at the Iranian mission. A few days later, the National Security Agency at Fort Meade, Maryland, reported that an Iranian official in

Vienna had changed his schedule abruptly and returned to Tehran. The assumption was that he had taken the trigger design with him.

The decision to provide the Iranians with such a critical design, even with built-in flaws, was disclosed in *State of War*, the 2006 book by James Risen. "The Russian's fears about the operation were well founded," Risen wrote. "He was the front man for what may have been one of the most reckless operations in the modern history of the CIA, one that may have helped put nuclear weapons in the hands of a charter member of what President George W. Bush has called 'the axis of evil.'"

Operation MERLIN was not the only reckless operation carried out by the CIA in its desperation to derail Iran's nuclear program. There were other efforts to insert sabotaged equipment into the Iranian procurement pipeline, and evidence would emerge later that the Iranians proved themselves fully capable of discovering the flaws and correcting them.

In fact, about the time the Russian defector was turning over the firing block design in Vienna, scientists at the Los Alamos National Laboratory in New Mexico were at work on another secret project; this one was designed to insert sabotaged equipment into the nuclear programs of Iran and Libya. The assignment was given to a weapons expert at Los Alamos known within the CIA as "the mad scientist." Working with Kinsman and others, he came up with a scheme to make slight alterations in a type of vacuum pump that was indispensable for the operation of a uranium enrichment plant. The scientist was confident that he could make undetectable changes in the pumps that would cause them to malfunction at random intervals after they were installed.

Though today Los Alamos is a sprawling complex of modern buildings housing about fifteen thousand employees and contractors, the lab was once among the most secretive places in America. It was founded during World War II as a secret community where scientists and engineers developed the first nuclear weapons as part of the Manhattan Project. In those days, it was known as "Site Y," and its only mailing address was a post office box in Santa Fe, thirty-five miles to the southeast. After the two atomic bombs developed there were dropped on Hiroshima and Nagasaki, Los Alamos became the most famous nuclear facility in the world. These days it is home to scientists working on a variety of projects, ranging from nanotechnology to fusion power. But along with Lawrence Livermore National Laboratory in California, Los Alamos remains the U.S. government's primary classified facility for developing nuclear weapons.

Scientists at Los Alamos often work closely with the CIA and other U.S. intelligence agencies. Back in the late 1980s, they had used designs obtained by the CIA to build a model of Pakistan's atomic bomb as part of an effort to convince Benazir Bhutto, then the prime minister of Pakistan, that her country was indeed building nuclear weapons. So there was nothing unusual about the request from Kinsman and his colleagues in the agency's Counter-Proliferation Division for help in sabotaging some equipment destined for Tehran and Tripoli.

Two major challenges remained. First, the plan could not use vacuum pumps manufactured in the United States because they would be likely to attract undue attention from the Iranians and Libyans. Second, the altered devices had to be inserted smoothly into the flow of equipment that the Khan network was shipping to both countries.

To solve the first problem, the scientist suggested using pumps manufactured in Europe. They would fit in with much of the rest of the equipment supplied by the network. When the CIA agreed, the lab ordered seven vacuum pumps from the American subsidiary of Pfeiffer Vacuum Technology, a well-known German company. The order specified that the pumps should be equipped with motors that operated on a 50-hertz frequency, an electronic network that would be more common in places like Libya and Iran than the United States. In mid-April, seven pumps, bearing serial numbers from 22003324 to 22003348, were shipped from the PVT plant in Hesse, Germany, to Los Alamos National Laboratory, Bikini Atoll Road, Building SM30, Los Alamos, New Mexico, USA. They cost forty thousand dollars. Once the pumps arrived at Los Alamos, the scientist there made small adjustments in the mechanisms. He assured the CIA that the pumps would malfunction and that the sabotage was so subtle it would be impossible to detect.

To get the pumps to Libya and Iran, Kinsman planned to use the CIA operative who had worked for Friedrich Tinner back in 1998 and had set up a new business in Dubai. In a shady operation like nuclear smuggling, people sometimes overlook past transgressions; Marco ignored his father's advice and started buying pumps from his old friend. Six of the Pfeiffer pumps were combined with an order that the operative sent to Libya; a seventh went to Iran with another shipment out of Dubai.

The sabotage of the pumps and the altered nuclear firing block were only part of a highly secretive effort by the CIA to make sure that neither Iran nor Libya developed the capacity to build a working nuclear weapon.

One of the other efforts involved tampering with devices known as "uninterruptible power supplies," or UPS. These devices control the flow of massive amounts of electricity required to run the centrifuges. They are calibrated to precise power levels to ensure smooth operations of machines spinning near the speed of sound. The Khan network was relying on a manufacturer in Turkey to provide the UPS for both Libya and Iran. Less is known about how the UPS devices were sabotaged. This time, the CIA could not get the equipment shipped to Los Alamos for alterations. So the sabotage was carried out at some point before the devices were shipped to Iran and Libya. One scenario is that CIA technicians managed to gain access to the devices at the plant in Turkey and alter them slightly. More likely, however, the power supply regulators were sabotaged while in one of the network's warehouses in Dubai while awaiting shipment to Iran and Libya. The goal was to disrupt the steady flow of electricity that was essential to the consistent operation of the centrifuges. The resulting interruption would cause the centrifuges to spin out of control and explode when they reached critical speeds, creating havoc inside any enrichment facility where they were installed.

When Urs Tinner told Kinsman that the network would soon be producing usable components for centrifuges at its new factory in Malaysia, the CIA case officer dusted off yet another aspect of the agency's sabotage plan. Collaborating with the same ingenious weapons scientist at Los Alamos, the agency's counterproliferation experts developed a list of incremental changes that the scientist promised would render centrifuges useless when they reached the high velocity required to enrich uranium. Centrifuges used to enrich uranium must spin flawlessly at well above the speed of sound for months on end. That means all of the hundred or so components that make up a centrifuge must be manufactured to the strictest tolerances. Even the oil left by a single fingerprint could be enough to push a machine out of balance and bring down an entire cascade of centrifuges. Sabotaging them would not take more than the most incremental adjustment. The trick was to make changes that were too subtle even for the trained eye to detect. If the plan worked, thousands of imperceptibly flawed centrifuges would be manufactured and installed in the Libyan enrichment plant. Only after the machines were spinning in concert would the tiny flaws cause the centrifuges to crash. The Los Alamos scientist who had designed the sabotage could envision centrifuges flying out of balance and careening through a giant cascade hall, destroying everything in their path. Even in the aftermath of such a catastrophe, it would take a master forensic scientist to detect the tiny alterations responsible for the failures.

Kinsman took the list back to Malaysia for a meeting with his spy near the end of 2002. Sitting down with Tinner, Kinsman went over the precise changes he wanted made to the specifications for some of the components that would soon be manufactured at the SCOPE factory. The instructions were very specific. In one modification, he was told to substitute steel for part of a centrifuge component that was supposed to be manufactured entirely from high-strength aluminum. The result was that the component would malfunction as it heated up from the spinning of the centrifuge, sending the machine out of balance and causing it to career through the plant, knocking over other centrifuges like a bowling ball knocking down pins. This was one of several nearly imperceptible alterations that Tinner was asked to make.

By this time, Tinner had grown more comfortable living a double life. He was a master technician and he envisioned no difficulty in making these minor adjustments. He agreed to Kinsman's plan.

THE OPPORTUNITY TO SABOTAGE THE parts arose not long after the meeting. Tinner was training the workers on the new lathes and other machine tools. Khan had sent one of his technical experts from Pakistan to show Tahir and Tinner the drawings for the centrifuge components that would be manufactured at SCOPE. The Pakistani also brought some sample components. Tahir knew nothing about the mechanics of manufacturing a part. Still frightened by the episode in Dubai, however, he insisted on cutting off all the markings that identified the designs as coming from Khan's lab.

Looking over the drawings sent by Khan, Tinner recognized that he could make the alterations for the sabotage on the documents themselves. Doing so would provide insurance in case any of the technicians at the SCOPE plant were smart enough to compare the components to the drawings. The first part of his plan was to tell Tahir that the drawings were smudged and incomplete. "These are dirty drawings," he complained. "Not all the dimensions are here." Tinner said he needed to scan the designs into the computer system. That way, Tinner explained, he could clean them up and begin turning out the precision components required by machines as sophisticated as a centrifuge. Tahir had no reason to challenge the Swiss technician, and he did not have the technical capacity to evaluate the drawings himself, so he agreed. But Tahir remained on guard and each time Tinner finished scanning a design into the computer, Tahir took the original and shredded it.

Tinner followed most of the instructions from Los Alamos as he reworked the designs for various components on his computer at SCOPE. In one case, he altered the diameter of a hole by less than a tenth of a millimeter. In another, he manufactured a centrifuge component out of steel instead of aluminum, which meant that it would malfunction before the centrifuge reached maximum speed. But Tinner understood the workings of a centrifuge at least as well as any American scientists, so he added some of his own alterations, too. Because the tolerances are so fine, the internal works of centrifuges must be cleaned in an ultrasound bath before they are assembled; Tinner skipped that step, allowing abrasive dust to remain and ensuring that the machines would wear out faster. Before the first component was manufactured, Tinner was sure that the centrifuges emerging from his factory would never enrich uranium to the weapons-grade requirements of an atomic bomb.

Kinsman kept tabs on the progress as the plant began to manufacture the components for the ten thousand centrifuges that were to be installed eventually in the Libyan enrichment plant. In the summer of 2002, the first shipment of parts was sent by sea to Tripoli, the capital of Libya. Despite the sabotage, Kinsman and his superiors began to wonder if the time was approaching to close down the network. Libya was moving closer to building an enrichment plant. If Kaddafi could not be persuaded to give up his plans, Libya would have received much of the material and technology to build an atomic bomb while the CIA stood by and watched.

Concern rose in August when an Iranian opposition group held a press conference in Washington and disclosed that Iran was engaged in a large-scale, clandestine nuclear program. The group, the National Council of Resistance of Iran, provided the first public evidence that the Iranians were building a huge underground enrichment plant near Natanz, in the central part of the country, and planning for a heavy-water reactor near Arak, in northern Iran. The origin of the group's information was unclear. Its representatives said that they had obtained the intelligence from sources inside Iran who were opposed to the regime. But there were strong suspicions that either the Americans or the Israelis had used the exile group to publicize the information without leaving their own fingerprints.

Certainly, the existence of the two supposedly secret nuclear sites was known to senior members of the Bush administration and the American intelligence community. "When they held that press conference, I wasn't personally unhappy about it," said John Bolton, who was undersecretary of state for arms control at the time. "I wanted people to know some of what we knew because I wanted to dramatize in this country and Europe the threat that I thought Iran's nuclear weapons program posed. I had to kind of bite my tongue at the time, but I was perfectly happy to have it treated as news."

The news shook the International Atomic Energy Agency, which opened an immediate investigation into the allegations. Khan's role in providing critical centrifuge technology to the Iranians was still secret and he took immediate steps to cover his tracks. Khan telephoned one of his contacts in the Iranian government and advised him to tell his associates to lie to the IAEA if his name came up. He also suggested that the Iranians claim that key figures who had dealt with Khan's operation had died. In an effort to tighten the security on his end, Khan instructed Tahir to destroy all records of the sales to Iran. The network's dealings with Iran had decreased sharply earlier in the decade, but Tahir flew back to Dubai from Malaysia to shred documents and erase computer files connected to the Iran project.

It remained business as usual for the Libyan project. Throughout the remainder of 2002, SCOPE was receiving monthly shipments of raw material such as high-strength aluminum and steel alloys and turning out thousands of components for the Libyan centrifuges. In November 2002, a shipment of more than one hundred thousand components left Malaysia, bound first for Dubai and then Tripoli. A third shipment, which included rotors manufactured from the aluminum, went the following month. Along with the turning out of components, the training of Libyan workers had shifted from Dubai to Malaysia. At the SCOPE factory in Shah Alam, they learned to operate the sophisticated machinery that Khan envisioned would one day be installed at an enrichment facility in Libya.

Tinner continued to submit regular reports to Kinsman at the CIA about the shipments. The Americans had enough information to close down the Malaysian operation and arrest Tahir and a host of other network participants on three continents. They knew about an operation under way in South Africa to build an elaborate system to feed uranium hexafluoride gas into the Libyan centrifuges and extract the enriched uranium at the end of the process. They knew that Khan had delivered the Chinese nuclear warhead plans to the Libyans more than two years earlier. And they were aware that Khan had used an airline controlled by retired Pakistani military officers to ship highly controlled uranium hexafluoride gas to feed the centrifuges from North Korea to Tripoli.

By this time, the CIA had learned an enormous amount about where the Khan network was producing equipment for enriching uranium and to whom it was selling this equipment. But senior CIA officials right up to the director, George Tenet, continued to argue that acting prematurely would only set back Khan's operation, allowing him and possibly others to resume their activities later. This approach dated back to 1975, when the CIA first decided not to stop Khan, and it was as flawed in 2002 as it had been nearly three decades earlier. The truth is that the CIA was addicted to information, not action. From case officers like Kinsman in the field to senior officials providing daily intelligence briefings to the president of the United States, intelligence was the source of power that kept them in the game. Recruiting spies, developing nifty tricks to sabotage equipment, watching as Libya accumulated nuclear technology and Iran made steady progress toward enriching uranium for its bomb, all of these activities became an end in themselves. The result was that the game of espionage overshadowed any inclination to take direct action to stop the spread of this dangerous technology as quickly as possible. The objective was not action but information.

The road to getting more intelligence would run through the Tinner family. Back at Langley, Kinsman and his colleagues in counterproliferation had assembled an extensive dossier on Friedrich, Marco, and Urs Tinner. There was more than enough evidence to arrest all three of them, though Kinsman had promised to protect Urs. But the decision was made at the top levels of the CIA to keep the game going and recruit the rest of the family. Each of the Tinners was involved in slightly different aspects of the nuclear trafficking business. Therefore, Friedrich and Marco could add to what the CIA was already getting from Urs, especially since he was tucked away in Malaysia. Friedrich had remained close to Khan, and the agency assumed that he would have useful information about the expanded workings of the network. For his part, Marco had been manufacturing some of the more sophisticated components for the centrifuges in Libya. He also appeared to be the central record keeper for the family business, including its dealings with the network.

The CIA did not want to trespass on Swiss soil. Recruiting a Swiss citizen as a spy was illegal under Swiss espionage law; doing so on Swiss territory would compound the problem. Further, if Friedrich objected, he might blow the whistle and bring in the police before his would-be spymasters could get out of the country. So in December 2002, a CIA officer contacted Friedrich. It is unclear what Tinner was told, whether he was threatened with prosecution or offered money. It is even uncertain whether Friedrich knew that Urs was already working for the CIA. Whatever the threat or inducement, Friedrich showed up as requested at the American embassy in Vienna in December. Kinsman flew to Vienna for the meeting. Before the day was over, Friedrich agreed that he and Marco would join Urs on the CIA payroll.

Urs had been a good asset, but signing up an entire family at the heart of Khan's network was an enormous coup. In March 2003, a few days after the American invasion of Iraq, President George W. Bush and British prime minister Tony Blair met at Camp David, outside Washington, to discuss the unfolding events in the Middle East. Room was found on the busy agenda to brief the two leaders about a recent feeler from Libya's Colonel Moammar Kaddafi, who was sounding like he might be willing to give up what CIA chief George Tenet later referred to as his "very expensive flirtation with WMD." Tenet and his British counterpart, Sir Richard Dearlove, provided intelligence updates to Bush and Blair about the fledgling talks with the Libyans. Tenet said that American and British intelligence were working together to increase the pressure on Kaddafi. Bush and Blair debated Kaddafi's motivation. They recognized that Kaddafi wanted to find a better place for his country in the world. They also did not discount the effect that 150,000 U.S. troops in Iraq might be having on the Libyan leader.

The CIA chief explained that the primary supplier for Libya's nuclear project was A. Q. Khan, and he explained that the CIA had recently recruited an entire family of Swiss engineers who were trusted participants in Khan's nuclear network. The agency expected to have enough intelligence soon to shut down the supply chain and expose Libya's clandestine nuclear ambitions. Tenet was told by Bush to take advantage of the opening with Kaddafi. When he returned to CIA headquarters from Camp David, he handed the assignment of persuading Kaddafi to turn in his nuclear weapons to Stephen Kappes.

By the summer of 2003, the CIA and MI6 were preparing for the endgame. Kinsman and his team had met several times with all three Tinners, and they were determined to learn as much as possible about every nook and cranny of the Khan enterprise. In June, Kinsman summoned the Tinners to the lengthy debriefing session in Liechtenstein.

CHAPTER SIX

VADUZ, LIECHTENSTEIN

The Tinners had been receiving relatively small payments from Kinsman for several months. The total for all three of them didn't amount to much more than pocket change for the CIA, a few hundred thousand dollars at the most—Urs had received the most because he had been working with the agency for the longest and had taken the biggest risks. As he prepared for the lengthy debriefing session, Kinsman knew he would have to come up with more cash. The stakes were high. The long pursuit of Khan and his accomplices was nearing its conclusion. The CIA was willing to pay a substantial sum to its spies to try to get as much intelligence as possible to close down every known element of the network. If action were taken against the nuclear black market without identifying all of the individuals and companies involved, there was a high risk that they would start up again in some new iteration.

The plan called for using a CIA front company to launder the first large payment to the Tinners. The company was called Big Black River Technologies, and it came complete with an address, phone number, website, and business cards for its phony employees. According to the cover story, the company was located in Washington, D.C., at 1825 I Street Northwest, an office building that occupied a full city block not far from the White House. Listings for the company had been inserted in various business directories and its website, www.bigblackriver.com, boasted that it provided "top quality products and services" to the aerospace and defense industries. Anyone who went looking for the office, however, would find an empty suite and mailroom clerks who said the company had never received a letter or a package.

A million dollars was wired to Traco Group International, a subsidiary of his Swiss company that Marco had set up on Tortola in the British Virgin Islands. The transfer was made on June 21, the day after the midnight intrusion at his apartment. As part of the cover story, Marco had signed a fictional contract with Big Black River Technologies. The contract claimed that the Tinners were selling the rights for manufacturing vacuum equipment and proprietary information about the valves and other devices. The two agents who signed on behalf of Big Black River used cover names, W. James Kinsman and Sean D. Mahaffey.

The CIA has a long history of using fronts, called proprietary companies, to support secret operations. The phony companies work as mail drops, provide apparently legal means of making payments to assets, and support false identities for the CIA's most clandestine frontline agents, who work without diplomatic immunity and are known as "nonofficial cover officers," or NOCs. During the Vietnam War, the CIA set up an entire airline, Air America, to ferry shipments and troops for the secret war in Laos. At one point more than three hundred pilots and mechanics were working for the CIA's secret airline in Laos and Thailand. Later, after the terrorist attacks on New York and Washington on September 11, 2001, the agency established dozens of front groups around the world to arrange flights for detainees in the war on terror and to run the "black" prisons where many of them were tortured.

Most fronts are more prosaic. In 1994, the Counter-Proliferation Division had established a company called Brewster Jennings & Associates to provide cover for NOCs working in Europe. Its address was an elegant downtown office building in Boston and it had a listing under Dun & Bradstreet, the business credit agency. But the company was nothing more than a post office box and a telephone number connected to an answering machine. One of the NOCs who used Brewster Jennings & Associates was the case officer Valerie Plame.

Recruited by the agency straight out of Pennsylvania State University in 1985, Plame had trained as a covert officer in the Directorate of Operations and was eventually posted to Athens, a dangerous assignment for a CIA officer. In 1975, the CIA station chief in Athens, Richard Welch, was gunned down outside his home there by the terrorist organization known as 17 November. It was the beginning of a campaign by the group to target American and British intelligence agents and diplomats. In Athens, Plame posed as a State Department employee and her job was to spot and recruit spies for the agency. In the early 1990s, she moved deeper into the clandestine world when she began working under nonofficial cover, the most secretive of the agency's frontline officers. NOCs do not pretend to work for the U.S. government and, if arrested, they face jail because they do not have diplomatic immunity. It is a high-wire act, only for the smartest and most unflappable of officers. By 1997, Plame had joined the Counter-Proliferation Division, where she posed as a businesswoman working for the energy consulting firm Brewster Jennings & Associates.

In the summer of 2003, Plame was gathering information on Iraq's supposed nuclear weapons program when her world was turned upside down. Her husband, former ambassador Joseph Wilson, had written an opinion piece in *The New York Times* accusing the Bush administration of twisting intelligence about weapons of mass destruction to justify the Iraq War. The White House retaliated with a whispering campaign to reporters aimed at undercutting Wilson's credibility by exposing his wife as a CIA officer. On July 10, the conservative columnist Robert Novak wrote a column identifying Plame as a CIA officer, effectively ending her ability to work undercover and endangering her and the sources she had developed over the years. The incident eventually led to an investigation by a special prosecutor and the conviction of I. Lewis "Scooter" Libby, chief of staff to Vice President Dick Cheney, for perjury and obstruction of justice for his role in revealing Plame's CIA role.

The CIA was at the heart of the debacle over the failure to find weapons of mass destruction in Iraq. The episode showed that the CIA had become deeply politicized during the Bush administration, damaging its credibility and threatening its independence. The accusations angered agency veterans, who were determined to demonstrate that the CIA still had a significant role to play in American foreign policy. Jim Kinsman was trying to bring home the kind of victory that might repair the agency's tarnished reputation. His ultimate success depended heavily on squeezing every possible piece of intelligence from the Tinners. And in case the Tinners were not forthcoming, Kinsman and his colleagues had developed an insurance plan.

For the meeting with the Tinners, Kinsman chose Vaduz, the capital of Liechtenstein, the tiny principality of about sixty square miles bordered on its west by Switzerland and on the east by Austria, for the meeting with the Tinner family. The city sits along the Rhine River and the royal family lives in a medieval castle high above its restored houses and quiet streets. The location was selected because it was outside Switzerland and convenient for the Tinners, who lived just a few miles across the border.

The strategy was straightforward. Kinsman brought a team of CIA experts and a nuclear weapons specialist from the national laboratory at Oak Ridge, Tennessee, to Vaduz for the meetings. The sessions would continue until the Americans were satisfied that they knew the tiniest details of Khan's network and precisely what had been sold to Libya, Iran, and anyplace else the ring had done business. To persuade the Tinners to talk, Kinsman had the authority from his superiors within the Directorate of Operations to pay them a million dollars. It was an unusually large amount of money to offer to assets in one installment, but the stakes made it seem like a worthwhile investment.

Kinsman had met Friedrich and Marco several times since Friedrich agreed to work for the agency back in December. In January, Kinsman had spent two days eating, drinking, and skiing with both men at a resort in Innsbruck, Austria. Those initial sessions had been not so much to gather information as to make the Tinners comfortable with him. In meetings with Marco alone in March and May, Kinsman had worked hard to obtain useful intelligence from his new spy. But the early meetings were only the preliminaries to Vaduz. On the morning of June 16, when the Tinners drove the short distance to a quiet hotel in Vaduz, the intention was to keep them there as long as necessary to extract as much information as possible.

Despite their seeming cooperation, there were concerns that the Tinners might not be divulging all of their secrets; after all, the family had been involved in deceptive trafficking in nuclear-related technology for three decades. So Kinsman and his colleagues had hatched a strategy to verify what they were being told and to try to confirm that nothing was being withheld. As they sat in the hotel the first day, the CIA case officer explained that part of what the agency required for its million dollars was free access to their records. The payment would be conditioned on the CIA conducting a thorough search of the records of the family's dealings with Khan and the rest of the network. To protect the Tinners down the road, the search would be disguised as a burglary in case the Swiss authorities later discovered that the family had broken Swiss law by cooperating with American intelligence. Even with permission from the Tinners, the CIA would be breaking Swiss law. Discovery would lead to a huge scandal, and possibly even criminal charges against the agents who were operating without diplomatic immunity. Kinsman stressed the need for secrecy to the Tinners. In the unlikely event the CIA team was discovered, the Tinners were admonished to say they knew nothing of what the Americans were doing. The Tinners had no choice if they wanted to get their million dollars and remain under the protection of the CIA.

On the night of June 20, while the Tinners were tucked away in the hotel in Vaduz, a six-person team broke into Traco's offices. Along with Kinsman and four other CIA agents, the team included the nuclear expert from Oak Ridge who had been participating in the debriefing sessions. The team members copied the contents of the office computer and photographed documents from the file cabinets. The intrusion netted a fair amount of information, but the decision was made to take another step, one that might not have been disclosed to the Tinners.

The following night, the same six people broke into Marco's apartment in the holiday village of Jenins. The search at Marco's apartment yielded a far bigger cache. In the living room of the apartment, the Oak Ridge expert paused to examine some of the material on the computers. What he saw was enough to conclude that they contained potentially dangerous designs for nuclear weapons. As the team scoured the apartment and the computers, thousands of files and e-mails were downloaded onto portable devices, which the two technical specialists on the team immediately carried back to Langley for detailed evaluation.

For reasons that have yet to be explained, instead of taking the computers and these highly dangerous files, Kinsman and his colleagues left everything behind. They did so even though they had seen enough from the preliminary examination to understand that the computers contained some of the most sensitive proliferation information imaginable. There is no rational explanation for leaving the material in place. The job of the CIA, and of the agents who broke into Tinner's apartment, was to stop the spread of nuclear weapons. So why leave blueprints for nuclear weapons in an unsecure location, in the hands of known traffickers? Even the fleeting first glance at the documents had confirmed the fears that the Tinners had not been telling the CIA everything. It was a conclusion that would be even clearer after the copies were evaluated by experts back at Langley.

THE DEBRIEFINGS CONTINUED FOR FOUR more days, but the investigation's momentum had shifted to Langley. There, analysts were poring over the thousands of computer files, e-mails, documents, and CDs that the burglars had copied from Marco's computers. Many of the e-mails were written in code and work was still going on to crack the system because the Tinners had not been asked to provide the CIA with the keys to the encryption. But the files had already yielded important information, some of which the Tinners had neglected to mention. As expected, the files contained the designs for two types of centrifuges that Khan had stolen from Urenco in the 1970s and developed in Pakistan, called the P-1 and P-2. The CIA already knew that he had provided prototypes and designs for both types to Iran and Libya. But the analysts were surprised to find that the computers also held designs for a third, more advanced centrifuge known as the G-4. The version bundled four of the slender cylinders together, providing a faster, more efficient means of enriching uranium. Nuclear experts from the national weapons labs and the CIA analysts had no idea that Khan possessed plans for this type of centrifuge, and the discovery caused a stir. The basic model was similar to the designs for the two types of centrifuges he had stolen from Urenco. The best guess was that Khan had also gotten away with an even more advanced version, which was under development at Urenco at the time. Somehow Khan had managed to keep it secret for nearly thirty years. The discovery in Switzerland raised a number of troubling possibilities, including the prospect that the G-4 design had been sold to Iran and was under development at a secret facility there. If that were true, the Iranians could be closer than the outside world knew to enriching enough uranium to build its first nuclear bomb.

Even more troubling than the ghost centrifuge were indications that centrifuge components and manufacturing equipment were being siphoned off for an unknown fourth customer. As the CIA analysts evaluated the files taken from the Tinner computers, they confirmed that the greatest danger in the espionage world is often not what you know but what you don't know. It was apparent that, despite years of monitoring by the CIA and MI6, the Khan network may have provided nuclear equipment and know-how to a still-unknown customer.

Some of the files contained invoices for shipments that had escaped the monitoring by American intelligence—and that the Tinners had failed to mention in any of their many debriefings. In fact, no one back at Langley could be certain that there were not multiple additional buyers, possibly including other countries, perhaps even a terrorist organization with deep financial resources like Al Qaeda. As the analysts reconstructing the transactions from the computers built their new portrait of the Khan network, they found that several thousand centrifuge components had disappeared. The stuff could have gone almost anywhere. Outposts of the network were strung across the globe, from the centrifuge factory in Malaysia to an engineering firm in South Africa where veterans of that country's nuclear program were at work on the Libyan project, from the high-tech operations in Switzerland and Germany to the hermit kingdom of North Korea, which was also contributing to the long shopping list. The Tinners were only one part of the network with their own business operations in Switzerland, Dubai, Italy, Singapore, and Russia.

The banking records on the computers hinted at the sums involved—tens of millions of dollars passing through accounts in Dubai, Zurich, Liechtenstein, and even Macao, the semiautonomous Chinese city. There was still more information on the computers that Marco or someone had encrypted, waiting for the experts at the National Security Agency to crack the code.

Then there was the matter of the designs for nuclear weapons, which had popped up on the hard drive of the laptop that belonged to Urs that Kinsman had found on the closet shelf. The first impression of the nuclear expert inside Marco's apartment was accurate: These were blueprints for a sophisticated nuclear warhead. The plans appeared to be incomplete, but there was no way of knowing whether a more complete set existed somewhere else within the Khan network. Even the incomplete designs were deemed dangerous enough that experts from Los Alamos and Oak Ridge were summoned to Washington to examine them. The verdict was that they were portions of the design for a Pakistani nuclear warhead. Their origin was confirmed by the initials on each document, "PAB," which the analysts concluded stood for "Pakistani Atomic Bomb." The same hard drive also contained a more complete set of blueprints for a second nuclear device, one that experts said appeared to be from a 1960s-era Chinese warhead, which the CIA knew Khan had sold to Libya already. But the greatest concern was the Pakistani design; it was more sophisticated and small enough to fit on missiles already in the Iranian arsenal. There were two pressing questions: Did more of these designs exist on other computers connected with the network and had others already received copies?

The stakes had been high from the start. But now, the prospect of advanced nuclear weapons designs floating freely around the Internet made it more vital than ever to track down every element of the Khan network before moving in for the kill.

The new peek inside the Khan network was causing grave concerns within the CIA. They thought they had monitored the technology that the Pakistani was selling very closely, particularly in recent years. But the contents of the Tinners' computers were shaking that confidence. In addition to the bomb plans from the Pakistani arsenal, the computers contained designs for the G-4 centrifuge, which the CIA had no idea Khan was peddling, along with evidence that significant amounts of equipment had vanished. Most of the alarming disclosures were contained on the laptop that belonged to Urs Tinner, who had traveled widely.

In a later interview, Urs acknowledged that he had made copies on his personal computer of virtually every piece of information about the network's business that passed through his hands in Dubai and Malaysia. But he said that he had not bothered to read much of what he had copied, adding that he knew nothing of any designs for nuclear weapons.

"There were many documents on my computer that I did not know because they were copies of Tahir's files," he said. "I copied everything from Tahir and everything that I gave to the third party. I didn't read it all. I may have read the names, but I was not that interested and my English is not good enough to read all that." (The phrase "third party" was a reference by Tinner to the CIA; though he acknowledged working with the Americans, he refused to use the agency's formal name or discuss his relations with Kinsman or other individuals.)

At CIA headquarters, the contents of the computers in Jenins raised serious questions about what else may have gone to Iran, Libya, and North Korea—or to an unknown customer. For some within the agency, the decision to let the network operate for this long was beginning to look like a bigger gamble than anyone realized. Clearly more technology had been set loose than anyone had known. And there was no way to know where some of it might have wound up. Certainly American and Israeli intelligence knew at the time that Iran was working on a design for a nuclear warhead. Had Khan or someone else in the network sold the Iranians the blueprints from Pakistan? It was well-known that Khan had provided the centrifuge designs and components that jump-started Iran's uranium enrichment program in the late 1980s. Why wouldn't Khan have sold them the rest of what they needed to build an atomic bomb? No one would be able to answer that question until Khan was arrested and interrogated.

The new evidence demanded urgent action. But closing down Khan completely was still not a sure thing. In the years since Pakistan joined the world's nuclear powers, Khan had become a revered and influential figure in his homeland. Persuading any Pakistani leader to arrest the man known as "the father of the Islamic bomb" would be a tall order. When it came to the current leader, the military dictator Pervez Musharraf, it was a particularly big request. Musharraf was increasingly unpopular in Pakistan, where he was seen by many as a puppet of the American government in its war against the Taliban in Afghanistan. The U.S. invasion of Iraq a few months earlier had ratcheted up anti-American fervor in Pakistan and the rest of the Muslim world. It would take a rock-solid case against Khan to force Musharraf to risk further wrath from his own people by arresting a national hero. Finally, the Americans did not have unlimited leverage over Musharraf. The United States may have been providing billions of dollars in military assistance to Pakistan to keep the country on its side in the fight against the Taliban in Afghanistan and Al Qaeda, which had hunkered down in the lawless tribal belt of northwestern Pakistan bordering Afghanistan, but the sense in many quarters was that the United States needed Pakistan more than Pakistan needed the United States. Even if Washington wanted to force Musharraf to act against Khan, it might not be able to do so.

Along with the potential resistance from Musharraf, the agency was concerned about whether it could force Colonel Kaddafi to abandon his dream of possessing nuclear weapons. He had already spent tens of millions of dollars buying equipment from Khan's network, much of which was sitting in crates in warehouses around Tripoli. The CIA's nuclear weapons experts thought it was unlikely that Libya could build a weapon for many years, but Kaddafi had not survived more than three decades in power by being a pushover. He would have to be convinced that relinquishing his nuclear ambitions was in his best interests.

Over the years, the debate within the CIA and other branches of the U.S. government had focused on when to pull the plug on the Khan network. The step could have been taken on any number of occasions, and some members of the intelligence community and other agencies had argued for taking action sooner because they were alarmed by the growing reach of the black market. The discussion began during the second Clinton administration, when U.S. intelligence began taking Iran's nuclear ambitions seriously and finally understood the connection to Khan. It continued into the early years of the Bush administration.

No matter which administration was arguing, the debate was over the significance of what they did not know. Some within the CIA and others from different government agencies contended that the Khan network should be allowed to continue until they understood its full parameters. Others inside government were more concerned that a country secretly building a nuclear weapon might buy the technology required to put it over the finish line while the United States waited to get more information.

"We began talking about what to do about Khan almost from the beginning of the administration," said Bolton, the chief arms control official under Bush. "I would characterize the debate as between views of what to do. One view was, we need to watch this and learn more about it and find out where all its tentacles reach and we shouldn't take action prematurely. The opposing view was, this is very serious, we don't live in a perfect world, and we have to stop this as soon as we can. For that side, it means acting against what we knew, so we don't lose track of elements that, by definition, we don't know about."

In his memoir, *At the Center of the Storm*, former CIA director George Tenet described the conundrum facing the Bush administration in mid-2003. He said that taking action earlier against Khan "might have dealt a temporary setback to Khan's scheme but would not have prevented it from springing up again somewhere else. . . . We had the goods on A. Q. Khan and his cohorts and we had reached a point where we had to act, but there were still some important matters to resolve."

Not all of the pressure to act came from within the U.S. government. MI6 had played a key role in uncovering information about the network and British agents had been involved in the initial negotiations with the Libyans. In fact, not long after the discovery of Khan's mega-deal with Libya, the British intelligence service had pressed the Americans to move immediately to close down the network. Senior MI6 officers worried that too much highly sensitive information had leaked already, creating an urgent need to act. Despite the new threat, those who argued that they needed more time to gather more information carried the day. But pressure was mounting to take action—the more the CIA learned about the operation, the more concerned even the doubters became about the advisability of allowing it to operate longer. The discovery of the Pakistani nuclear weapon designs on Tinner's hard drive reinforced the urgency.

WITH THE NEW PARTNERSHIP BOUGHT and paid for, the Vaduz debriefings ended on June 25. Friedrich and Marco drove home to Switzerland while Urs headed back to work in Malaysia. He left with strict instructions from his contacts to gather as much information as possible in the coming weeks, and plans were made for a follow-up meeting the next month in Singapore. Before his departure, Urs received a symbol of his significance to the CIA. Kinsman provided him with a code name and a telephone number in northern Virginia. The arrangement was straightforward: Urs would call the number, identify himself by his code name, and ask to speak to Kinsman. The call would trigger a personal meeting or sometimes a follow-up telephone call. The CIA uses the system with vetted sources worldwide, maintaining more than five hundred dedicated telephone numbers at headquarters in Langley to handle the calls. By using only cover names and by not having to leave a message, callers minimize the possibility of unfriendly governments overhearing sensitive information over the phone lines. The phones at the other end of the five hundred numbers are answered twenty-four hours a day, seven days a week, by clerks who match the caller's name with the name of the person to whom he asks to speak. A match triggers a response, according to the prearranged code established between the case officer and his asset.

On July 16, Kinsman and one of his CIA colleagues, a counter-proliferation expert named Sharon who worked in the Vienna station, met with Urs in Singapore. Tinner insisted on meeting outside Malaysia because Tahir seemed to be growing more suspicious of him. The Sri Lankan had insisted on cutting off markings that linked technical drawings to Khan's operation in Pakistan before turning them over to Tinner. Tahir also tried to monitor the technical work that Tinner did in the factory, but he lacked the expertise to understand what was going on there. The fears might seem small taken individually, but as they built up over the months, Tinner was left struggling to control the strands of his double life even as the factory seemed to be humming along. He had a sense of always looking over his shoulder, wondering whether Tahir or someone else suspected he was a spy for the CIA. Later Tinner described the mental strain in physical terms, saying: "There was a physical stress in working as a spy. Working, always looking behind you to see who is coming, it makes you stronger."

Singapore was a perfect location for the clandestine meeting. The SCOPE factory in Malaysia was buying lots of specialty metals from a supplier there, and Tinner had his own trading company in Singapore, too, giving plenty of reasons to travel there. During the meeting, Tinner provided a rundown on plans for another shipment of centrifuge parts to Libya. He said the shipment would be leaving early the next month and it was likely to contain as many as twenty-five thousand components. Some critical components in the shipment had been secretly sabotaged by Tinner, but the CIA still wanted to stop this batch of material before it got to Libya. At Kinsman's urging, Tinner promised to provide as much detailed information as possible on the shipment.

As a potential bonus, Tinner said that Khan was planning to visit the factory in Malaysia on August 27. Khan wanted to see for himself how the production was progressing. Kinsman seized on the opportunity to record Khan discussing nuclear proliferation, exactly the kind of proof that would force Musharraf to act. They discussed having Tinner wear a concealed recorder to the meeting, but Tinner balked. As an alternative, Kinsman offered him a cellular telephone capable of recording conversations. Tinner took one look at the phone and knew it would not work. The model was at least five years old, and he was well-known for always carrying the latest mobile phone. "Tahir would say, what are you doing with that old thing?" Tinner told Kinsman. He refused to accept the CIA phone, saying he would find his own means of recording the meeting. Before Tinner left to return to Malaysia, Kinsman reminded him to press Khan for information about any unknown customers.

Tinner himself had pondered the existence of an unknown customer. Before the move to Malaysia, when Tahir had claimed to have sold off all the equipment in Dubai, Tinner wondered just where it might have gone. But Tinner said he had no idea whether there was another customer. His view of the network's undertakings, while essential to the CIA, was relatively narrow. He was cut off from his family and, after moving to Malaysia, from any regular contact with Khan, too.

Kinsman continued to fill in as many gaps as possible in the agency's knowledge of the Khan network through the other Tinners and additional intelligence assets. Shortly after Tinner returned to Malaysia, he sent Marco an encrypted e-mail instructing him to remind his brother to find out as much as possible about the unidentified customer. He also told Marco to have Urs question where Khan had gotten the two tons of uranium hexafluoride gas that he had supplied to Libya several months earlier. International supplies of the gas are limited and highly regulated, and the CIA could not figure out how the Pakistani scientist had come up with the material he had sold to Libya. Marco sent the message, instructing his brother to press "the boss" for any information about the unknown customer and the origin of the uranium gas in Libya. He was not worried that anyone who intercepted the message would have been able to decipher its contents. When it came to sensitive communications about their illicit business, the Tinners used an old-fashioned book cipher encryption system.

The method is simple and effective: The people corresponding with each other must have identical editions of the same book. The book forms what is called the key text. To an outsider, the message appears to be a random series of numbers. To the recipient, however, each number directs the reader to a specific page, line, and word in the book serving as the original text. Unscrambling the message can take some time for the recipient, but the Tinners generally kept their communications brief, often using only text messages between mobile telephones or short e-mails. The book they were using at the time was the newest thriller by John Grisham, *The King of Torts*.

Urs received his brother's coded message while the factory outside Kuala Lumpur was making final preparations for the August shipment to Libya. The demands from Kinsman, especially the request to record his upcoming meeting with Khan, increased the pressure on Tinner. He discussed the strain in a 2009 interview on Swiss television. His description was instructive about his mind-set and actions as he prepared the shipment for Libya, which was scheduled to leave Kuala Lumpur for Dubai and then travel on to Libya aboard a German freighter called the *BBC China*. "I had identified the last delivery of the *BBC China*, the biggest cargo," he told the interviewer, Swiss journalist Hansjuerg Zumstein. "I said to myself, we must prevent this material from reaching its destination."

As the date approached for the shipment to leave the factory, Tinner was desperate to get as many details as he could. He knew that he needed to provide the name of the shipping line and to identify the containers as completely as possible. As the Swiss technician pondered his assignment, he realized that the best item he could pass to Kinsman would be a copy of the shipping invoice. It would list the precise route for the shipment and the registration numbers of the crates holding the centrifuge components. But Tinner had no business with a copy of the invoice. Tahir, already suspicious of his Swiss colleague, kept tight control over all the paperwork.

The opportunity arose when Khan contacted the factory and demanded a copy of the invoice for the upcoming shipment.

"We have to send an urgent fax about the shipment," Tahir told Tinner. "Go tell the office lady."

In the hierarchy of an East Asian office, it would have aroused suspicion if Tinner had volunteered to fax the invoice himself. But it was not suspicious for him to supervise the secretary while she sent an important fax to Khan in Dubai. As the secretary began to feed the papers into the fax machine, Tinner reached forward and pressed the "copy" button. He immediately swore loudly enough for everyone nearby to hear.

"Why are you copying?" he said to the woman. "You have to fax it."

Tinner took the copy and threw it in the trash while the secretary faxed the originals to Khan.

A short time later, everyone in the office left for afternoon prayers. Tinner had only a few minutes, so he hurried back to the fax machine, retrieved the papers from the wastebasket, and folded them carefully into his pocket. Later he went to a public telephone shop and faxed the invoice to Kinsman at the CIA.

Tinner had taken a big risk. If he had been caught, Tahir's suspicions would have been confirmed. At the very least, Tinner would have been fired. But in his mind, he would have faced more dire punishment. The result was a major intelligence coup that would make it far easier for the CIA to keep track of the crates that were soon leaving Malaysia.

Keeping track of the crates on their journey was essential, and there had been a spirited discussion between the CIA and Tinner over how to do so. Normal practice at SCOPE was to pack the crates in a single, large shipping container for the voyage. The CIA suggested that Tinner attach a small GPS beacon to the container during the loading process. He objected on two grounds. First, he said Tahir was too careful not to spot even a tiny device. Even if the locator escaped notice, Tinner said the crates would probably be transferred to another container when the ship arrived in Dubai. The counterproposal was to drop the beacon inside one of the crates. Again Tinner objected. "There would be no signal," he said.

"On the inside, it would be surrounded by metal." In the end, the CIA would rely on observation, with the help of its eyes in the sky. Satellites would be tasked to track the shipment across the Indian Ocean.

On August 4, five crates labeled "agriculture parts" were loaded onto a freighter in Kuala Lumpur harbor. The forty-foot-long wooden containers were being shipped from SCOPE to Aryash Trading Company in Dubai, but that was not the final destination—and they did not contain agriculture parts. Instead, the massive crates contained roughly twenty-five thousand casings, pumps, tubes, flanges, and other parts, all manufactured to precise tolerances from high-strength aluminum and bound for warehouses in Libya. There the components would eventually be assembled into centrifuges for the clandestine enrichment plant. Two CIA agents watched as the ship left the port. Along its route, the vessel would be tracked by satellites through the Indian Ocean until it reached Dubai. There agents on the ground would be on hand to monitor the transfer to Aryash Trading and the subsequent loading onto a German-registered ship, the *BBC China*. Then the final leg of the journey would begin through the Suez Canal and across the Mediterranean Sea to Tripoli. If all went according to plan, the shipment would never reach Libya. At a point along its route that was still to be determined, the U.S. Navy would intercept the ship and remove the five wooden crates.

Back in June in Vaduz, Tinner had mentioned that Khan had taken two prototype rotors for the P-2 centrifuge from his stock in Pakistan and planned to use them for manufacturing the advanced version for Libya, and possibly Iran. The Malaysian factory had been manufacturing the more primitive P-1 model for the Libyans, but Tripoli was demanding that its enrichment plant be upgraded by stocking it with P-2s, which enriched uranium faster and more efficiently. One of the prototypes was still in a warehouse in Dubai, but the other one had been sent to Malaysia and work was under way to shift production to the advanced version. Once they were no longer necessary, Tahir told Tinner to destroy the rotors and to dispose of the remnants. Instead Tinner offered to sell both of the rotors to the CIA. He and Marco wanted another million dollars for them.

For Kinsman, getting hold of the rotors would accomplish two important tasks. First, it would allow the CIA's scientists to examine the more advanced centrifuge, which they suspected had been supplied long ago to Iran. Second, and at least as important, it would keep the prototypes off the black market. But the CIA accountants, already alarmed at the amount of money going to the Tinners, balked at the price, especially for something the Tinners had acquired at no expense. The CIA officer sent Urs a message telling him, "The people who must approve such a large expenditure doubt whether your price has been sufficiently justified." Urs and Marco cut their price in half, agreeing to take five hundred thousand dollars for the pair.

Jim Kinsman was riding high. He was on the brink of closing the biggest operation of his career, bringing down the world's most dangerous nuclear proliferation ring, fulfilling that boyhood dream of stopping the bad guys from getting atomic bombs. And the icing on the cake was that Kinsman was headed to the White House. Soon after the ship carrying the five containers left Kuala Lumpur, with the plans in place to intercept the merchandise before it reached Tripoli, Kinsman had the rare opportunity to join Tenet in briefing President Bush about the impending victory over the Khan network. "Mr. President," Kinsman said when he and Tenet met with Bush at the White House, "with the information we've just gotten our hands on—soup to nuts—about uranium enrichment and nuclear weapons design, we could make CIA its own nuclear weapons state."

Bush had been kept up to date on the pursuit of the Khan network and the ongoing negotiations with the Libyans over giving up their nuclear program. Now he was being told that the CIA had collected enough intelligence about Khan—the existence of nuclear weapons plans, the hundreds of tons of material already in Libya, and the shipment that the CIA intended to intercept—to finally bring down the Pakistani scientist and the nuclear black market he had created.

CHAPTER SEVEN

SINGAPORE AND KUALA LUMPUR

As the ship from Kuala Lumpur was steaming through the Indian Ocean and nearing the conclusion of the first leg of its voyage in the Persian Gulf port of Dubai in early September 2003, A. Q. Khan arrived in Singapore, the city-state at the southern tip of the Malaysia peninsula. Singapore is a bustling international financial and technology center, the sort of place where the Pakistani scientist felt at home and blended in easily with the thousands of foreigners who work and visit there. Indeed, his network had purchased material from Singapore and he had visited several times, so he was familiar with the country. Khan had come from Islamabad to get an update on operations at his Malaysian centrifuge factory from his site manager, Urs Tinner. Khan had initially planned to meet Tinner and B. S. A. Tahir in Kuala Lumpur and visit the factory. But his normal security concerns had increased sharply in recent months after the disclosure of the secret Iranian nuclear facilities. After years of operating with a wink and a nod from various Pakistani military and civilian regimes, Khan also had seen his relationship with General Musharraf sour in recent months. Musharraf had ordered an investigation of Khan not long after the general took power in a coup in late 1999. The results showed that the scientist had accumulated wealth far beyond his government salary, and it had turned up indications that much of that money may have come from selling nuclear technology abroad. But Musharraf had decided not to risk taking on a man of Khan's influence, so the only action he had taken was to demote the scientist and keep a closer eye on him. Khan was not sure that Musharraf would protect him if he were exposed by the international community, and he had been unsettled by the discovery of Iran's secret nuclear program and the search of Tahir's offices in Dubai. At the last minute he had changed his plans and told Tinner and Tahir to meet him in Singapore.

The late switch in locations made Tinner more nervous. He had complained a few weeks earlier to Kinsman about the risks that he was taking. The American had assured him that he would be protected. Now he was expected to record a meeting, the biggest risk he had taken. After rejecting the older cell phone that Kinsman had given him for recording his conversation with Khan, Tinner had bought a new one on his own. Using his mechanical expertise, he adjusted the inner workings so that the phone would record a conversation without the red "on" light signaling that it was even in use.

Telephone and e-mail communications among the participants in the network were always cryptic because of fears of eavesdroppers, so face-to-face meetings were crucial opportunities for Khan to determine how the various elements of his far-flung enterprise were working.

The meeting was in Khan's suite at one of those Singapore's and anonymous hotels. As he sat down in the room, Tinner pulled his cell phone from his pocket and put it on the coffee table. For the next hour or so, Tinner and Tahir provided the boss with a thorough rundown of production cycles at the factory, bringing him up to date on the latest shipment of components to Libya. Tinner sought Khan's advice about the modifications under way to shift production from the old P-1 centrifuge to the more advanced P-2 version, which the Libyans were demanding for their factory. Tinner assured the Pakistani scientist that he could handle the changeover and that the workers at SCOPE were skilled enough to follow orders. The last thing the Swiss technician wanted was for Khan to send one of his people from Pakistan to go over the designs. A competent engineer might spot Tinner's subtle sabotage.

Khan had an almost fatherly faith in the son of his longtime Swiss associate, so he was pleased to hear about the progress. For his part, Tinner struggled to control his nerves as he spoke with Khan about events that he knew would not happen. Tinner knew that the latest Libyan shipment would not arrive at its destination. He knew that the Americans were going to intercept the shipment somewhere along its journey to Tripoli, although he was not privy to exactly how the CIA would stop the shipment. He knew only that whatever they did would set in motion events that would shut down the network and rupture the bond that had been built over the years between Khan and the Tinner family. The CIA didn't want to spring its trap on Khan's network until after it had seized the cargo. The plan was to first use the evidence to convince the reluctant Moammar Kaddafi to abandon his clandestine nuclear program and turn over the information that could be used to indict Khan.

Even without knowing the details, Tinner knew his world would never be the same. Perhaps because of his anxiety, he could not bring himself to carry out Kinsman's instructions to press Khan for information about the fourth customer. Every time he started to ask, Tinner changed his mind. He said good-bye to his patron without raising the issue. As he stood to go, Tinner stuck the cell phone he rigged as a recorder into his pocket.

On the short flight back to Malaysia, Tinner went over a mental checklist of steps he needed to take in preparation for his exit. Much as he wanted to run, he could not just pack up and return to Switzerland; Tahir continued to watch him carefully and any deviation from his routine would set off alarms within the network. Kinsman had given him explicit instructions to stay in place as long as possible. Tinner was trapped as the days passed and he waited for word that he could escape his double life. While he waited, he began carefully erasing records from his computer that could implicate him in the production of nuclear technology. Transferring the recording to a digital file, he sent it to Kinsman via e-mail from his home computer. Before the *BBC China* arrived in Tripoli, Marco had flown to Miami to meet with Kinsman and a colleague from the CIA. They had told him about the plan to seize the cargo, warning that word of the missing material would find its way to Khan quickly once the ship arrived in Tripoli. Marco was concerned that fingers would be pointed at his brother because Tahir was already suspicious of Urs. Kinsman proposed a two-part plan to deflect suspicion from Urs. First, he told Marco to tell his brother that he should complain to Khan and others about Tahir's terrible security, accusing the Sri Lankan of attracting too much attention to the operation in Malaysia by his ostentatious lifestyle. Second, he said the CIA was already applying pressure on the Turkish government to go after the two Turkish electronics manufacturers involved in the Khan network. When word leaked about the Turkish investigation, it would be logical for Khan to assume that one of his partners there had turned on him.

Still, when Marco spoke with his brother after the Miami meeting, he warned Urs that his days were numbered and that he should get out of Malaysia as quickly as possible. Urs agreed, but before leaving he still needed to arrange a meeting to sell the P-2 rotor to the CIA.

As the net was beginning to close around Khan's enterprise, a leak demonstrated the dangers of what could happen if the CIA did not sweep up the entire operation. In September, someone alerted Gotthard Lerch, a key player in the Libyan project, that the Americans had gotten wind of what was going on.

Lerch was a German immigrant to Switzerland who had done business with Khan and the Tinners for more than twenty years. In the 1970s and early 1980s, Lerch had worked for Leybold-Heraeus, the big German manufacturer of vacuum equipment used in centrifuge plants and other machinery. In 1983, the German authorities discovered that Lerch had engineered the sale of a million dollars' worth of highly sophisticated valves and other components to Pakistan. The company pressured Lerch to leave, and he moved his operations to Switzerland. He set up his own business and lived in a tidy house in the village of Grabs, not far from Friedrich Tinner, and continued supplying Pakistan. In fact, some evidence indicated that Lerch had been involved in the network's original sale of centrifuge designs, components, and other equipment to Iran in 1987. When the Libyan project was hatched a decade later, he was in the thick of the operation, working closely with the Tinners to coordinate production of components and get the right material delivered to Tripoli. He also provided the overall schematic designs for the Libyan centrifuge plant and found an engineering firm in South Africa to do some of the most complicated work.

Lerch's involvement wasn't a secret, at least to the intelligence services of the countries that cared about such things. Shortly before midnight on Valentine's Day in 2002, someone had tacked a note on the door of his home in Grabs. Addressed formally to "Herr Lerch" and written in German, the note read: "After many years of watching your business efforts we are alarmed at your current plans to sell the P-2 design to Iran. . . . If you carry out these plans there will be grave consequences for all concerned. We have traveled many hours and come to your house to talk with you. Please take our advice! We will contact you soon to talk and perhaps to find a way to meet both your goals and ours." It was signed, "Your sincere friends."

Lerch did not take the threat seriously enough to report it to the police. His attitude changed sharply a month later when a second note was left at his house. "We are concerned," said this one, which was in French. "Police report they have found a body in a very bad state and it has a very small brain and a badly damaged penis. We are concerned it is you." This time he was frightened enough to go to the police and turn over copies of both notes.

The notes didn't amount to much in the way of evidence. Whoever had made the threats had not followed up by contacting Lerch, so the local police turned the matter over to the federal police. A senior Swiss intelligence official was called into the case. He suspected Lerch was involved in trafficking in nuclear technology, but there was no evidence that he had violated Swiss export laws. The intelligence official speculated that the note had been left by either the CIA or the Mossad, the Israeli intelligence service. The Swiss official leaned toward the Israelis, who had a history of both threats and actions against people perceived as dangers to its security.

In September 2003, Lerch got a different kind of message. He was tipped off that a shipment of centrifuge components to Libya was about to be grabbed by the Americans. Only a small circle of people within the American and British governments knew of the impending seizure. The CIA had kept the knowledge tightly compartmentalized. Within the Bush administration, only the president, vice president, and national security adviser, Condoleezza Rice, were aware of the details. The Tinners were among the very few outsiders who knew what was about to happen. It is possible that one of them alerted Lerch, as doing so would protect their long-standing business partner and keep their options open for the future. Lerch was concerned enough to pass on the warning to Gerhard Wisser, a German engineer who lived in South Africa and was overseeing work being done there for the Libyan project. Wisser later told German police that Lerch warned him that trouble was coming, urging him to destroy all evidence of the Libyan project, from the massive centrifuge piping system to computer designs provided by Khan and others. Wisser promised to comply. Destroying the extensive work that had been done in South Africa for the Libyan nuclear project would have eliminated a significant element in the Khan network before the CIA or any other authorities could have exposed it. The people involved there would have been able to cover their tracks, resurfacing later in another form.

When Wisser returned home after the warning from Lerch, he immediately destroyed three computer hard drives and other documentation related to the Libya project in the offices of his firm, Krisch Engineering, in a Johannesburg suburb called Vanderbijlpark. But when he tried to persuade one of his accomplices, Johan Meyer, to do the same, he ran into a wall. The huge system of pipes and valves to connect and operate the Libyan centrifuges was complete. It had been tested and dismantled for shipment. The system had been packed into eleven shipping containers that were each forty feet long and labeled "water purification" equipment, bound for Dubai and ultimately Tripoli. The containers were sitting in Meyer's factory when Wisser arrived with orders to destroy everything. Send it to the smelter and melt it down, Wisser said. The instructional videos from Khan and a stack of design documents, he said, should be committed to "an Easter bonfire." Meyer refused. He argued that he had not been paid his final installment of $150,000. Wisser promised to transfer the money to Meyer's Swiss account out of his own pocket. Meyer still refused, and Wisser left, angry and worried. The following day he sent a text message to Meyer's cellular phone. "The bird must be destroyed, feathers and all," he wrote. "They have fed us to the dogs."

- - - - - -

SEVERAL THOUSAND MILES AWAY, THE endgame was approaching. On September 24, George Tenet met with Pakistani president Pervez Musharraf in the president's suite at the Waldorf-Astoria hotel in New York City, where the Pakistani was attending a United Nations conference. It was what is called in intelligence parlance a "four-eyes" meeting, which meant that it was just Tenet and Musharraf, with no aides present. Tenet had brought copies of some of the designs and diagrams that had been obtained from the Tinner computers; they were clearly marked as property of the Pakistani government.

"A. Q. Khan is betraying your country," Tenet said to Musharaff. "He has stolen some of your nation's most sensitive secrets and sold them to the highest bidders. Khan has stolen your nuclear weapons secrets. We know this, because we stole them from him."

Tenet tossed the blueprints on the table. Musharraf showed no emotion as he examined the documents. "Mr. President," said Tenet, "if a country like Libya or Iran or, God forbid, an organization like Al Qaeda, gets a working nuclear device and the world learns it came from your country, I'm afraid the consequences would be devastating."

After asking a few questions, Musharraf said, "Thank you, George, I will take care of this."

But it would take more than a warning from the CIA director to prompt Musharraf to take action against an opponent of Khan's stature, no matter what secrets he had sold.

In late September, the Malaysian ship carrying goods to Libya arrived in Dubai's Jebel Ali Free Trade Zone. The crates marked "agricultural product" were never inspected and never left the free-trade zone. Instead they were offloaded and taken to storage in the warehouse of Aryash Trading Company. Two days later, the crates were back in the port and being lifted into the hold of the four-hundred-foot freighter *BBC China*. The ship was registered to a reputable chartering company based in Hamburg, Germany, and the captain had no idea he was being watched carefully by American spy satellites as the vessel steamed out the southern end of the Persian Gulf, through the Red Sea, and into the Suez Canal.

Midway through the canal, the *BBC China* captain was hailed on the ship's radio by a dispatcher in Hamburg. A senior official with the company that owned the freighter wanted to talk to him. The captain was given a puzzling new itinerary: After leaving the canal and entering the Mediterranean Sea, he was told to make way to the southern Italian port of Taranto. It was an unusual order and no explanation was offered. What the captain did not know was that the German security service had contacted the ship's owners and requested the course change. The ship's owners were told the ship was the unwitting carrier of a load of nuclear technology. They were ordered to keep the cargo secret, even from the captain of the *BBC China*.

The *BBC China* was shadowed on its journey across the Mediterranean by two frigates from the U.S. Navy. As the ship neared the port on October 4, the captain was directed away from the commercial section to an out-of-way spot under the control of the Italian naval operation. There the vessel was met by American and Italian naval officers and several men in civilian clothes. The civilians had a list of exact crates that they wanted removed from the ship's hold. The process took some time, but eventually the five forty-foot-long crates were lifted from the hold by one of the ship's twin cranes and deposited on the dock. The *BBC China* was sent on its way with a warning to the captain and crew not to discuss the detour with anyone.

The containers were loaded onto military trucks and the convoy drove directly to a secure warehouse within the navy compound. There the CIA agents watched as the crates were opened, exposing thousands of components for centrifuges. Word of the huge coup was sent immediately to headquarters at Langley, but there was no time to celebrate. Events were unfolding quickly. The CIA moved immediately into the next phase of the operation.

For months the United States and Britain had been trying to persuade the Libyans to shut down their once-secret nuclear program. The Libyan leader's eldest son, Saif, had initiated the negotiations back in March as part of his father's efforts to rejoin the international community, which had considered his country a pariah because of its involvement in terrorism incidents like the bombing of Pan Am Flight 103 over Lockerbie, Scotland. The Libyans seemed willing to give up their stocks of chemical weapons, but Saif was refusing to even acknowledge the existence of the nuclear program. As a result the talks had been stalled for several weeks.

Giving up the chemical program would be easy compared with sacrificing Moammar Kaddafi's nuclear ambitions, which had already cost tens of millions of dollars and were central to his outsize ambitions to be recognized as the leader of the Arab world.

The CIA now had evidence that would prove beyond any doubt that Libya was pursuing a nuclear weapon. Kaddafi would face a stark choice: He could either give up his nuclear ambitions as a first step toward rejoining the international community or he could refuse to do so and find himself to be an even greater outcast and possibly the next target of a preemptive strike by the Bush administration. Inside the CIA, Stephen Kappes and other senior officers believed that they had the proof to convince the Libyan leader that his plans to build a nuclear weapons factory were doomed. He would have no choice except to give up.

The day after the crates were opened, Mark Allen, a senior member of MI6 and fluent Arabic speaker who had been leading the negotiations, telephoned Musa Kousa, the Libyan security chief. He asked for an immediate meeting to discuss new developments on the nuclear front. Kousa agreed, and two days later Allen and Kappes, his American equivalent, were on an unmarked CIA jet headed for Tripoli. Kousa met them at an isolated portion of the military airfield and ushered them aboard one of Kaddafi's personal jets. They flew to an airstrip in the desert about two hours away, where they found the Libyan strongman waiting for them in an ornate tent.

As far as the brash Kappes was concerned, the time for negotiations was over. The proof that Kaddafi was engaged in a nuclear weapons program was already on its way back to the national weapons laboratory at Oak Ridge, where experts would piece together the centrifuges that had been intended to enrich uranium to fulfill the Libyan's dream of joining the nuclear elite. If Kaddafi refused to abandon the program, negotiations would end and there would be consequences for him and his country. The neoconservatives of the Bush administration would later argue that Kaddafi didn't need to imagine what those consequences might be. In April 1986, the United States launched an air attack on Kaddafi's compound in retaliation for Libya's involvement in the bombing of a Berlin nightclub that killed two American servicemen. The strike killed sixty people, including Kaddafi's fifteen-month-old adopted daughter.

In their view, he needed only look north to Iraq, where American troops were scouring the country for Saddam Hussein, another Arab leader who once had nuclear ambitions of his own. Never mind that the Americans had failed to find evidence of any nuclear program in Iraq. The image of another strongman on the run in his own country was a strong one for Kaddafi. But Kaddafi was a shrewd man whose survival over the years had depended on accurately reading the intentions of the United States and other adversaries. He recognized that the supposed existence of weapons of mass destruction in Iraq was little more than a pretext and that Bush's decision to oust Saddam Hussein and occupy Iraq was a foregone conclusion. No such predetermination had been made for Libya, something that Kaddafi must surely have known. Rather than the specter of American forces prying him from a spider hole in the desert, Kaddafi was driven by a desire to regain Libya's place in the international community and put his country on a sounder footing for his eventual succession by his son.

Still, the American intelligence official played the role of tough guy when he encountered Kaddafi in his tent.

"You are the drowning man, and I am the lifeguard," Kappes told the man referred to by six million Libyans as "the guide of the revolution" and "brotherly leader."

Kaddafi knew when to fold his hand. So he agreed to be "saved." Kaddafi said that he would renounce his nuclear program. He sent Kappes and Allen back to their respective capitals to begin preparations for the announcement, which would give much-needed political boosts to their own leaders, President Bush and Prime Minister Blair, who were weathering heavy criticism for the failure to find weapons of mass destruction in Iraq.

Secrecy was important before, and it was vital now. The Americans and British did not want word of Kaddafi's decision to leak before everything was in place, out of fear that the mercurial Libyan might change his mind if he were faced with a barrage of criticism from the Arab world. Secrecy was also important as the CIA began preparations for rounding up the participants in Khan's global nuclear network. But news that something was afoot would not be kept from Khan and his associates for long.

A few days after the meeting in the desert, the *BBC China* arrived at its berth in Tripoli. When Libyan military personnel arrived to take control of the containers from Malaysia, they were surprised to find that five of the seven containers expected from the network were missing. The missing crates were the ones from Malaysia; two containers of electrical components, including the sabotaged regulators, from Turkey had arrived safely. The ship's captain and his crew offered no explanation, suggesting that the cargo must not have been loaded in Dubai. Word of the missing containers quickly spread up the chain of command in Libya. The senior Libyan nuclear official, Mohammad Matuq Mohammad, telephoned Khan and told him about the missing containers. It made no sense that five containers had gone missing. The Pakistani scientist had no idea what had happened, but he promised to find out.

Since the disclosure of the Iranian nuclear program the previous year, Khan had been on alert for security breaches. He knew that five crates had left Malaysia. When he checked with the freight forwarders at Ayrash Trading in Dubai, they swore that the containers had been loaded onto the *BBC China*. Somewhere along the line, five huge containers, with thousands of dollars' worth of components, had vanished. Khan suspected a leak in his operation, but he didn't know who it might have been.

SITTING IN HIS OFFICE AT the SCOPE factory in mid-October, Urs Tinner got a telephone call from Tahir, who was in Dubai. The Sri Lankan was in a frenzy, saying he had terrible news. Khan had just called. The containers from SCOPE never made it to Libya. They had arrived safely in Dubai, but somewhere after leaving the Persian Gulf port, the crates had disappeared. No one knew what exactly had happened, but Khan feared that the British or the Americans had gotten them.

"Why were they looking for those five containers?" Tahir demanded. "There must be a spy somewhere in our operation."

"Why are you asking me?" said Tinner.

The two men argued. Tahir's long-held suspicions about Tinner seemed to be coming true. Tinner claimed that he was innocent. He maintained that he had not known the containers were going beyond Dubai. So how, he demanded, could he be responsible for something that happened on a part of the journey he didn't even know about?

"Tahir, if I'm the spy, then the goods would have been found before Dubai, not after," Tinner said.

Tahir was not persuaded. He ordered Tinner to get on the first plane to Dubai. Tinner did as he was told.

When Tinner arrived in Dubai the next day, he went directly to the SMB offices. Tahir was still shaken by the disappearance of the crates. He was suspicious that someone within the network was a spy, and those suspicions pointed at the Swiss technician. Tahir was waiting for Tinner at SMB and he angrily repeated the accusations. But Tinner had had time on the flight to rehearse his responses.

Once again Tinner suggested that the problem was in Dubai, not Malaysia. Someone at the shipping company could have been working for one of the Western intelligence agencies. He said there had been rumors in the past week or so that the two Turks involved with the network had come under scrutiny from their government. Perhaps they had provided the tip to save themselves. Why else would their two containers have gotten through and SCOPE's been seized?

Tinner did not know if Tahir believed him, but it was apparent that his colleague was unnerved and suspicious. Rather than stay in Dubai, where he feared he might fall into the hands of MI6 or the Americans, Tahir went home to Kuala Lumpur. There he and his wife lived in one of the city's most secure buildings. He also expected that his political connections would protect him. Before leaving, he told Tinner to stay in Dubai until he got orders from Khan.

The person who mattered most still trusted Tinner. Khan was rattled by the missing containers, though he did not know the Americans had them. He wanted to get rid of as much evidence as possible in case more trouble was on the way. Khan telephoned Tinner and told him to go to SMB and help scrub the computers there. Most of the information was to be destroyed outright. But Khan told Tinner to make electronic copies of the weapons plans and e-mail them to him before erasing them from the computers. Tinner also was told to dispose of any equipment left in Dubai, including the second P-2 rotor.

Tinner followed Khan's instructions, though not to the letter. He destroyed most of the evidence, but not all of it. Instead of throwing the rotor in the sea, as he would later claim to Tahir and others, he turned it over to a CIA agent. When it came to the nuclear weapons designs and other critical information, he sent copies to Khan—and to his brother, his father, and his own Yahoo e-mail account. Later, he would boast to investigators from the International Atomic Energy Agency that he posted copies of the information "out in the ether where no one can find them." Many of those records were already on the laptop that Urs had left behind at Marco's apartment in Jenins and on other computers owned by the Tinners, and Tinner knew that the CIA had copied them weeks earlier. But the claim by Urs that he had posted some of the material on the Internet, if true, raised the stakes to a higher level. It meant that he could retrieve the records at any time from any place—and sell them to anyone.

After carrying out the assignment from Khan, Tinner returned to Kuala Lumpur. When he encountered Tahir, he could not tell if the Sri Lankan still suspected he was the spy. A few days after his return, Tinner's fears increased when one of his coworkers at SCOPE told him that someone at the shipping company in Dubai had died under mysterious circumstances. "It was very scary and I was afraid," Tinner said later. "After that, I did not live at home. For a couple weeks, I stayed in hotels where no one knew I was staying. At least I could sleep."

Tinner knew his days in Malaysia were numbered. At work he continued quietly cleaning out his desk and removing as much evidence as possible. One day he risked returning to his house so that he could hide some documents and a flash drive under the floorboards of the house he shared with his Malay girlfriend, a young dancer named Ang.

On the night of October 27, Tinner carried out another assignment from Kinsman. Shortly before ten o'clock, he drove his car to a country club on the outskirts of the Malaysian capital. He pulled into the far end of the parking lot, away from any lights, and waited. A few minutes later, Tinner saw a second car pull into the lot and make its way toward him. Eventually the driver pulled alongside Tinner's vehicle and rolled down his window. Tinner recognized him. He was one of the CIA officers who worked with Kinsman in Kuala Lumpur.

The man got out of his car and motioned for Tinner to do the same. Both of them popped the trunks of their cars. Tinner took out a slender cylinder and passed it to the American, who put it in his trunk. The cylinder was about the size of a set of golf clubs and didn't weigh much. A casual observer might have assumed two golfers were repacking their gear after a round and a few drinks. But Tinner had just given the CIA the second P-2 rotor, which he had been instructed by Tahir to destroy.

On November 10, four days after Tinner's thirty-eighth birthday, two intelligence agents, one from the CIA and one from MI6, arrived at the headquarters of the Malaysian Special Branch, the country's security service. The world still did not know about the material removed from the *BBC China* or Libya's decision to renounce its nuclear program. The two intelligence officers told the director of the agency, Bukit Aman, that the SCOPE factory in Shah Alam was part of a nuclear black market that had been supplying material to Libya. They asked for his help, suggesting that B. S. A. Tahir, one of the officers of the factory, be placed under surveillance and not allowed to leave the country.

It is unclear whether the intelligence agents raised Tinner's name in their conversation with Aman. A police report issued later by the Malaysian government made no mention of any request regarding the Swiss technician at the time. But Tinner later said that he was telephoned by a Malaysian security officer and told that he should leave the country as soon as possible. In case Tinner doubted the urgency of the request, the security officer said he was canceling Tinner's work permit and his visa, effective immediately. About the same time, a director at SCOPE telephoned and told Tinner that he was being fired for stealing material from the company's computers.

Tinner was frightened and furious. He later complained that he had no time to pack his belongings. He did not even retrieve the material hidden under the floorboards of his house before boarding the next flight to Switzerland.

When he arrived home, Tinner hoped he was outside the reach of Tahir and Khan. The tension and fears of his double life had taken a toll. Before he had a chance to settle in, Marco called. He said he was in New Orleans with some friends and they wanted Urs to join them.

The trip turned out to be part holiday, part debriefing, part payday. Over the course of five days, Urs and Marco met in a hotel suite with Kinsman and the nuclear weapons expert from the national lab at Oak Ridge. The parts from the five containers were being examined at the lab and the expert had lots of questions for Urs. They went over the events of the past two months carefully and thoroughly. Urs provided a detailed inventory of material left behind at the SCOPE factory in Malaysia and in the various warehouses and offices in Dubai, providing the CIA with an idea of what its agents would need to do to mop up that part of the network. He and Marco described once again the entire setup in Libya, outlining the extensive enrichment facility that was planned. They identified the components from photos that the expert had brought along.

They also explained again, as they had in Vaduz, that the most complex components for the centrifuges had been manufactured by the Tinners at their own factory in Switzerland. Thousands of them were still stored there; the inventory represented a substantial investment by the Tinners. It also would be evidence against them if the Swiss government investigated their role in the network. Marco wanted the CIA to buy the components; he demanded the same price that Libya would have paid. After the meeting with Urs and Marco in New Orleans in November, the CIA spymaster came up with a strategy to help them get rid of the evidence of their involvement in the Libyan project and get paid for the material.

Even though the Tinners were outliving their usefulness to the CIA, the case officer retained a strong loyalty to his spies. They had taken risks and performed admirably in his eyes, even if they had withheld information. He cautioned Urs that, if his role in Khan's operation surfaced in public, he should take care not to leave Switzerland. Kinsman said he remained committed to protecting all three Tinners, but he warned that the CIA's ability to keep them out of the hands of law enforcement officials was limited. They would all be safer sticking close to home in the coming months. Before the Tinners departed from New Orleans, they received confirmation that another five hundred thousand dollars—payment for the two rotors—had been deposited in Marco's account in the British Virgin Islands.

On December 19, a little more than a month later, with the Tinners tucked away at home, Libya's foreign minister went on national television and announced to the world that the country would disclose and dismantle its nuclear and chemical weapons programs. The Americans had insisted that Kaddafi himself participate in the announcement to drive home that it was endorsed by the country's leader. He appeared briefly on television, calling it a "wise decision and a courageous step."

In Washington and London, Bush and Blair held their own press conferences to praise Libya's decision and bask in the glory of a much-needed political victory. The full repercussions of Libya's action were not evident yet. Tahir had been taken into custody by the Malaysian security service and he was being interrogated. Khan, however, remained free while Musharraf pondered what he could get away with politically when it came to dealing with the popular scientist.

For Kinsman and his colleagues in the Counter-Proliferation Division, the announcement in Tripoli was the culmination of what they regarded as a textbook example of a successful intelligence operation. They fully expected that authorities around the world would begin rolling up the nodes of the Khan network, and that Khan himself would finally face justice in Pakistan. But unforeseen complications were about to arise. They would raise troubling questions about just how great an intelligence victory had been achieved.

On one hand, the seizure of the material from the *BBC China* exemplified the integration of intelligence collection and policy initiatives. The CIA and MI6 finally had obtained the evidence required to fulfill the policy objective of persuading Kaddafi to abandon his nuclear program and return to the norms of the international community. And certainly in the months to come, the operation would be touted as a significant intelligence success, especially by the Americans. But viewed more skeptically, or some would say more pragmatically, the operation against Libya represented an intelligence and policy failure that exemplified the long-term refusal of the CIA and MI6 to shut down A. Q. Khan. The intelligence agencies of both the United States and Britain had known for years that the Khan network was providing sophisticated nuclear technology to Libya. Key policymakers in both governments knew at least the broad outlines of what was occurring. Yet shutting down the flow of nuclear technology and critical secrets to Tripoli had been delayed over and over, allowing delivery of the Chinese warhead designs to people in Libya who had little reason not to either share them or sell them to other parties. And while the CIA had waited for the right time to strike, the Khan network had sent far more dangerous nuclear secrets to unknown points and Iran had continued its steady progress toward developing the capacity to construct a nuclear weapon. The lessons of 1975, when the CIA helped persuade the Dutch to let Khan go, had gone unobserved and the world was more dangerous because of it, even if the CIA was determined to portray the entire episode as an intelligence victory.

PART II

THE COVER-UP

CHAPTER EIGHT

VIENNA AND TRIPOLI

On the morning of Saturday, December 20, Olli Heinonen was shopping with his family at Vienna's famed Christmas Market outside City Hall. Heinonen was a senior inspections official with the International Atomic Energy Agency, the nuclear watchdog for the United Nations. Libya was one of about twenty countries that he monitored to make sure its small civilian nuclear program was not used for military purposes. In the rush to finish the family's holiday shopping, Heinonen had left the house that crisp and cloudy morning without reading the newspaper, so he had missed the announcement by Libya the night before. As he was looking through a shop filled with ornaments, Heinonen's cell phone rang. Mohamed ElBaradei's secretary was calling. The IAEA director general wanted Heinonen to come to his office for an emergency meeting. He left his family in the midst of the market and drove the short distance to the IAEA's horseshoe-shaped complex overlooking the Danube River.

Late the previous night, ElBaradei had received a telephone call from an American government official who informed him of Kaddafi's announcement. ElBaradei's relations with the United States had been touchy since he had criticized the decision to invade Iraq earlier in 2003. ElBaradei had pleaded with the United Nations and the United States to give his inspectors more time to prove that Iraq did not have a nuclear weapons program. So it was not a big surprise that the Americans had failed to tell ElBaradei or the IAEA anything about the operation against

Libya in advance of the announcement. The American who telephoned ElBaradei with the last-minute news had said that two British intelligence officials would arrive in Vienna the next morning to brief the IAEA on the Libyan operation. The director general, a veteran diplomat and international lawyer, had waited until Saturday morning to gather his senior staff to meet with the British agents.

The IAEA team was joined by two diplomats from the British embassy and two from the American mission to the IAEA. Together, they listened as the intelligence agents presented an hourlong description of the types of nuclear technology discovered in Libya and the number of hidden installations inspected by a joint British-American team earlier in December. They said the inquiry was preliminary, but the Libyans had acknowledged that the technology had come from A. Q. Khan and suppliers working with him over the past four or five years. Some of the equipment was still in crates marked KHAN RESEARCH LABORATORIES, they said.

The agents said that Kaddafi had agreed to give up his entire program, including the hundreds of tons of equipment sitting inside various warehouses in and around Tripoli. The Americans would pack up the material and ship it back to the United States for a careful examination, they said, but the IAEA would have a chance to take a look at the inventory before it left Libya. They said the Libyan government planned to invite ElBaradei to Tripoli to see for himself what they had been up to for the past few years.

The disclosure of the secret Libyan weapons program, and the indications of the scope of the material they had purchased on the black market, was a stunning setback for ElBaradei and his team. Unfortunately for the director general, it was only the most recent in a string of surprises that had embarrassed the IAEA, dating back to the discovery of Iraq's secret nuclear project in the early 1990s. In truth, the IAEA was set up as a paper tiger, without the authority to fight the spread of nuclear weapons effectively.

When the IAEA was created in 1957, its mission was to promote the peaceful uses of nuclear energy. The agency's responsibility for making sure the technology used to generate electricity was not diverted to military programs was almost an afterthought. From the outset there were questions about whether the agency had the powers to stop the diversion of nuclear technology to weapons. Leery of ceding power over nuclear technology to an international organization, the U.S. Congress had demanded that the agency's authority be watered down. Among the elements that were stripped away from the original concept of the IAEA was an independent intelligence arm. As a result, the agency would be more lapdog than watchdog, dependent on the United States and other countries in looking behind the closed doors of nuclear research facilities around the world.

The decision to weaken the agency came despite early reports by the CIA and other American intelligence agencies, which warned that the spread of nuclear expertise was creating the capability for small-scale nuclear weapons programs in many countries. France, China, West Germany, Japan, Sweden, and Israel were identified in early intelligence reports as the countries most likely to develop nuclear weapons. India and Pakistan were added a few years later. The danger was that the barrier between peaceful nuclear energy and its military uses was turning out to be an illusion. The clearest example of the dual nature of the technology was the centrifuge; the machines could enrich uranium to about 5 percent to fuel a civilian reactor or, with slight adjustments, to 90 percent or more for use in weapons.

The IAEA had plodded along in its promotional role for more than three decades. But the agency awoke from its slumber after the Persian Gulf War in 1991, when it was discovered that Saddam Hussein had moved frighteningly close to producing a nuclear weapon. In the years that followed, first under the leadership of Hans Blix and later under ElBaradei, the agency had been struggling to assume a more aggressive stance toward possible diversion of nuclear technology. The process was moving slowly, inhibited by the continued unwillingness of its member nations to grant inspectors the broad access necessary to find hidden weapons facilities and by its own bureaucratic inertia.

For the past year, the agency had been struggling to understand the scope of Iran's nuclear program. Now the Libyan discovery brought another challenge, and another black eye to the efforts to the IAEA's image. As soon as the British and Americans left his office on December 20, ElBaradei said that he wanted to go to Libya as soon as possible. The agency's inspectors needed to understand what the Libyans had acquired and where it had come from. Khan's name had already surfaced in the Iranian inquiry, and ElBaradei was beginning to develop the idea that the Pakistani scientist was at the epicenter of an entirely new and extremely serious type of nuclear proliferation. In the past, concerns had been focused on state-to-state transfers of technology. Khan appeared to signal a deeper involvement of private individuals and companies, which could multiply the threat.

As he pondered Khan's potential role, ElBaradei concluded that the agency needed to open a far more sweeping inquiry into the nature of the Pakistani's operation. Khan's name had now popped up in Iran and Libya. Who knew where else he might have sold his technology? To head the new inquiry he chose Olli Heinonen. ElBaradei and Heinonen had worked together for many years at the agency, and Heinonen had been at the center of the IAEA's inquiry into Iran's nuclear program since its exposure in the summer of 2002.

Heinonen had spent nearly twenty years at the IAEA. He had a doctorate in radiochemistry from the University of Helsinki and he had worked as a researcher at Finland's nuclear research center before joining the IAEA out of a commitment to stopping proliferation. Thanks to a keen intellect, he had risen through the ranks and was now head of Division B, one of three groups within the safeguards department that monitored compliance with international nuclear treaties. ElBaradei told him he would have whatever resources he needed to conduct a full-scale inquiry into what the director general feared was a new breed of proliferation threat.

A WEEK LATER, AN AUSTRIAN Airlines jet touched down at Tripoli's airport. Stepping off the plane onto the tarmac were ElBaradei, Heinonen, and a handful of other senior IAEA officials. They were escorted to a line of black BMWs and whisked out of the airport, past billboards proclaiming the greatness of Kaddafi, and on to the Corintha Bab Africa Hotel.

What they found over the next few days was sobering. Libya had not bothered to conceal its secret program in bunkers or buried complexes in the Sahara. Instead the delegation toured a series of nondescript warehouses and innocuous-looking school buildings around the city. There they saw components for five thousand centrifuges. Twenty machines had been set up and tested at one site. At other sites, crates had not even been unpacked. In all, there was more than a hundred tons of equipment, all of it purchased from Khan and his suppliers.

As Heinonen wandered among the stacks of machinery in one location, the Libyan technician named Karim pointed to dozens of four-foot-high metal cabinets that contained UPS regulators to govern the flow of electricity to the centrifuges. They were marked with the label of a Turkish company. Karim, who had acknowledged to Heinonen earlier that he had negotiated the early deal with Khan, said, "That firm is owned by Jews. Nothing is holy in this world."

The Libyans appeared to hold back little. They acknowledged many meetings with Khan and described how equipment was shipped to Tripoli with false invoices and through various middlemen. They calculated that they had paid about $80 million to the network so far. They said they had no idea what the final price tag would have been—$500 million? $1 billion?

In the weeks that followed, IAEA officials made several trips to Libya to try to understand how the startling amount of material had gone to Libya without the IAEA's knowledge. Previously its infrequent inspections had not turned up any evidence of the secret program. There had been no credible tips from companies selling the equipment. And the American and British intelligence agencies had kept the international nuclear watchdog in the dark. But the new inspections had another purpose, too. From the first visit, Heinonen and others from the agency had noticed striking similarities with what they had been seeing in Iran over the past year. The same P-1 centrifuges that inspectors had seen at Iran's pilot plant were present in Libya. The same electronic assemblies used in Iran were stacked in a warehouse in Tripoli. There were enough parallels to convince Heinonen and others at the IAEA that Khan and his partners also had been the sources of much of the equipment and designs in Iran.

But Khan appeared to have sold the Libyans some crucial equipment and blueprints that had not yet been uncovered in Iran. For instance,

Libya possessed five prototypes for the advanced P-2 centrifuge, which enriches uranium about twice as fast as the P-1. More alarming, the Libyans had showed two IAEA weapons experts, Jacques Baute and Bob Kelley, a shopping bag with the logo of a tailor shop in Islamabad, filled with documents, which Khan had given to them. When Baute and Kelley opened the bag and started sorting through the hundreds of documents inside, they found designs for a Chinese nuclear warhead. The plans were dated, and appeared to be those developed by the Chinese in the 1960s. Markings on the copies indicated that Khan and his technicians had used them in Pakistan before passing them on to the Libyans. The blueprints were not complete, but it was clear that Khan was selling not just his expertise in enriching uranium. He was peddling blueprints that could enable Libya or other customers to build a workable nuclear warhead. The plans were so sensitive that the Americans insisted on taking them back to Oak Ridge after the two IAEA officials examined them.

Since its secret nuclear program was exposed in 2002, Iran had maintained that its only interest in nuclear power was to generate electricity. The government said it had kept its efforts secret for fifteen years by making its purchases on the black market to evade sanctions by the United States and other Western governments. For its part, the IAEA was having difficulty proving otherwise. The Iranians allowed inspectors to visit suspicious sites but only after the sites had been scrubbed of all evidence of illicit nuclear activities. The material uncovered in Libya raised critical new questions about both the origins of the Iranian program and about how much they were still hiding from the IAEA. The most serious question was raised by the existence of the weapons designs in Libya. Why would Khan have sold those Chinese blueprints to the Libyans and not the Iranians? Heinonen was eager to find the answer.

The IAEA was not the only agency spurred to action by the Libyan disclosures. Rumors had appeared in the press that Swiss engineers had played a role in the Libyan nuclear project, and the authorities in Bern began asking U.S. intelligence if they had any information to offer. Many of the same concerns were coming to light in Germany and Turkey, where the authorities were looking into allegations that domestic businesses might have sold equipment to Libya. In Malaysia, B. S. A. Tahir remained in custody. He was undergoing extensive questioning, and his answers alarmed the Malaysian authorities. It seemed that Tahir and SCOPE had some potentially embarrassing political connections and the Malaysian intelligence agency was uncertain what to do with this information.

The multiple investigations presented an opportunity and a problem for the U.S. government. The State Department and arms control experts in Washington wanted to make sure that everyone associated with the Khan network was prosecuted as fully as possible. But the CIA and some of its backers in the White House worried that prosecutions could expose ongoing intelligence operations. More significantly, a thorough investigation of the events leading up to the Libyan decision might tarnish the portrayal of Kaddafi's decision as a major intelligence victory. What would the world think if it realized that extremely sensitive nuclear weapons designs had been spread across the globe while the CIA watched and waited? What would the world think if it knew that American intelligence had been complicit in allowing sophisticated nuclear-related technology into Iran?

CHAPTER NINE

WASHINGTON

No one had a greater interest in preserving the idea that Libya's abandonment of its nuclear ambitions was a major intelligence victory than George Tenet. By early 2004, the CIA director's star was tarnished. He and his agency had been criticized sharply for failing to act on clues about Al Qaeda's plans before the 2001 attacks. Some experts had even gone so far to suggest that the plot could have been disrupted if the CIA had taken the Al Qaeda threat seriously. While the failures of 9/11 may have been the result of not connecting the dots, the controversy swirling around Tenet in early 2004 was based on seeing dots that didn't exist. The agency, with Tenet as a willing cheerleader, had provided the president with deeply flawed intelligence before the start of the Iraq War in March 2003. The president's public justification for the war, a mantra repeated over and over by administration officials and by Tony Blair in Britain, was that Saddam Hussein possessed chemical, biological, and nuclear weapons, which he was likely to unleash on his enemies at any moment. Tenet had repeatedly assured Bush that Saddam harbored weapons of mass destruction, reaching a climax when he told the president it was a "slam dunk" that Iraq possessed the banned weapons. As the months passed after the invasion and America's massive inspection efforts turned up no evidence of active WMD programs, the pressure mounted on the CIA and its director. Some thought that Tenet would be forced to resign.

Kaddafi's announcement offered him a life raft. The efforts of Jim

Kinsman and his colleagues had shut down the world's most dangerous proliferator and his network. Tenet was justifiably thrilled, and he later saw to it that the agent known as Mad Dog and the entire team were awarded the Distinguished Intelligence Medal, the agency's highest and most coveted honor. Even before those honors were bestowed, however, Tenet was determined to use the episode to burnish his image and that of the agency. In an unusual step, he enlisted Kinsman and half a dozen senior intelligence officials to craft a major public speech that would showcase the Kaddafi decision and the penetration of the Khan network.

In early February, Tenet and his crew got some good news from half a world away. For years American officials had lobbied Pakistani leaders to take action against A. Q. Khan because of his proliferation activities. But Khan was the proud public face of the country's nuclear arsenal, and a long line of Pakistani leaders had refused to take him on. The demise of the Libyan program changed the situation. The Libyans had turned over reams of documents and tons of equipment, which all traced back to Khan and his network. Some of the material had come directly from Khan's government-funded enrichment complex outside Islamabad. The Libyans had gone a step further, explicitly identifying Khan as their main supplier. When Tenet himself flew to Pakistan and laid out the evidence for President Pervez Musharraf in late 2003, the Pakistani dictator had realized that he had no choice. Khan, who was sixty-six years old and living on a comfortable estate on the outskirts of Islamabad, was arrested and, after several days of interrogation, he agreed to sign a written confession and make a public apology. In exchange Musharraf agreed to pardon Khan for his crimes and reduce his sentence to an indefinite term of house arrest.

On February 4, Khan appeared on national television in Pakistan. Reading from a script prepared by the government, the scientist appeared somber and even contrite as he expressed his sorrow and regret for passing nuclear weapons secrets to other countries without government authorization. He didn't explain why he had sold them. For many people, his remarks raised as many questions as they answered. But within the Counter-Proliferation Division at the CIA, the confession was cause for celebration, a signal victory in the war against the spread of nuclear weapons. All they needed now was for Tenet or someone else to persuade Musharraf to grant them access to the disgraced scientist so that they could complete their picture of his operation and roll up the outliers, including the mysterious fourth customer.

The next day, Tenet delivered his speech. The location was chosen carefully to guarantee both a prestigious and receptive audience—students and the press at Georgetown University in northwestern Washington. Tenet was a graduate of Georgetown's School of Foreign Service, and he used the friendly confines of his alma mater to defend the CIA and presumably try to save his own job.

"I have come here today to talk to you and to the American people about something important to our nation and central to our future: how the United States intelligence community evaluated Iraq's weapons of mass destruction program over the past decade, leading to a national intelligence estimate in October of 2002," he said, launching into a spirited and detailed defense of the CIA and its methods in assessing Iraq's weapons of mass destruction programs. Over the course of nearly an hour, he spoke in unprecedented detail about the agency's operations. At one point he acknowledged that "we may have overestimated the progress Saddam was making," but he never apologized for the mistakes that had led the nation to war. Instead Tenet sought to explain the complexity of intelligence work and extol the courage of his officers. "The risks are always high," he said. "Success and perfect outcomes are never guaranteed. But there's one unassailable fact: We will always call it as we see it. Our professional ethic demands no less."

Near the end of the hour, Tenet sought to leave his audience with a positive image of America's intelligence professionals at work by highlighting Libya's abandonment of its nuclear program and the shutting down of the Khan network. "Let's talk about Libya, where a sitting regime has volunteered to dismantle its WMD program," he said. "Somebody on television said we completely missed it. Well, he completely missed it. This was an intelligence success. Why? Because American and British intelligence officers understood the Libyan programs." Tenet praised what he called "the powerful combination of technical intelligence, careful and painstaking analytic work, operational daring and, yes, the kind of human intelligence that people have led the American people to believe we no longer have."

Then the CIA director singled out Khan and his network, accusing them of "shaving years off the nuclear weapons development timelines of several states, including Libya." He boasted about delivering a "crushing blow" to the network, saying that several of Khan's senior officers were in custody and its operations had been shut down worldwide.

"What did intelligence have to do with this?" Tenet asked rhetorically. "First, we discovered the extent of Khan's hidden network. We tagged the proliferators, we detected the networks stretching across four continents offering its wares to countries like North Korea and Iran. Working with our British colleagues, we pieced together the picture of the network, revealing its subsidiaries, its scientists, its front companies, its agents, its finances and manufacturing plants on three continents," he said. "Our spies penetrated the network through a series of daring operations over several years."

Few in the audience challenged the implications of that final phrase— "a series of daring operations over several years." Tenet's acknowledgment that the CIA and British intelligence had penetrated Khan's operation years earlier should have raised questions about why it had taken so long to close it down, and how much damage had been done during the time that the CIA was collecting its information.

The CIA could have stopped Khan before he had even begun to help Pakistan build its nuclear arsenal, and before he ever provided the technology and expertise that was even then leading Iran to the brink of possessing a nuclear weapon, further destabilizing the Middle East. In his memoir, Tenet would go so far as to brag about how much the CIA knew about the Libyan nuclear program before it was shut down. "Sometimes we knew more than the Libyans themselves did," he wrote. "At one point we told them, 'Hey, we know you guys paid a hundred million dollars for all that stuff from A. Q. Khan.' There was a puzzled silence on the other side. 'A hundred million? We thought the price was two hundred million!' Apparently someone had made a heck of a profit on the side." Tenet also discussed the internal debates over the right time to take down Khan. He would defend the decision to wait until the agency had built what he regarded as an airtight case.

TENET'S CLAIM THAT BRINGING DOWN the Khan network was a major intelligence victory, and his later assertion that the agency had acted at the optimal moment, hinged on the CIA's ability to shape the events that followed the speech. Agency experts, or at least someone from the outside world, needed to interrogate Khan to understand the full extent of his perfidy. Among the most pressing questions was exactly what Khan and his accomplices had sold to Iran. CIA and Pentagon nuclear experts poring over the seizures in Libya had reached the same conclusion as the IAEA: Khan had sold much of the same material and designs to Iran, from extensive plans for building an enrichment plant to blueprints and prototypes for the P-2 centrifuge. But there was at least one critical discrepancy: The Libyans had turned over plans for a Chinese nuclear warhead that Khan had delivered to them in a shopping bag from a tailor shop in Islamabad, and no similar plans had been uncovered in Iran by the IAEA inspectors who had been examining Iran's nuclear facilities for several months. Ever since its secret enrichment program was exposed by an exile group in mid-2002, Tehran had maintained that its program was designed solely to develop civilian reactors to generate electricity. Iranian officials denied repeated accusations by the United States and other countries that it was developing a nuclear weapon, and they denied receiving any weapons blueprints from Khan. So far, neither the IAEA nor the CIA had come up with proof to contradict the Iranian claims. But it was logical to assume that, if Khan had provided weapons blueprints to Libya, he had also offered them to Iran. The stakes were raised dramatically by the discovery of electronic versions of the Chinese warhead and the more advanced Pakistani warhead design on Urs Tinner's computer. The Tinners had told Kinsman that they knew of no weapons plans that had been provided to Iran, but Khan was the only person who could provide the definitive answer. He could provide the ultimate proof of the true goal of Iran's nuclear program. In addition to developing a complete understanding of what Iran had obtained, only Khan could identify every major element of the network and the missing customer—or customers.

In order to protect the idea that this had been a major intelligence victory, the agency devoted to uncovering the secrets of other governments and individuals had to mount its own massive cover-up to make sure the world never found out how much critical information, from nuclear weapons designs to missing equipment, had gotten loose while the CIA waited for the right time to act. Even as Tenet spoke at Georgetown, Kinsman was already working to manage the disclosures that would shape what the world would come to know about how the network was brought down and what lethal secrets were revealed before that happened. The challenge would soon grow more difficult and require enlisting senior officials of the Bush administration to subvert the laws of a foreign government.

The first task was protecting the Tinners. As he had promised Urs and Marco back in New Orleans in November, Kinsman had come up with a way for them to destroy evidence and collect more money. In the middle of January, he contacted Friedrich Tinner and laid out his plan: Destroy the remaining cache of valves and components. The CIA would pay the Tinners as if they were actually sold to the U.S. government. He even provided details for the fake shipping records. On January 16, Friedrich's daughter signed customs documents to ship thirty-two packages containing high-tech vacuum valves to a CIA front in Chicago called Deramo Systems. Four days later, she signed paperwork for a second shipment of ninety-four boxes of centrifuge components to Deramo. The shipments were valued at a total of $1.5 million, roughly the amount the Tinners said they would have gotten from Libya. The CIA wired that amount to the Traco account in the British Virgin Islands.

The substantial payment was authorized for the Tinners despite doubts about their truthfulness and even though they were no longer essential to the intelligence agency. Kinsman had long suspected they weren't telling him everything. But there is no indication that Kinsman or his associates ever took the standard step of hooking the Tinners up to a polygraph machine to determine just how much information they were withholding. Instead, suspicions about the gaps in the story had led to the break-in at Marco's house in Jenins, which had proved that critical information was being withheld. With each meeting, the CIA officer peeled back another layer of the onion, but the Tinners were shrewd enough to realize that information was money and leverage. The ongoing attempt to get the full story was why the CIA paid for Friedrich, Urs, and Marco to travel to the British Virgin Islands at the end of January. The meetings occurred on Tortola, the largest of the sixty inhabited and uninhabited islands that make up the archipelago in the Caribbean Sea. The Tinners were more than happy to get a break from the Swiss winter, and they were familiar with Tortola. And they could visit their money at Marco's bank.

From January 26 to 30, Kinsman and a couple of his colleagues met with the Tinners at a luxury hotel on Tortola. The days were spent going over the details of the network's operations with the Tinners. The CIA debriefers pushed them to recall details of what had been produced at the Malaysian factory and to identify every other supplier and manufacturer involved with the network. One topic of discussion was how the network obtained maraging steel, an alloy that is on restricted export lists worldwide, for use in the P-2 rotors the factory was gearing up to produce for Libya.

As the conversation continued, the CIA agents kept circling back to what worried them most—the possible existence of other customers. They asked whether the Tinners were aware of any dealings with other countries or terrorist organizations like Al Qaeda. They pressed them on what had happened to equipment that had gone missing. Each time, the Tinners said they knew nothing about any other customers and they knew nothing about the final destination for any missing material. Khan kept much of what he did to himself, they said repeatedly.

What Kinsman and his colleagues could not know was whether the Tinners were withholding information for their own purposes, either to sell it down the road or as insurance in case the CIA abandoned them. The Tinners clearly remained concerned about what might happen if their involvement in the network were exposed by the Swiss government or the investigators from the IAEA in Vienna who were using information provided by Libya to try to unravel Khan's operation.

After consulting with his superiors back at Langley, including a senior agency officer who had served as Vienna station chief, Kinsman proposed that the Tinners cooperate with the IAEA investigation, at least up to a point. The idea was to win some immunity by helping the

IAEA. Before the Tinners returned to Switzerland, they agreed to the plan. Kinsman said he would set up a time and place for a meeting. He cautioned the Tinners to sit tight and promised to get back in touch as soon as the arrangements were set.

Like every other big government agency, the CIA is a bureaucracy, with rules to obey and turfs to be protected. In order to put his plan in motion, Kinsman had to get the approval of the chief of the agency's European division, who controlled the Vienna station. The two men were old friends and the European division chief readily agreed to instruct the Vienna station to quietly reach out to the IAEA on behalf of the Tinners. Before any arrangements were made, however, events veered way outside the CIA's control and threatened to upset all of the plans.

Tahir had remained in Malaysian custody since his role in the network was disclosed to the authorities there back in November. The Malaysians were alarmed by the disclosure that a factory in their country was associated with a nuclear black market that was now generating headlines around the world. The concerns focused not only on the proliferation aspects but also on the potential political fallout. The SCOPE factory was partly owned by the son of the country's prime minister, Abdullah Badawi, though there is no evidence the son was involved in the nuclear trade.

Under an agreement with the Americans and British to avoid tipping their hand, the Malaysians had not arrested Tahir immediately. Instead he had been placed under twenty-four-hour surveillance until Libya's announcement. Only then was he taken into custody and held incommunicado on vague charges of violating the national security act. He could be held indefinitely without the embarrassment of a public trial that would embarrass the prime minister's son. During his detention, Tahir described the extent of his involvement in the Khan network. He named names, implicating more than two dozen participants worldwide. The Americans and the British pressed the Malaysians to keep the wraps on Tahir's disclosures while they went around the world trying to roll up portions of the network in their own time. The Malaysians agreed reluctantly.

On February 11, President Bush delivered what the White House billed as a major address on weapons of mass destruction at the National

Defense University in Washington. Still defensive about the failures in Iraq, Bush emphasized the success against Khan and his network. "A. Q. Khan is known throughout the world as the father of Pakistan's nuclear weapons program," the president said. "What was not publicly known until recently is that he also led an extensive international network for the proliferation of nuclear technology and know-how." Instead of disclosing the full scope of Khan's operation, however, Bush singled out the factory in Malaysia and Tahir, whom he accused of being "the network's chief financial officer and money launderer." The president, who had already demonstrated his resolve by invading Afghanistan and Iraq, vowed to wipe out the entire Khan network. "We will find you and we're not going to rest until you are stopped," he said.

Back in Kuala Lumpur, the president's speech hit like a bomb. The Malaysian authorities had been playing ball and keeping Tahir under wraps, but senior officials were angered by the shift in focus to the SCOPE factory, and fearful of its political implications. Their response would be swift and orchestrated for maximum exposure worldwide. It would make Kinsman's damage control efforts much harder and much more urgent. Defying requests from the CIA and MI6, the Malaysians were going to identify key participants in Khan's network to deflect criticism from their own role. Among the names would be all three Tinners. All that remained was for the Malaysians to determine the best way to get the message out.

CHAPTER TEN

VIENNA

On February 18, 2004, a week after Bush's big speech, Friedrich, Urs, and Marco Tinner checked into a suite at the InterContinental hotel in Vienna. Waiting for them were Kinsman, Sharon, and two technical agents from the Vienna station who would operate the recording equipment in the room next to the suite. After operating in the shadows for so long, the Tinners were about to meet investigators from the IAEA. All three were nervous as Kinsman rehearsed the script for the session, coaching them on what to say and what to withhold. He assured them that he and Sharon would be there, ready to intervene if anything went awry.

Kinsman had heard from colleagues that the Malaysians might be releasing information about the network in the coming days, and he knew that it would be difficult to contain the fallout if the Tinners and other participants in the ring were identified. So he was under pressure to enlist the assistance of the IAEA, trading access to the Tinners for the agency's future help in protecting the Swiss family—and ultimately the CIA. Fortunately for the CIA, the atomic energy agency was in the market for some help.

Two weeks earlier, the thirty-five countries that comprise the IAEA board of governors had voted unanimously to open a formal inquiry into the worldwide activities of the Khan network, which ElBaradei referred to as a "nuclear Wal-Mart." It was an unusually aggressive step for a generally timid agency, but ElBaradei had persuaded his board to formalize the inquiry he had authorized Heinonen to start right after the Libyan disclosure in December. Still, the IAEA had no legal authority to demand that individuals or companies cooperate with its inquiries. Instead Heinonen and his colleagues would have to rely on persuading people to cooperate with them—and on information parceled out to it by the world's intelligence and law enforcement agencies.

A few days after the board approved his inquiry, Heinonen got a major break. A woman with an American accent called his office. She did not identify herself, but she seemed strangely familiar with his investigation. When the woman said she had valuable information and proposed meeting him at a Starbucks near the State Opera House on Vienna's Ringstrasse, Heinonen agreed. The next day he found himself sitting across from an attractive young Asian woman who said her name was Jackie. Heinonen suspected she was from the CIA. There was no casual conversation to break the ice. The woman got straight to the point. She said she was willing to set up a meeting between Heinonen and the Tinners to help the IAEA understand the inner workings of the Khan network. She said that the Swiss businessmen were cooperating with the U.S. government and that they were willing to assist the IAEA, too. Jackie, who actually worked in the counterproliferation section at the CIA station in Vienna, made no mention that the plan was to provide the IAEA with enough information to later enlist the agency's assistance in protecting the Tinners from possible reprisals in Switzerland.

Friedrich Tinner had long been on the agency's radar screen for his proliferation activities. Swiss authorities had warned the IAEA as early as 1979 that Friedrich Tinner was helping Pakistan. But the agency had never had any solid information about his involvement in nuclear trafficking. Since he started investigating Iran's nuclear program the previous year, Heinonen's interest in the emerging picture of a worldwide nuclear black market had ratcheted up. The Iranians never volunteered anything, however, and extracting evidence of their ties to Khan required time-consuming and often maddening negotiations. The Americans and the Israelis had been feeding bits of intelligence to the IAEA about Iran's program, but Heinonen knew there was more to the network than he had been told. So when Jackie offered up the Tinners, he jumped at the chance to meet with participants in the network.

On February 18, Heinonen knocked on the door of the InterContinental suite. It was opened by a man who appeared to be in his late sixties. He introduced himself as Friedrich Tinner. Seated in the room were his two sons, Urs and Marco. There also were two Americans who introduced themselves only by their first names, Jim and Sharon. Heinonen assumed they were from the CIA. Before the conversation began, the Americans insisted that Heinonen agree to treat the information as highly confidential. They said it could not be shared beyond a small circle within the IAEA. It could not be disseminated to other countries that were part of the agency's governing board. Heinonen agreed to what he later called "rules of the game." One rule was unspoken: The CIA would expect the IAEA to go to bat for the Tinners with the Swiss authorities if it came to that.

Over the next two hours, the Tinners revealed the architecture of Khan's operation. As the names, dates, and transactions gradually unspooled, the IAEA official learned that the Tinners were not just suppliers to Khan. They were at the heart of the network, aware of shipments to Libya and Iran, the identities of other participants, the nuts and bolts of the enterprise's day-to-day operations. They could lead the agency deep into the network, provided Heinonen played his cards carefully. The IAEA official listened intently as the Tinners described the massive enrichment and bomb-making facilities that the network had been building in Libya.

According to the Tinners, the enrichment plant was based on drawings that Gotthard Lerch had taken from Leybold-Heraeus nearly twenty years before and schematics of Pakistan's plant provided by Khan. The Pakistani scientist had also sold the Libyans technical data on enriching uranium for nuclear weapons, data drawn from years of his own experience and tests. The plant was designed to produce highly enriched uranium through 5,832 centrifuges arrayed in four levels of cascades. The Tinners described how the uranium would be enriched to progressively higher levels as it passed through the four tiers of cascades, ending with a final product that would be 90 percent enriched—perfect for weapons. They said that the thousands of centrifuges, and tens of thousands of components required to build the machines, had been built at the SCOPE factory and at the Tinners' own plant in Switzerland. Additional equipment had been bought secretly from suppliers across Europe and Asia, they explained. Some of the most technical work had been contracted out to engineers in South Africa who were veterans of that country's nuclear weapons program more than a decade earlier. Some of the equipment had been flowing directly from Khan's facilities in Pakistan to Libya, but most of it had been shipped to Dubai first and then forwarded to Libya, according to the Tinners.

The scope of the operation described by the Tinners was far beyond anything that Heinonen had imagined. He and his team knew nothing about the South African end of the network, and they had no idea that such detailed plans had made their way to Libya. This was more than the Libyans had disclosed, and it raised new questions about whether Kaddafi was concealing material. The disclosure also focused new concerns on Iran. Had Khan and his accomplices shared far more knowledge with the Iranians than anyone knew? When Heinonen expressed his alarm at the sophistication of the enrichment setup planned for Libya, Urs Tinner said the situation was not as bad as it appeared. He said the Libyans would never have been able to make the crucial leap of getting their centrifuges running at the ultrahigh speeds required to enrich uranium to weapons grade. "I sabotaged the machines at the factory in Malaysia," he said, providing details of the steps he had taken to ensure that the centrifuges would not operate properly.

Heinonen did not have the technical background to understand the significance of the sabotage that Tinner was describing. He stopped the proceedings and said that he wanted to bring in a colleague who could verify whether Tinner's supposed alterations were feasible and whether they would have an impact on the operation of the centrifuges. Heinonen asked Jim and Sharon if he could come back the next day with the IAEA's top centrifuge expert. The CIA officers agreed.

No one at the IAEA was better positioned to understand what Tinner was saying about the centrifuge components and the broader concept of building an entire enrichment facility than Trevor Edwards, a British engineer who had worked at the IAEA for several years. In the 1970s, Edwards had been a project manager for Britain at the Urenco plant in the Netherlands, helping develop advanced centrifuges for enriching uranium for civilian electric plants. While working at Urenco, he had met a young scientist named A. Q. Khan. They had even exchanged a few words in English.

When Edwards and Heinonen returned to the hotel the next morning, Urs Tinner was asked to go over his sabotage efforts again, in greater detail. Much of what he heard sounded right to Edwards. Tinner had a grasp of the architecture of the components, and he seemed to understand the impact of his alterations. Still, Edwards wondered whether the subtle changes would lead to malfunctions. It was possible the machines would run, albeit more slowly or for a shorter period of time.

Heinonen and Edwards spent the second day pushing the Tinners to try to fill gaps in their knowledge. The Libyans had turned over copies of thousands of invoices for nuclear equipment to the IAEA. Using them, Heinonen's team was assembling a vast matrix of the companies involved in the network and trying to determine the precise quantities of equipment sold to Libya. The goal was to use the Libyan information to understand the full extent of the network's reach, and to confront Iran down the road. In reconstructing the shipments to Libya, one of Heinonen's colleagues had discovered that Khan had shipped seven rotors for the P-2 centrifuge from Pakistan to Dubai, but only five had made it to Libya. The missing rotors were significant for several reasons. Could they have gone to Iran? Were they an indication that there was a still-unidentified customer?

"Two P-2 rotors seem to missing," Heinonen said. "Do you know what happened to them?"

"As the network started to fall apart, I took those remaining rotors out into the gulf on my boat and threw them overboard," Urs said, following Kinsman's script. "I was worried that they would fall into the wrong hands."

After several hours on the second day, Kinsman suggested that the IAEA officials return for a third day to complete the debriefing. Heinonen said that he could not be there. He would send Edwards back alone.

The next day, Edwards brought his laptop computer and a computer disk that the IAEA had been given by the senior Libyan nuclear technician, Karim. The disk was an instructional manual for planning and constructing a centrifuge plant. Most of the information appeared to have originated at Khan's research lab in Pakistan. Some of it, however, had come from other sources. As soon as Edwards played the disk on his computer for the Tinners and the two CIA agents, Urs interrupted. "Oh, that isn't my latest," he said. "I gave another to Karim that was more up to date."

Edwards was surprised. After Kaddafi's public mea culpa, the Libyans had asserted that they had turned over everything from the network. There were suspicions that they had held back information and possibly equipment in case their leader changed his mind about closing down the program; Tinner's revelation seemed to confirm that the IAEA had not gotten everything, as promised. As he thought about the existence of the second disk, Edwards caught a glimmer of a far bigger threat. How much information had the Tinners and others involved with the network transferred to digital formats?

Edwards did not know it, but the CIA was already well aware of the danger that bomb plans and centrifuge designs were floating around the electronic world. The Khan network had digitized and distributed the blueprints to enrich uranium and construct a nuclear device. The CIA had known that Khan was selling nuclear plans as early as 2001, when Urs Tinner had copied them from the black cases in Khan's Dubai apartment. Two years later, the CIA had discovered digital copies of those same construction plans as well as more advanced Pakistani weapons plans at Marco's home in Jenins. Where else could those plans have gone in the intervening years? Even now, with much of the network shut down, the CIA had ordered the Tinners not to mention electronic copies of the weapons designs to the IAEA or anyone else. American intelligence officials were determined to keep the lid on how much highly sensitive technology and information the Khan network had loosed on the world, even if it required lying to the international agency charged with stopping the spread of nuclear weapons, even if it meant efforts by the IAEA to understand the reach of Khan's enterprise would be undermined. The CIA had its own interests to protect.

By the time Edwards was wrapping up the third day at the InterContinental, Heinonen and one of his assistants, Miharu Yonemura, were making plans to go to Dubai to check out the information from the Tinners. They contacted the Dubai police and, after several calls higher and higher up the chain of command, they reached an agreement for escorts to several locations that had been mentioned in the debriefing.

A few days later, Heinonen, Yonemura, and Edwards boarded an airplane and flew to Dubai, a sunny and warm respite from the bone-chilling cold of Vienna. After checking into a hotel and meeting with the police officers who would accompany them, the group drove to the free-trade zone where SMB Computers had its office and warehouses. This was, according to the Tinners, the hub of the network's shipping operation. Essential equipment had been stored there over the years, and the IAEA team hoped to at least get some sense of the operation's scale. Urs Tinner had said the locations were cleared out, but Yonemura had brought along a technical kit that would allow her to take samples from the warehouses to determine whether any radioactive material had been on the premises. The results would answer the most critical question of all: Had Khan sold Libya or Iran not only the means to produce fissile material for a bomb, but the actual material itself?

Chapter Eleven

Bern

Zurich is world famous for its banks and Geneva is known for diplomacy. But the capital of Switzerland is Bern, a beautiful city of about 130,000 nestled along the banks of the River Aare near the center of the country. While Zurich and Geneva are sophisticated, Bern is quaint. A bear park dating to 1513 was modernized in 2004 and is a source of pride for locals. The skyline is dominated by the green dome of the Bundeshaus, the highly decorative parliament building completed in 1902. Arrayed around Parliament Square are elegant, low-rise buildings housing the various ministries. In one of the more nondescript structures, a good walk from the Bundeshaus, are the offices of the State Secretariat for Economic Affairs, the agency in charge of issuing export licenses.

On the morning of February 21, 2004, Othmar Wyss, a trim man in his fifties, was sitting in his office when he first read about Tahir's accusations against the Tinner family in a newspaper. The day before, the Malaysian government had released a twelve-page statement that identified the Swiss engineers as participants in the worst proliferation network in history. It was all over the newspapers and television. The accusations were startling, and it was not the first time Wyss had heard the Tinner name in a suspicious context. As the head of the Swiss export regulatory agency, he had come across the Tinners several times.

Wyss had been regulating exports for a decade. Over the years his agency had approved many licenses allowing the Tinners to export so-called "dual use" technology, which had both civilian purposes and military applications. Switzerland ranked among the leading nations for exports of dual-use technology, which can be among the trickiest equipment for regulators to evaluate. Discerning how a particular piece of equipment will be used once it arrives in a country is difficult. Places like Pakistan and Iran have created numerous front companies with innocuous names or associations with universities to fool regulators over the years. They claim that a particular piece of dual-use technology is destined for a university for research purposes or a hospital for medical care when in truth, the equipment is for a secret nuclear program.

Swiss authorities had long suspected that the Tinners were involved in nuclear trafficking, but they had never proven any illegal activity. The closest they had come was in 1996 when, after a request from the IAEA, Swiss authorities had questioned Friedrich Tinner about how some of his specialized valves licensed for export to Singapore had ended up in Jordan, marked for forwarding to Iraq just before the Gulf War. The case appeared to be a classic case of a false end-user certificate. "No, no, I sent those to Singapore," Tinner told his Swiss inquisitor, digging the legal export license for the Far Eastern country out of his records. "I have no idea how they ended up in Jordan." The suspicions were never followed because Switzerland's two-year statute of limitation on export crimes had expired by the time the shipments came to light. But the suspicion had stayed with Wyss.

At the office that morning, Wyss checked the license records. He found that Tinners operated two companies, now called Phitec and Traco. They had received twenty to thirty licenses to export dual-use technology since 2000. As with the Singapore transaction, the license applications specified that the equipment was for civilian purposes and was destined for countries that rang no alarm bells. "Tinner never exported to Iran, Libya, or North Korea," Wyss said later. "He always exported to countries like Malaysia or Dubai, which were not suspicious at the time."

A few days earlier, the IAEA had sent Wyss a list of fifteen people and four Swiss companies suspected of participating in the Khan network. The list was dated, going back fifteen years, and the people were identified only by surnames. The only names that Wyss recognized were

Tinner and two Tinner companies, Phitec and Traco. But the newspaper article Wyss read on February 21 was a different story.

On February 20, the Malaysian police released a summary of Tahir's confession to the press and posted it on the Internet. The action came nine days after President Bush had singled out Malaysia as a hub of the Khan network. The Internet posting was arranged to ensure maximum publicity. The summary essentially exonerated the Malaysian government and the factory. Tahir was being held without charges under a tough national security law. His claims could have been buried for years, perhaps forever. But the Malaysian government had been angered when Bush cast the country in such a bad light.

The Malaysians pointed the finger almost exclusively at Europeans and urged the IAEA to focus its investigation there. The report identified two Germans, Gotthard Lerch and Heinz Mebus, and said they were involved in providing centrifuge designs and technology. Peter and Paul Griffin, a British father and son, were accused in the statement of arranging for the shipment of equipment to Libya through their business in Dubai. Also named were Gunes Cire and Selim Alguadis, the owners of the Turkish factories involved in sales to Libya.

The most detailed and damning allegations were reserved for the Tinners. According to the police report, Tahir had described Friedrich as a long-standing supplier for Khan. It singled out Urs as the person who provided technical expertise to the SCOPE factory and oversaw purchases of specialized machinery and material for the project. It described how he had tried to cover his tracks by destroying material before fleeing Malaysia. "In Oct 2003, URS TINNER ended his term of service at the SCOPE factory and just before this, is said to have taken the hard disk of the company's computer that was designated for his use," the report said. "URS TINNER is also said to have taken his personal file from the SCOPE factory's records. This gave the impression that URS TINNER did not wish to leave any trace of his presence there." To prove otherwise, the police released a photocopy from the page of Urs's passport with his picture and his Malaysian work permit. According to the statement, Tahir told the police that Friedrich had arranged for the manufacture and production of advanced centrifuge components in Europe for the Libyan nuclear project. He said that Marco had arranged for SCOPE to import sophisticated machinery and restricted technology from Britain, France, and Taiwan through his Swiss company, Traco Holdings.

The Malaysian report caused a sensation in the world's press. Enterprising reporters began tracking down people like Lerch and the Tinners, knocking on doors and demanding answers to questions raised by the statement. Governments reacted, too, launching their own investigations into the allegations against their citizens.

In Bern, Wyss immediately got in touch with the federal police. Before the day was over, he and a senior police official had discussed a preliminary investigation into whether the Tinners had exported controlled goods without proper licenses, whether they had exported noncontrolled items with the knowledge they were intended for use in a nuclear weapons program, and whether Urs Tinner had knowingly assisted a foreign nuclear weapons program, the most serious potential charge.

AT CIA HEADQUARTERS, THE MALAYSIAN report caused an altogether different reaction. The American government had never expected the Malaysian authorities to release such a detailed report on Tahir's confession. The CIA was caught flat-footed when the statement named so many names and singled out the Tinners as central players in Khan's nuclear black market. With their names published in newspapers around the world, it would now be much harder to persuade the Swiss government to ignore the role the Tinners had played. Some evidence against them had been destroyed, and the Malaysian statement said nothing of their role in helping the CIA. But plenty of incriminating information was still stored on computers left behind at Marco's apartment and other locations. Faced with potential prison terms and hefty fines, the Tinners might tell all. Jim Kinsman needed a new plan to keep the lid on.

The first step would be persuading Swiss intelligence to block any investigation. Within days, a team of senior CIA officers was dispatched to meet with their counterparts from the two Swiss intelligence agencies, the domestic arm known as the Secret Service and the external arm, Strategic Intelligence Service. The cover-up would be shrouded in the vague language of "national security" and "ongoing intelligence operations." If that didn't work, there was always the veiled threat that the CIA had been forced to do the job because the Swiss had endangered the world's security by failing to police their own nuclear exports. The CIA team would have to reveal that the Tinners had helped them, but they would disclose only enough to motivate the intelligence officials to persuade the police to back down. And of course, any word that the Tinners were assets would be kept within the kinship of the intelligence world. The goal was to keep the details of the episode "in the family," as one senior CIA official described it later.

The crew from Langley, joined by the agency's station chief for Switzerland, told their Swiss colleagues the truth, just not the whole truth. They stressed that bringing down the Khan network had stopped a major threat to world security, a threat that carried particular weight in the aftermath of the attacks on the World Trade Center and Pentagon less than three years earlier. They acknowledged that the Tinners had helped the CIA and MI6 by providing information on various shipments, particularly those related to the Libyan project. But, they said, dismantling the Khan network was not over. Putting the Tinners on trial risked exposing critical aspects of the ongoing intelligence operations. Among the secrets that had to be protected, they said, were the identities of people in other countries who were cooperating with the Americans and the British. Some of those spies were still in place, they hinted, and were sabotaging the Iranian nuclear program. The CIA officers admitted that the agency had broken Swiss law by recruiting Swiss citizens as spies, but they justified their actions by pointing to what they regarded as the greater good—shutting down a black market that represented a genuine security threat to the West. In case the Swiss missed the point, the Americans said that they would not have been forced to solicit help from Swiss citizens if Swiss authorities had acted forcefully in the previous years and stopped the Tinners and other Swiss manufacturers who had supplied nuclear technology to countries like Pakistan, Iraq, and Iran.

The Americans had plenty to hide themselves. They conveniently left out anything that might have made their interlocutors less receptive to the idea of blocking any inquiry into the Tinners. They did not mention the break-ins at Marco's office and house. They did not describe the extensive records copied from his computers. They said nothing about the detailed blueprints for nuclear weapons still in the possession of the Tinners. Nor did they suggest that the Swiss authorities act as quickly as possible to seize those same computers, which had remained in place now for more than a year. Despite the fact that the Tinners still had access to those records, and could conceal them or ship them anywhere in the world, the CIA was unwilling to share, even with members of the intelligence family.

For the most part, the CIA officers found their Swiss counterparts receptive to the explanation. Even though the Americans had broken Swiss law by recruiting its citizens, there was an unspoken bond within the intelligence world that such transgressions were best dealt with in a way that did not draw attention from outsiders. And some of the Swiss officials nodded knowingly when the Americans described the failure of the Swiss government to crack down on the trafficking in nuclear technology. One of the Swiss intelligence officials acknowledged that his agency had been frustrated by its inability to act on tips about suspicious exports from the Americans and others dating back to the late 1970s. Senior government officials, often more interested in economics than stopping proliferation, had blocked him by dismissing the allegations as American propaganda, he said.

"We were speaking the same language," the senior Swiss official said later. "We had been cooperating for many years, with multiple successes in the war on terror, so we trusted each other. We had the advantage of being old comrades in arms. . . . I got the feeling that the main goal on the U.S. side was really to try to get the Tinners out, to get hold of the information they still might have, and to try to dismantle the rest of the Khan network. They had nothing to hide. I could be wrong, but I have a good feeling for the people I was dealing with."

Not every Swiss official would be so understanding, particularly when it came to leaving highly sensitive nuclear blueprints unguarded on the Tinner computers. In a reference to the staged break-in at Marco's office and apartment, Swiss senator Claude Janiak, head of a parliamentary commission that subsequently investigated the Tinner affair, said later, "The United States knew at least in 2003 that the Tinners had all these materials when they paid a visit. They informed the Swiss government in 2004 only that the Tinners had worked for them and that they were good guys. They didn't tell the Swiss, 'Careful, you have dangerous material at home.'"

On March 4, the day after the CIA delegation left the country, two senior officers from the Swiss Secret Service went to the Ministry of Justice to meet with the justice minister and the director of the federal police. Much as the Americans had withheld important details from the Swiss, the intelligence officers presented a sanitized version to their own officials. They acknowledged that the Tinners had probably broken Swiss export laws through their involvement with the Khan network. They argued that the Tinners' crimes were mitigated because they had helped shut down the black market. Yes, they said, the Americans had broken Swiss law by recruiting the Tinners, but they had acted out of necessity. Echoing the CIA, the Swiss officers argued that pursuing a case against the Tinners at the time could damage ongoing intelligence operations, which they were not authorized to discuss in any detail.

The justice minister who heard these revelations was Christoph Blocher, a larger-than-life figure in Swiss politics. Blocher bears a striking resemblance to a cheerful Dick Cheney. And his politics run in a similar direction. In a country where consensus rules and savvy politicians practice the art of self-effacement, Blocher was a brash billionaire industrialist who had used his fortune to finance various right-wing causes.

When the intelligence officers laid out the American position for him, Blocher's inclination was to bow to the demands. He didn't want to be accused of disrupting intelligence operations, particularly those involving a nuclear threat. He also could see the political dangers in going against the wishes of the Americans. Near the end of the meeting, he said he would recommend to his colleagues on the Federal Council, the executive branch of the Swiss government, that they not investigate the Tinners. Still, ceding authority to the Americans was hard for such an ardent nationalist. When the federal police director, Jean-Luc Vez, countered that the preliminary investigation should continue, Blocher relented slightly. The inquiry could proceed, he said, but it should be carried out quietly, with regular progress reports directly to him. He wasn't prepared to give in to American pressure quite yet, though he was clearly leaning toward agreeing to the cover-up.

IN THE WEEKS THAT FOLLOWED, Wyss and the federal police assembled a clearer picture of the technology that the Tinners had exported. They compared it with the information in the Malaysian report and with press accounts of what had been discovered in Libya by the Americans and British. The Tinners were summoned for questioning, but their answers were vague and unhelpful. The investigation was only preliminary, so the police could not subpoena evidence from the Tinners and they could not raid their offices or homes, where incriminating information was still stored. "The problem is that they only gave us what they thought would not be problematic," Wyss said later.

For help, the Swiss Secret Service turned to the CIA. They asked for more information about the role played by the Tinners in the Khan network and for specifics about any Swiss-origin equipment that had been found in Libya. The Swiss were not operating blindly. For instance, in examining the export records of Phitec and Traco, Wyss had found that the companies had shipped sixty-six steel containers to Dubai and then on to Singapore. The containers had been exported without a license because the invoices specified that the contents were not restricted technology. But Wyss learned from a German customs official that the containers were manufactured from specialized steel to precise specifications that meant they were suitable for transporting uranium hexafluoride, the highly corrosive gas used to fuel centrifuges in the enrichment process.

The new information was important because it indicated that the containers had a use specific to a nuclear program, which meant they were subject to Swiss export regulations. For Wyss, this was the first solid clue that he could use to build a case against the Tinners. But he could not rely on information from a German official. He would need to examine one of the containers himself and, if possible, retrieve one for use as evidence in court.

The first American and British team into Libya had found a large number of such containers. They had been crated up and sent to the

American weapons laboratory in Oak Ridge, Tennessee, along with hundreds of tons of other material from Libya's nuclear program. There American nuclear experts had determined that the containers had actually been used to transport uranium hexafluoride. Documents recovered along with them had enabled the Americans to track their strange voyage from Switzerland to Dubai and Singapore to Pyongyang, the capital of North Korea. In the final piece of the puzzle, financial records from a bank in the Chinese territory of Macao indicated that the Libyans had paid about forty thousand dollars into an account belonging to the government of North Korea about the same time invoices showed the steel containers were shipped from Pyongyang to Tripoli. The evidence indicated that Khan had used his long-standing connections with the communist nation's nuclear scientists to purchase a significant quantity of uranium hexafluoride, which was critical to his nuclear effort in Libya.

Through the Swiss Secret Service and a formal government-to-government request, the Swiss attorney general's office asked the Americans to send one of the containers to Switzerland for tests to confirm that it had been manufactured to transport uranium gas. A single container could constitute proof that the Tinners had violated Swiss export laws. But the Americans refused to even reply to the request. Wyss was frustrated. "The United States knew at least since 2000 that the Tinners had exported to the Libyan nuclear program, but we were not told," he said later. "And we authorized shipments to Malaysia and Dubai because we had no information that these Swiss companies were critical."

On September 22, Wyss and his police colleague sent their preliminary findings to the attorney general's office. The attorney general would make the final recommendation to Blocher on whether to proceed with prosecution of the Tinners. Though couched in careful language and avoiding legal conclusions, the analysis made clear that there was enough information to investigate the Tinners for violating Swiss export laws and knowingly shipping goods for use in a foreign nuclear program. As one example, it mentioned the sixty-six steel containers, though the Swiss had still not been granted access to them by the Americans. There also was evidence that the Tinners had exported noncontrolled items to Dubai, Malaysia, Turkey, and Singapore that they probably knew were intended for use in nuclear weapons programs. Stymied by the lack of cooperation from the Tinners or the CIA, the report said there was no proof yet that Urs Tinner had committed the most serious crime by violating the Swiss War Material Act, which specifically prohibits assisting foreign countries develop nuclear, chemical, or biological weapons.

Blocher had been getting progress reports on the slow-paced investigation of the Tinners and their connection to nuclear proliferation from the Swiss intelligence service and police. When the attorney general's office presented the findings to him, he was angry and demanded to know why Swiss export regulators had not stopped the shipments by the Tinners. As a politician, he recognized the potential embarrassment if Swiss ineptitude came to light on the international stage. As justice minister, however, he had legal responsibilities that made it difficult to block the prosecution of lawbreakers.

For many years, the Swiss had failed to respond to formal inquiries, called demarches, from the American and British governments that Swiss companies were trafficking in nuclear technology. German, Dutch, and French companies also had been implicated, but little action had been taken by those governments either. "I got sick and tired of sitting back all those years, demarching all those countries, seeing how they ignored the demarches, sort of mocking the whole process," said a former CIA officer who worked in Europe and specialized in nuclear proliferation issues. "If you are a CIA officer anywhere in the world, you always try to be the little gray man. You never flaunt local customs or laws. I am just saying, theoretically, that the CIA is the CIA. We are not social workers. We will work with countries, but when that doesn't work, we will do what we need to do."

Blocher believed that the CIA had done what it thought it needed to do. The Secret Service officers who attended the meeting told him that the Americans had recruited the Tinners in violation of Swiss law. They also appeared to have conducted operations on Swiss soil, though exactly what they had done remained unclear.

Blocher was in a tough spot.

CHAPTER TWELVE

INNSBRUCK, AUSTRIA

The disclosure that Libya had received the warhead designs from Khan in early 2000 was especially troubling to the IAEA. Given Khan's central role as chief supplier to both Iran and Libya, it was logical to assume that he would have provided the same designs to Tehran. But asked whether they had received the warhead blueprints, Iranian officials were adamant in their denial. They said there was nothing in the material they had bought from anyone on the black market related to nuclear weapons. Their program was, after all, strictly civilian.

By the fall of 2004, nearly a year after the discoveries in Libya, Heinonen was trying to talk with as many participants in the Khan ring as possible; he did not want to depend solely on the Tinners. He believed that his investigation was gaining traction. The evidence turned over by the Libyans was a virtual inventory of what the network had on offer. There was no doubt that Khan had provided critical technology and expertise to the Iranian program, too, but the inventory provided by Libya had allowed the IAEA inspectors to ask tougher, more pointed questions. Some of the results were surprising.

From the first inspections of Iran's previously secret enrichment efforts in early 2003, the IAEA had known that Iran was building a version of the P-1 centrifuge. The Iranians initially tried to claim they had designed the centrifuges themselves, but Trevor Edwards was familiar enough with the P-1 design from his days at Urenco in the 1970s to recognize a replica when he saw one. Eventually the Iranians acknowledged obtaining designs and components for the P-1 from the nuclear black market. Still, they denied any dealings with Khan.

In Libya, the IAEA team had seen plenty of components for P-1 centrifuges, and some assembled machines. But they also had found rotors for the P-2, the more advanced machine. The Libyans freely acknowledged that they had bought the improved version from Khan. In fact, they said they intended to eventually switch entirely to the P-2 because it enriched uranium much faster. The logical question was whether Khan had provided the same advanced version to Iran. It was an important issue: If Iran had bought designs, components, or actual P-2 machines, it meant they were hiding something from the IAEA inspectors. When confronted by the IAEA, the Iranians claimed to know nothing about any advanced version. Several weeks passed. Letters were sent back and forth. Heinonen pressed the Iranian Atomic Energy Organization for a straight answer. The Iranians maintained their position. Finally, after several weeks, Iranian officials admitted that they had acquired designs for the P-2 in 1994. But they once again denied getting them from Khan. Further, they claimed the early research had gone nowhere, stalling after a private company that had been asked to do the work could not buy the specialized metal for the P-2 rotors. The Iranians said they had abandoned the effort and concentrated on the P-1.

After nearly two years of trying to pry information out of Iran, this pattern of denial, confrontation, and admission was familiar to the IAEA and Heinonen. The opening position from Iranian atomic energy officials was invariably denial. When presented with hard evidence, they eventually backed down, bit by bit. Inevitably they returned with a claim that they had never used a particular technology or followed up on a certain line of research. Even when faced with the discovery of nearly identical technology in Libya, which the Libyans had acknowledged buying from Khan, the Iranians continued to deny that they had had any dealings with the Pakistani scientist. The denials continued even after Khan's televised confession in which he acknowledged selling nuclear secrets to Iran. Since Khan was under house arrest in Islamabad and quarantined from outside interrogators, there was no way to completely disprove the Iranian assertion.

Heinonen and his colleagues could only speculate on why the Iranians were so determined to distance themselves from Khan. One possible reason was that admitting buying centrifuges and other material from him might lead to questions about what else the Pakistani scientist had sold to them, such as blueprints for a Chinese nuclear warhead. But the foot-dragging on the admissions was a central part of the overall Iranian strategy in dealing with the IAEA and the international community. Iran was playing a shrewd game, buying time to develop its capacity for enriching uranium by denying the obvious and giving ground slowly and grudgingly when confronted.

One topic on which Iran refused to budge, however, was the motive behind its nuclear program. Over and over, the country's military and religious leaders publicly denied that they intended to build a nuclear weapon. Instead they said they were preparing for the day when their vast oil and natural gas reserves were gone and they could switch to nuclear power for electricity. So Heinonen was surprised by the response when he started asking Iranian atomic energy officials whether they had received information for producing a nuclear weapon from the network. Two participants in Khan's network had told Heinonen that the Iranians had received written material from the network in 1987 that included instructions on casting uranium metal to form the hemispheres required for the core of a nuclear weapon. Heinonen initially wrote a letter to Iran asking about the written material. He got no response. When he raised the matter on a visit to Tehran, however, a senior Iranian nuclear official acknowledged the 1987 offer and produced a file containing several documents. Among them was a fifteen-page document detailing the procedures for casting enriched natural and depleted uranium into hemispheres for a weapon. It appeared to be the clearest evidence to date that Iran had obtained weapons-related designs. But the Iranian said the document had never been used, and he refused to identify the suppliers who had provided it and the rest of the material in the file. Heinonen asked to see the rest of the casting document, and the Iranian said no. He would only allow the agency officials to see the top page, and he refused to let them copy anything. One of the IAEA inspectors, however, could read upside down. While Heinonen discussed the document with the Iranian official, one of his colleagues took the opportunity to take notes from the single visible page. It was nothing like the nearly complete set the Libyans had obtained, but the existence of the instructions deepened concerns among the IAEA contingent that Iran had nuclear ambitions beyond generating electricity. Heinonen had no way of knowing that the CIA had discovered Pakistani nuclear warhead plans on the Tinner computers, so he was unable to ask Iran whether these designs had made their way to Tehran.

Whether Iran had received a full set of weapon designs was not the only mystery confronting the IAEA. By reconstructing invoices and shipping records obtained in Dubai and Libya, Heinonen's team had identified two—and possibly three—forty-foot shipping containers of centrifuge components, raw materials, and top-line machine tools that had disappeared. These containers were not part of the *BBC China* shipment. They were in another batch of equipment sent from Malaysia and they appeared to have gotten as far as Dubai, but there was no sign that they had ever arrived in Tripoli. There was no evidence of them in the warehouses and transshipping companies that had been used by the network. The containers seemed to have simply vanished. The components and other material in the containers was not enough to build a bomb. It was, however, enough to feed Heinonen's nagging sense that there could be another customer out there. But where to search?

From his conversation with the Tinners, Heinonen understood that Khan had kept secrets even from his most trusted associates. The Tinners had described how the Pakistani never assembled the main players of the network at one time, insisting instead on individual meetings. So this made it evident that in order to find the suspected fourth customer it would be necessary to talk to Khan himself. But the Pakistani government had firmly rebuffed formal and informal requests from the IAEA for access to Khan.

For its part, the U.S. government was not even asking for access to Khan. At the time, Pakistan was considered a key ally in the fight against Al Qaeda and the Taliban. The administration determined that pushing to question Khan would endanger Musharraf's tenuous hold on power; from the Pakistani perspective, Khan remained a national hero despite his prime-time confession. Allowing outsiders to interrogate him would have inflamed the country. Musharraf and other Pakistani military leaders had their own reasons for keeping Khan in the quarantine of house arrest. The government was maintaining that Khan's illicit activities had occurred without the knowledge or approval of anyone in authority, a plausible fiction only so long as Khan was kept incommunicado.

Without Khan's help, Heinonen's first step in finding the potential fourth customer was to reconstruct the Pakistani's travels. The IAEA had managed to obtain some of his travel records from some cooperative foreign governments. Additional information about Khan's comings and goings was culled from material collected in Libya and Dubai and from interviews with the Tinners. A handful of other network participants were also sharing bits and pieces of information with the IAEA. Assembling the records into a matrix, Heinonen's team found that Khan had made forty-one trips from Islamabad to Dubai and traveled to ten other countries in the decade before he was placed under house arrest earlier in 2004. Muslim nations were a particular concern because over the years Khan had been increasingly outspoken in his criticism of the United States and Israel for possessing nuclear weapons while trying to thwart Pakistan and denying the technology to other Islamic nations. Among the places he had gone were several Muslim countries regarded as potential customers—Saudi Arabia, Syria, Egypt, Sudan, and Turkey.

SAUDI ARABIA WAS AT THE top of the list of suspects. When Pakistan began work on its nuclear bomb in the mid-1970s, the Saudis had helped with the financing. Zulfikar Ali Bhutto, the prime minister at the time, was so grateful for the help that he renamed Lyallpur, the country's third-largest city, as Faisalabad in honor of Saudi King Faisal. It was the start of what Bruce Riedel, a former CIA officer and presidential adviser, referred to later as the "unacknowledged nuclear partnership" between the two Sunni countries. In 1998, when Pakistan was trying to decide whether to match India's nuclear tests with its own, the Saudis promised fifty thousand barrels of free oil per day to help Pakistan cope with the expected economic sanctions. The next year, the Saudi defense minister became one of the few foreigners ever allowed into Khan's enrichment plant at Kahuta, where the Pakistani scientist himself provided a guided tour. On one of his trips to Saudi Arabia, Khan acknowledged the Saudi role in Pakistan's nuclear progress, telling an audience at the Hyatt hotel in the capital, Riyadh, "Thanks to the kingdom's assistance for various development projects, we were able to divert our own resources to the nuclear program."

American intelligence agencies had long-standing worries about whether the Saudis were developing a nuclear arsenal. In 1987, the CIA established a task force to try to determine whether the Saudis were trying to acquire nuclear weapons. The group was small and operated under the highest levels of security. Nothing could be transmitted through the agency's computers, and no one outside the task force was to be told about its existence. The task force was run by Saudi specialists from the Directorate of Operations, with the help of a single nuclear expert from the analysis side of the shop. The ultrasecrecy was required because no one wanted to risk upsetting the largest supplier of oil to the Western world.

The task force started with plenty of circumstantial evidence. The most public clue came in 1988 when it was disclosed that Saudi Arabia had purchased thirty-six nuclear-capable missiles from China. The Saudis and the Chinese maintained that the missiles, called CSS 2s, were equipped only with conventional warheads. But because the missiles were notoriously inaccurate, they were of little use in striking specific targets with conventional payloads. Despite anger from the U.S. Congress, the Saudis refused to permit outside inspection of the missiles, which were maintained by Chinese engineers at remote sites around the country.

In defending the purchase, General Khaled bin Sultan, the Saudi military commander who negotiated the deal, told a journalist that the Saudis "needed a weapon to improve the morale of our armed services and our people, a deterrent weapon not intended to be used, except as a last resort when it should be able to demoralize the enemy by delivering a painful and decisive blow . . . a weapon that would make an enemy think twice before attacking us." Khaled was educated in the United States and Britain, and he had a clear understanding that nuclear weapons are the ones described by strategic military thinkers as "deterrent weapons" and "weapons of last resort." It was not an admission of a nuclear program, but it was pretty close.

Few people outside the Kingdom of Saudi Arabia knew that the Saudis had given serious consideration to starting a nuclear weapons program a year earlier, at the very time Khan was beginning to make his rounds of the Islamic world. In 1987, a prominent Saudi living in Britain had written a letter to King Fahd ibn Abdul Aziz suggesting that the country needed a nuclear arsenal to improve its security in the region. The neighborhood was growing more dangerous. Israel possessed a nuclear arsenal and there was widespread speculation that Saddam Hussein had continued his nuclear program after the Israelis attacked his reactor at Osirak in 1981. King Fahd took the proposal seriously enough to refer it to Prince Sultan, the defense minister.

Prince Sultan set up a committee of military leaders and scientists to explore the prospect of building a nuclear weapon. The man put in charge of the effort was Rashid Abdul Aziz Al-Mubarak, a professor of nuclear chemistry at King Saud University. On May 10, 1987, Mubarak sent the prince a four-page outline of the political and national security reasons to pursue a nuclear weapon. The outline described the scientific and economic challenges of developing a nuclear arsenal, and proposed a strategy to build the required industrial base and technological expertise. Mubarak suggested bringing experienced scientists from other countries and recruiting Saudi physicists living abroad to jump-start the nuclear efforts.

"Some states have made remarkable progress in nuclear technology and joined the international nuclear club, including some states that bear hostility toward the Kingdom, such as Israel," Mubarak wrote. "The situation is further complicated by concerns that states like Iran and Libya may be concealing nuclear weapons programs." The knowledge that Iran and Libya were pursuing nuclear weapons is one indication that the paper's author had enough authority to have access to the highest levels of Saudi intelligence.

Muhammad Al-Massari was a young physicist working at King Saud University when he was approached by Mubarak about joining the nuclear project. "It was definitely a good idea," Massari said later. "You cannot have two neighbors who have nuclear weapons and you do not unless you are inviting them to invade you one day."

Planning continued for several months, but Massari noticed a cooling of support from the upper levels of Saudi royalty. He said that some members of the royal family were concerned that the CIA had learned of the nuclear project, raising concerns that to stop the effort the United States might take action that could damage the country. "We waited a long time for feedback, expecting a general approval," he said. "Weeks, months went by. Nothing happened." Eventually Massari got word from Mubarak that King Fahd had pulled the plug on the program, though Massari never understood the exact reasons.

Over the years, there have been hints that the clandestine project was not abandoned. Robert Baer, a former CIA case officer who served in the Middle East and specialized in Saudi Arabia, said two employees of the American embassy in Riyadh were camping in a remote region of the country in the early 1990s when they came across what appeared to be a secret weapons facility. Baer said the CIA had no real sources inside Saudi Arabia, but that the agency ordered spy satellites to photograph the suspected site. Whatever they discovered remains buried inside the intelligence agency. At the time, Baer said, the CIA was "willfully ignorant" of such activities inside Saudi Arabia.

A few years later, indications that the program might have continued became public. Muhammad Al-Khilewi was a Saudi diplomat posted to the United Nations, where his responsibilities included nuclear proliferation issues. In 1994 he asked for political asylum in the United States, claiming that he possessed documents proving that the Saudis had tried to buy research reactors from the Chinese in 1989 as part of a clandestine nuclear weapons program. In August, *The New York Times* published an article based on a letter from the Chinese Nuclear Energy Industry Corporation informing a nephew of King Fahd that it was willing to sell the country small reactors. The Saudi government claimed the letter was a forgery that Khilewi had created on government letterhead.

The existence of a Saudi nuclear weapons program has never been proven, but the speculation has never quite disappeared, despite the denials from the kingdom and public scoffing from U.S. officials. In 2006, a German magazine, *Cicero*, published an article that said Saudi Arabia was working on a secret nuclear program with help from Pakistani scientists. During the Haj pilgrimages to Mecca in Saudi Arabia between 2003 and 2005, the article said, Pakistani nuclear scientists posing as pilgrims slipped off to spend several weeks working at a secret weapons facility in an isolated mountainous region of the country. The article also said that Pakistan had trained Saudi scientists since the mid-1990s at Kahuta, the complex outside Islamabad run by Khan.

Saudi Arabia has long been regarded as rich but vulnerable to security threats from inside and outside its borders. An analysis of its military published by the U.S. Army Foreign Military Studies Office said the Saudis emerged from the Persian Gulf War "sobered by the realization that their force structure development goals were not commensurate with the regional threats that they confronted. Accordingly, they candidly identified shortcomings, and carefully planned for their elimination. Witnessing firsthand the technological advantages of modern warfare, particularly those possessed by the United States, they aspired to the deterrent capabilities that they afforded." Since then, the threats have multiplied. Richard Russell, a former CIA analyst who teaches at the National Defense University in Washington, D.C., argues that the security concerns facing the Saudis, plus their rocky relationship with the United States, could drive them to seek their own nuclear deterrence. "The acquisition of nuclear weapons and security delivery systems would appear to be rational and logical measures, and perhaps even necessities from the Saudi point of view," Russell wrote in *Weapons Proliferation and War in the Greater Middle East.*

THE IAEA HAD LIMITED ABILITY to gather its own intelligence, which meant that Heinonen's means of identifying other customers were extremely limited. The agency depended on voluntary information from member countries and the results of its inspections. Much of the information Heinonen was getting in 2004 was coming from the Tinners. They may have been stonewalling the authorities in Switzerland, where they faced potential criminal charges, but at the encouragement of the CIA, the Tinners were continuing to meet with Heinonen and members of his team and provide leads about the network and its participants. Still, the Swiss family of traffickers were operating under CIA instructions not to tell everything to the IAEA.

There had been a lull in meetings after the two-day session in Vienna in February. The next meeting did not occur until July, when Heinonen and Miharu Yonemura, one of his colleagues, drove to the Austrian mountain village of Innsbruck to see the Tinners and their CIA handlers, Jim Kinsman and Sharon. Innsbruck is a famous ski center and hosted the Winter Olympics in 1964 and 1976, but in summer it is far less crowded and so provided the necessary privacy for the meeting. Once again, niceties were exchanged. The IAEA team listened patiently as Friedrich described his orchid collection and pretended to be interested when Urs complained about his two divorces. Still, the conversations provided the officials with important insights into the material sold by the network and how the tens of millions of dollars were moved around the world to pay suppliers and participants alike. The Tinners provided a list of banks in various countries, including Switzerland, Liechtenstein, the United Arab Emirates, and the Netherlands, where members of the network conducted business. The description of the payment system was a lesson in how thieves do business. Most of the goods were shipped with false invoices, so the suppliers would take photographs of the equipment as it was being crated. The images served as proof of purchase in lieu of written receipts.

At one point, Friedrich sought to justify his decades-long relationship with Khan and his more recent dealings with Libya. "Just because someone makes a pistol, it doesn't mean he is a murderer," he shouted at Yonemura, who had questioned his rationale. "Just because we help build centrifuges, it doesn't mean we are making a bomb."

In September, Heinonen and Trevor Edwards flew to Innsbruck for two days of debriefings with Urs and Marco Tinner. As always, the Tinners were accompanied by Kinsman and Sharon, who sat in the suite to monitor the conversations but said little. Heinonen had a couple of specific items on his agenda, and they were about to lead him into the heart of the CIA's penetration of the network that provided equipment, material, and assistance to the Iranians and Libyans.

First he asked about several specialized vacuum pumps that his inspectors had seen in Libya and Iran. Such pumps are indispensable components of a centrifuge system for enriching uranium to fuel a nuclear weapon or civilian reactor. IAEA inspectors had discovered six of them, still in their packing crates, at one of the Libyan nuclear sites that Kaddafi had opened up for inspection before the Americans packed up everything for transfer to Tennessee. The pumps bore stamped labels showing they had been manufactured by Pfeiffer Vacuum Technology, a German company known by the initials PVT. Heinonen had not been surprised to find a German company supplying material to Libya, since many German firms sold nuclear-related technology.

But the presence of the pumps took on more significance when inspectors discovered an identical pump at Natanz, the vast underground enrichment plant being constructed by the Iranians in the central part of the country. Even stranger, the IAEA inspectors noticed that the pump bore a sticker from Los Alamos National Laboratory, the place where the Americans built the first atomic bombs. They were so surprised by the potential involvement of America's most famous nuclear weapons lab, the birthplace of the first atomic bombs, that Edwards was summoned from Vienna to examine the pump at Natanz.

After inspecting the equipment for himself, Edwards returned to Vienna and compared its serial number to the ones found in Libya—all of them were consecutive, indicating that they had come from the same batch at PVT. He sent the the serial numbers of all seven pumps to the German customs service, asking for help in tracking how they got from the manufacturer to Libya and Iran. Just a few days before he and Heinonen had left for Innsbruck, the Germans had reported back that the pumps had been sold by the German manufacturer, but the client had not been Iran and Libya. All of the pumps bearing those serial numbers had been bought by the Los Alamos National Laboratory in New Mexico and shipped there in April 2000.

The IAEA's discovery of the pumps in Iran and Libya was troubling. The only plausible explanation seemed to be that an American company, and possibly even someone associated with one of the most secure facilities in the American nuclear weapons complex, had provided critical equipment to Iran and Libya.

Heinonen brought up the pumps and the mysterious connection to Los Alamos as he and the others sat in the hotel suite in Innsbruck. The two CIA officers remained silent. The Tinners offered no suggestion about how the devices had gotten from the United States to the network. Undeterred by the silence, Heinonen explained that the German customs service had reported a few days earlier that the pumps had been sold to the weapons lab at Los Alamos. Pressing his point, he said records obtained by the IAEA in Dubai and Libya showed that the same pumps had been shipped to Iran and Libya by the same company. Had anyone heard of this company? he asked, naming the outfit involved in the shipment.*

This time Urs spoke up. He said that the company was run by someone who once worked for the IAEA in Vienna. He said the man had later worked for his father for a year or so in the late 1990s before setting up his own business. He acknowledged that the network used the company to ship some material to Libya and perhaps elsewhere. Tinner did not mention that his father had fired the employee because he suspected he was connected with the U.S. intelligence.

The explanation did nothing to clear up the mystery. Instead Heinonen and Edwards looked at each other in wonder. They seemed to have evidence not only of a potential leak from Los Alamos, but also indications that a former IAEA employee had been implicated in the shipment of pumps to Libya and Iran. With no further information coming from the people in the room, Heinonen said that he and his team would have to take a more serious look at the company in Dubai.

As Heinonen and Edwards started to leave the hotel at the end of the day's session, Kinsman came dashing down the stairs after them.

"Don't investigate that company too much," he said to Heinonen.

"We have to follow every lead, especially one that involves a former agency employee," Heinonen replied.

Kinsman had to make a snap decision. The CIA had used the company to move the sabotaged pumps into the pipeline for Iran and Libya. The last thing he wanted to do was to allow IAEA investigators or anyone else to blunder into an ongoing intelligence operation. The only way to stop Heinonen was to explain that the company was working with American intelligence. Still, the next question from the IAEA official would be, why would the CIA send vital pumps to these two rogue nu-

---

* The name of the company is being withheld to avoid exposing a CIA front operation.

clear programs? Answering him would require Kinsman to share details of the CIA's sabotage program with foreign nationals without proper security clearances. Weighing his options, Kinsman decided there was less risk if he told Heinonen and Edwards enough to kill their inquiries.

Pulling the two men into a corner of the lobby, Kinsman said that the company had shipped the pumps to Libya and Iran with the CIA's knowledge. The company, he said, was part of the ongoing intelligence operation against the remnants of the Khan network. He did not identify its owner as a CIA asset, but Kinsman left the clear impression that the former IAEA employee was helping their investigation and that this was a no-go area for the IAEA.

Heinonen and Edwards were shocked that the CIA had a role in supplying Iran and Libya. Why, they asked, had the CIA sent these sophisticated pumps to Iran and Libya? And how could he explain the Los Alamos sticker?

Kinsman hemmed and hawed before exposing another secret. Finally he explained that the pumps had gone first to Los Alamos. There, he said, almost invisible alterations had been made to the pumps that would cause them to fail when the centrifuge systems reached a critical point. The sabotage was designed to set back the Iranian and Libyan programs in a way that their experts would never figure out. He said the subtle modifications had been made by a "mad scientist type" who assured the CIA that his changes would render the pumps inoperative.

Heinonen depended heavily on the access to the Tinners provided by the Americans. He told the CIA officer that he understood the sensitivities involved. In fact, he was enthralled to finally be getting a glimpse of the massive intelligence operation that the Americans had under way. He had no intention of wrecking an ongoing investigation by the Americans. Nor did he want to damage his relationship with the CIA and risk losing his conduit to the Tinners. Still, he could not back away completely from the inquiry into the pump found in Iran because too many people at the IAEA knew it had been discovered.

"We have to appear to inquire about it," Heinonen said to Kinsman. "Otherwise it would look weird. But we'll make sure it doesn't go too far."

Edwards was not as comfortable with the action of the Americans. He had a far better working knowledge of centrifuge systems than Heinonen. After hearing Kinsman's explanation, he didn't doubt that the American scientist had altered the pump enough so that it would not work properly. But he had seen enough of the ingenuity of Iranian scientists to suspect they might be able to figure out what was wrong and correct the problem. The Americans seemed to have taken a huge risk.

The concern that the Iranians might figure out what was wrong with the pump was underscored by another discovery that Edwards and some IAEA inspectors had made several months earlier in Iran. For a period at the end of 2003 and early 2004, Iran had bowed to international pressure and suspended work on its enrichment pilot plant at Natanz. During the suspension, the inspectors had found several Iranian technicians replacing the O-rings on valves that were part of the centrifuge system inside the pilot plant. When the inspectors told the Iranians that there was not supposed to be any work under way, the Iranians had replied that they were simply replacing O-rings that had not been working properly. The rings, they said, had been manufactured from material that was too soft to withstand the pressures created in the feed-and-withdrawal system. The system kept crashing during testing, and the technicians had traced the reason to the faulty O-rings. They showed one of the flawed rubber rings to the inspectors—it was made in Britain. Edwards had suspected at the time that the British company had purposely shipped faulty rings to Iran. After hearing Kinsman's explanation of the pumps, Edwards wondered whether the rings, too, were part of an elaborate strategy to sabotage and slow down the Iranian and Libyan nuclear programs.

CHAPTER THIRTEEN

JOHANNESBURG, FRANKFURT, BERN, AND WASHINGTON

The failure to find weapons of mass destruction in Iraq was fresh in the minds of officials in South Africa, Malaysia, and even some European countries. Because the Bush administration had relied on bad intelligence regarding weapons of mass destruction to justify its invasion of Iraq, American credibility on nuclear issues was at an all-time low, even though the stakes seemed to be at an all-time high. Still, with time and hard evidence emerging from other sources, law enforcement and intelligence officials outside the United States were beginning to act.

South Africa had voluntarily given up nuclear weapons more than a decade earlier. Officials there believed that they had attained the moral high ground on the topic. At IAEA board meetings, the strong-willed South African ambassador, Abdul Minty, was an outspoken leader of the nonaligned movement. He was fond of buttonholing American diplomats to lecture them about their double standard. So when the Americans came knocking on South Africa's door with a request to go after a major arm of the Khan network in early 2004, they had been cautious.

When the South Africans asked for proof, the Americans provided them with details about a flow-forming lathe that they said had been imported illegally by a South African company to manufacture centrifuge rotors. The lathe had been built in Spain, shipped to Dubai, and forwarded to South Africa through the network's shipping hub. The Americans turned over the names of the participants—two veterans of South Africa's defunct nuclear program, Gerhard Wisser and Johan Meyer, and their companies, Krisch Engineering and Tradefin Engineering, both of which operated in suburbs of Johannesburg. South African export officers questioned Wisser about the lathe. He acknowledged importing it from Dubai, but he said it had nothing to do with any nuclear project. And he insisted that it operated at specifications below those that required an import license. Wisser explained that the project for which he planned to use the lathe had not worked out, so he had returned it to Dubai months earlier. Without evidence, the South Africans dropped the inquiry.

The Americans had also provided the German intelligence service with extensive information about the involvement of Gotthard Lerch, a German living in Switzerland, and Wisser, a German citizen who had lived for years in South Africa. In August, Wisser had gone to Germany for a holiday. As he was leaving the country on August 25, he was detained by the police and taken into custody for questioning. He was confronted with a detailed recitation of his work for the Libyans, his involvement with Lerch and other members of the Khan network, and the Swiss bank accounts where he deposited his payments. Told that he faced charges of trafficking in nuclear technology for Libya and accessory to treason, Wisser waived his right to an attorney and offered an answer for every accusation. Certainly he knew Lerch, he said. They had worked together many years earlier and Wisser managed some real estate for him. Yes, he had done some work for B. S. A. Tahir, but it was for a water purification system. He said there was nothing illegal about the deal and that he had contracted the work to another firm, Tradefin Engineering. Yes, he had spent considerable time in Dubai, but it was because the weather helped his arthritis. As for helping Moammar Kaddafi build a nuclear weapon, he replied indignantly, "I swear to God I did not supply anything to Libya." The police sent out for pizza and the interview continued until almost midnight. As the night wore on, the sixty-five-year-old Wisser began to fade. He asked for a lawyer. An attorney arrived, and the questioning continued in his presence. When he was pressed again on the Libyan connection, Wisser acknowledged that he had suspected that the system being built at Tradefin had something to do with a nuclear program. That was why, he claimed, he had urged the owner of Tradefin, Johan Meyer, to destroy the system a year earlier.

Even after his lengthy statement, the German prosecutors were not sure they had enough evidence to charge Wisser. They decided to hold him for a couple of days to give the South African police a chance to check out his story. A transcript of the interrogation was prepared the following day, but it had to be reviewed and signed by Wisser before it could be considered evidence under German law. By the time it was ready to be sent to the South African embassy in Berlin, it was late on the afternoon of August 27, a Friday. The embassy was closed, so the transcript and accompanying information were not transmitted to South Africa until Monday, August 30. Once it was delivered, police and prosecutors in Pretoria, the administrative capital of South Africa, read the transcript, which contained far more evidence than the Americans had provided months earlier. Search warrants were obtained immediately for Krisch and Tradefin. Wisser was being released from jail in Germany. If there was any physical evidence there, they wanted to beat him to it.

On the morning of September 1, armed with their search warrants, the police arrived at Krisch's nondescript offices in Randburg, about twenty miles northwest of Johannesburg. There wasn't much to find; nearly a year earlier, Wisser had destroyed his computer hard drives and records of the Libyan transaction after the warning from Lerch. But it was another story when the team arrived at Tradefin's workshop and offices in Vanderbijlpark, an industrial city about thirty miles southwest of Johannesburg.

Tradefin was located behind a metal fence, inside a massive blue metal warehouse on a dusty road lined with small factories manufacturing nothing more sophisticated than paint, tiles, and tires. At fifty-three years old, Johan Meyer was a moderately successful engineer, but he had never built anything as spectacular and complex as the system he affectionately called "the beast." After the system had been tested and deemed workable a year earlier, Meyer and his workers had dismantled the two hundred tons of pipes and valves, carefully numbering each part so that it could be reassembled in Libya. The works were then packed into eleven shipping containers, and the forty-foot-long containers were stacked three high behind some tall metal shelves. The plan had been to truck the containers to a port and ship them to their destination, but the final shipping notice had never come. The beast, which Wisser had urged Meyer to melt into oblivion, would turn out to be Wisser's downfall.

When the South African police entered Tradefin, they initially saw the mundane workings of any tool-and-die shop. There were rusting tanks and idled machines. But they also noticed something behind the shelves. Two police officers scaled the shelving and looked down on the eleven containers. After moving the shelves aside, the police opened the first container and found what they had been told to look for—an elaborate system of pipes. Then they sealed the containers so they could not be opened again without their knowledge and secured the premises. The search also turned up extensive records of transactions with other members of the network, including the Tinners and Lerch. Shipping documents indicated that plans had been made months earlier to send the containers to Dubai and on to Tripoli. In an old trunk in Meyer's office, they found blueprints for the piping system from Khan's laboratory in Pakistan and an instructional video filmed at Kahuta—proof that this was no water purification system and a direct link to Khan.

The South African authorities were now moving fast. On the same day as the searches, they took Wisser, Meyer, and a third man who worked for Krisch and Tradefin on the project, Daniel Geiges, into custody. A judge agreed to hold them without bail as flight risks. On September 7, after authorities studied records taken from Tradefin and made a cursory examination of the contents of the containers, all three were charged with violating export laws and illegally manufacturing equipment for use in a nuclear weapons facility. Within days, Meyer began cooperating, laying out the history of his dealings with Lerch, Tahir, and Wisser. He described receiving designs from Lerch, which he was told had been prepared by a Swiss technician named Urs Tinner, along with the additional help from Khan's lab. He said that the Libyans had sent two nuclear experts to inspect the work just a few months earlier. He acknowledged that the elaborate system had nothing to do with water purification and everything to do with uranium enrichment.

The South African authorities shared their haul with the Germans and the Swiss. The hard evidence provided new momentum for the investigations in both of those countries, creating a new set of problems for the CIA's cover-up.

WATCHING EVENTS UNFOLD IN SOUTH Africa from CIA headquarters, Jim Kinsman had repeated his warning to Urs Tinner to stay put in Switzerland. The Germans were preparing evidence to seek the arrest and extradition of Lerch from Switzerland and Wisser from South Africa. The American government had set those events in motion by providing evidence against both of those men to the Germans. Helping the Germans and others, however, was risky from the CIA point of view. The agency would no longer be able to control the flow of information once arrests began. Protecting the Tinners would be harder if the Germans started gathering evidence against other participants in the Khan ring. The CIA suspected that the Tinners might already be on the German radar. Some of the network's goods had moved through German ports, which meant the Germans could assert jurisdiction. The CIA and the German federal intelligence service, or BND, had a close working relationship. The Americans had asked them not to seek arrest warrants against the Tinners because of what the CIA described as an ongoing intelligence operation. Kinsman didn't know if the request would hold.

Tinner may have felt that his work for the CIA conveyed more immunity than it did. Despite his handler's warnings, in October he flew from Zurich to Frankfurt to visit a friend. When he passed through passport control, his name was flagged on the computer and he was taken aside by the customs police. In a way, it was a mistake. The BND knew enough to keep hands off Tinner, but his name had gotten into the national police computer system and he found himself in a German jail.

Tinner's arrest constituted the biggest threat yet to the CIA. Kinsman and his colleagues would have to do everything in their power to stop the Germans from putting Tinner on trial, particularly in an open courtroom where all their secrets would be bared to the public. One strategy was to persuade the Swiss not to share any evidence about Tinner with the Germans. CIA representatives met again with their Swiss counterparts, arguing that they should not cooperate with the German investigation. "The Swiss were going to turn over documents to the Germans, but we convinced them not to do so and to extradite him instead," a former CIA officer said. The Swiss investigation was still going slow, operating under restraints imposed by the Justice Ministry. They had not gotten to the point where anyone had been arrested, and no search warrants had been issued. But the Wyss report and information provided by the IAEA and other agencies filled several folders, and the information was being prepared for transfer to the Germans.

As expected, in November the German police filed an arrest warrant for Gotthard Lerch with the Swiss government. Based on information from the Americans and the South Africans, the Germans were charging the longtime trafficker with export violations and treason for his role in the Libyan nuclear project. Lerch was taken into custody at his home in Grabs and held for extradition proceedings. The two arrests offered a chance for the CIA and its allies in the Swiss government to get Tinner back on Swiss soil and limit the potential damage of putting him on trial in Germany. The idea of a prisoner swap was broached with the Swiss: Lerch would be extradited to Germany in return for Tinner coming back to Switzerland. Negotiations were slow, but Kinsman saw a chance to save his cover-up.

The American ambassador to Switzerland, Pamela Willeford, was a political appointee with no experience in diplomacy. She was a longtime friend of first lady Laura Bush, had served on a statewide education committee in Texas, and contributed to various Republican committees from 2000 to 2004. She would later become famous as a witness when Vice President Dick Cheney accidentally shot a lawyer during a quail hunt on a Texas ranch. But by late 2004 she had been on the job in Bern a little more than a year and had not had to deal with anything more troubling than the persistent anti-American attitudes of the Swiss and other Europeans angered by the Iraq War and the detentions at Guantanamo Bay.

In early December, the CIA asked Willeford if she would meet with Christoph Blocher to discuss the Tinner case. It was a sensitive task, but the hope was that she could convince the Swiss justice minister that the relationship between the Tinners and the CIA was too sensitive to risk exposure in the German case against Urs Tinner. Willeford wasn't given a full briefing, but she was told enough to make what the CIA hoped would be a good case. On December 4, she went to the Justice Ministry to meet with Blocher and the head of the federal police, Jean-Luc Vez. When she returned to the embassy, Willeford reported back to the CIA station chief that she believed she had convinced the Swiss to restrict any information sharing with the Germans.

The arrest of his son had outraged Friedrich Tinner. He told Kinsman and Sharon that there would be no more debriefing sessions with them or with officials from the IAEA. He felt betrayed by the CIA, which had promised to protect Urs and the rest of the family. He was no longer sure that the Americans would even provide a defense for them if he and Marco were arrested, too. He worried that Kinsman and Sharon might crawl back into their secret world, leaving him and his family to face arrest and conviction.

Tinner also blamed Olli Heinonen for the arrest of Urs. He telephoned the IAEA official and accused him of leaking the information to the Germans that led to his son's incarceration. But despite his anger at the IAEA, Tinner was desperate for protection. He expected nothing from the Americans; their sole interest seemed to be pretending they had never heard of the Tinners, since they had no further use for them. Instead he clung to the hope that he might find salvation with the IAEA in Vienna. The international nuclear agency could explain to the Swiss and German authorities that the family had cooperated with its investigations of Khan and the other participants. In the best possible scenario, Heinonen would confirm to the other authorities that the Tinners had worked with the CIA for several years, in case his friends from America really had abandoned his family.

Tinner telephoned Heinonen, asking for a meeting as soon as possible. He refused to say what he wanted to talk about. Heinonen had never fully trusted Friedrich Tinner, and he wasn't sure why Tinner wanted to see him when the Swiss engineer called. He had agreed to meet with Tinner, but he insisted that he come to the agency's headquarters in Vienna this time. Out of an abundance of caution, Heinonen arranged for one of the IAEA's senior lawyers, a no-nonsense American named Laura Rockwood, to join him.

Rockwood had been one of the primary forces behind the IAEA's attempts to become more aggressive in its inspections in recent years. She had drafted an addendum to the international Non-Proliferation Treaty that required signatories to permit more intrusive inspections of suspicious facilities by the IAEA. But she was not always content to work behind a desk. On a couple of occasions, Rockwood had accompanied inspectors on trips to see clandestine nuclear facilities in Iran. And she had kept a close eye on Heinonen's inquiry into the Khan network, helping negotiate with reluctant governments over access to records and advising Heinonen and others on how far they could push to get information.

Tinner flew into Vienna on December 10 and went directly to the IAEA. He was processed through the guard station on the perimeter of the agency's complex and given directions to Heinonen's office on the twenty-sixth floor of one of the towers. Heinonen met him at the security door outside the hallway of offices and escorted Tinner into his office. Rockwood was already there.

Tinner wasted no time. He said Urs had been arrested in Germany, which the IAEA officials already knew, and he said he feared that he and Marco were next. The key to their defense, Tinner said, would be that the family had begun providing information to the CIA long before the Khan network was exposed, that they had initiated the contact with the Americans out of concern about proliferation, and that their intelligence had played a central role in bringing down a threat to world security. Tinner said he was worried that the CIA would not defend him and his sons, that they would not tell anyone what an important role he and his sons had played in bringing down A. Q. Khan. Tinner said the only way out was for Heinonen to go to Bern and tell the appropriate Swiss authorities how the family had helped the IAEA. At the same time, Tinner said, Heinonen could tell the Swiss about the assistance they had provided to the CIA, too. Heinonen could even tell them about Urs sabotaging equipment.

But Heinonen explained that he could not corroborate such a story. He reminded Friedrich that he had not met any of the Tinners until February 2004. That, he said, was after the exposure of Khan's operations. He pointed out that he knew nothing about when the family started working with American intelligence.

Tinner interrupted, explaining that he had started providing information to the Americans long before he met with Heinonen in Vienna. He described how he had personally gone to the U.S. Embassy in Vienna in December 2002 to offer his help. Surely, he insisted, the CIA had told Heinonen of that early contact. But the CIA had never told Heinonen more than it thought he needed to know. He repeated that he had no idea when the Tinners had started cooperating. Indeed, Heinonen was adamant that he knew nothing about the relationship between the Tinners and American intelligence until February 2004. Tinner left the meeting dejected and more concerned than ever that he and his sons would be abandoned.

HEINONEN HAD HAD LITTLE CONTACT with the CIA in recent weeks, and no contact with the man he knew as Jim Kinsman. So he had no way of knowing that the CIA case officer had no intention of abandoning his spies. Throughout his career spotting and recruiting assets, Kinsman had told every person he signed up that he would protect them as long as necessary. Even the stupid decision by Urs to travel to Germany had not caused his commitment to waver. But the CIA was in turmoil. The case officer was having trouble getting the right people to listen to his pleas.

In June, George Tenet had abruptly announced that he was resigning as head of the CIA. He had been under attack for months over a series of intelligence failures, ranging from the missed clues to the September 11 attacks to his own promise that finding nuclear, chemical, and biological weapons in Iraq was a "slam dunk." On June 3, President Bush had just completed a press conference with Australian prime minister John Howard in the White House Rose Garden and he headed for the helicopter waiting on the South Lawn. While reporters were still milling around on the lawn, Bush returned and told them that Tenet had resigned. It almost seemed like an afterthought. Later that morning, a teary Tenet told employees at the agency's headquarters in Langley that the resignation was "the most difficult decision I have ever had to make." He said he would be leaving in early July.

Tenet's departure had left Kinsman without a key ally. And worse was coming. The new CIA chief was Porter J. Goss, a former covert operative for the CIA who had gone on to serve in Congress and eventually as chairman of the House Intelligence Committee. Goss had taken the CIA director's job after promising to increase the number of case officers in the field in the battle against Al Qaeda. But he soon found himself at loggerheads with the clandestine side of the spy service. First he installed several cronies in key positions. For instance, he handed the number-three position at the CIA to Kyle "Dusty" Foggo, whose previous job was chief of the agency's logistics office in Germany. But Foggo had ingratiated himself with Goss by funneling inside information to him while he was a congressman. There were other appointments that smacked of favoritism, but the anger among old hands at the agency boiled over when Goss pushed out the popular chief of the directorate of operations, Stephen Kappes. After the Libyan episode, people had expected that Kappes might eventually become director of central intelligence. But he got into a dispute with Foggo and Kappes was fired. Several other top operations officers followed him out the door, either voluntarily or with a shove. The last laugh would belong to Kappes: A year later, Foggo was indicted for steering CIA procurement contracts to a friend and he was later convicted and sentenced to three years in federal prison.

As Kappes and others left, Kinsman watched helplessly as his support network was decimated. He found himself without the patrons who are essential to operating in a bureaucracy as big and sometimes vicious as the CIA. With only a year until he could retire with his full pension, Kinsman wondered whether he could hang on to his job. He also wondered whether he had the backing he needed to protect the Tinners.

On the one hand, keeping the Tinners quiet had been complicated by Urs's arrest in Germany. There was a chance that he would begin talking to try to save himself. Part of his story would no doubt be that he had helped the CIA. The agency could deny it. Criminals often tried to win leniency by concocting tales of assisting various intelligence and law enforcement agencies. There was no way a German court could get to the bottom of the relationship between the CIA and the Tinners. But Tinner could name names. He could provide dates and places for meetings that would, at the very least, create an embarrassing media sensation. If that happened, the Swiss authorities would start to get more interested. So far, the investigation there was moving slowly, and Kinsman was certain it could be contained before any damage was done. But if the headlines started coming, and the Swiss started digging, it would be harder for the CIA to maintain the stone wall it had erected around the real story of how the Khan network was brought down—and how much nuclear know-how had gotten out before it happened.

CHAPTER FOURTEEN

JOHANNESBURG AND BERN

Pelindaba means "be silent" in Zulu. It is an appropriate name for the heavily guarded facility in northern South Africa where the country's apartheid regime built its nuclear arsenal in the 1970s and 1980s. Shortly before the collapse of the apartheid government, South African president F. W. de Klerk terminated the weapons program, but Pelindaba remains the country's primary nuclear research center and it is closed to outsiders. There is only one road to the complex and visitors must use it to drive up a mountain to a guard station. After stopping at the guard station, visitors are allowed into a vast compound, which covers thousands of acres and contains dozens of buildings. The complex where six atomic weapons were once hidden is now used for civilian nuclear research.

Early on the morning of January 17, 2005, a Monday, a convoy of vehicles carrying representatives of three countries and the International Atomic Energy Agency passed through the checkpoint and onto one of the interior roads. Little more than a dirt path, the road meandered through hills, past factory buildings and more guards until it reached a dirty brown building six stories high and two football fields in length. The building is called Area 26, and it is the most secretive and secure facility within Pelindaba. Stored within that cavernous structure that day were eleven shipping crates, which contained the fantastically complex and beautifully engineered system that Johan Meyer had created to run the centrifuge plant planned for Libya. Stacked alongside the giant containers were six trunks of documents seized at Meyer's factory and at the offices of his accomplice, Gerhard Wisser. The documents offered the most complete road map to date of the scope of the Khan network's nuclear plans for Libya.

Experts from the IAEA, the United States, Britain, and Germany had been invited to Area 26 by the South African government. They were there to examine the records and the web of polished tubes and specialized vacuum valves and pumps inside the containers as part of the ongoing international investigation of Khan's network. After the discovery of the illicit nuclear operation on their soil, the South Africans were working hard to pursue this case quickly. They had conducted a thorough investigation, interviewed dozens of people, and arrested Meyer, Wisser, and a third man, Daniel Geiges, back in September. Meyer had since been released after agreeing to cooperate, but Wisser and Geiges remained in jail.

Though the South Africans were opening their doors at their most secret facility to other investigators and the international regulators, there were rules. The visitors were restricted to opening one shipping container at a time to inspect the equipment. They were allowed to open only one of the trunks at a time. The South Africans had prepared an index and summaries of the material in the trunks to make the review easier for their guests.

While everyone had agreed to the restrictions the night before at their hotel in Pretoria, the investigators from the German federal prosecutor's office balked when they saw the massive accumulation of evidence. They were interested solely in building their case against Gotthard Lerch, who had been fighting extradition from Switzerland since his arrest the previous year. Waving the index and some of the summaries, the Germans insisted on opening all of the trunks simultaneously so that they could cherry-pick the material that was relevant to Lerch's involvement with the work in South Africa on behalf of the Libyan nuclear project. They said they feared they would not have time to gather the evidence they needed if they had to pick through the trunks one by one. After consulting with his colleagues and the IAEA officials on the scene, the senior South African official relented.

The documents at Pelindaba shed new light on the beginnings of

Khan's nuclear black market, showing that the Pakistani and some of his confederates offered centrifuge technology to South Africa at the same time they were selling it to Iran. In one of the trunks, an IAEA official found records showing that Khan had offered to sell designs for the P-2 centrifuge to the South African government in 1988, just a few years before the shutdown of its nuclear program. The records were from government files and they showed that Khan and Lerch had made the offer, using Wisser as the middleman. The proposal provided new insights into how the network operated in its earliest days and raised new questions about the timing of Khan's transactions with Iran, too. As one of the IAEA officials reviewed the records showing that Khan and Lerch had offered the more advanced centrifuge to South Africa in 1988, he wondered whether Khan had sold the P-2 to Iran even earlier than the Iranians admitted.

The question about when Iran got the P-2 went to the heart of the mystery surrounding the Iranian program. The Americans and others had been trying to prove for months that Iran was engaged in secret weapons work, possibly at hidden nuclear facilities and inside military complexes that were off-limits to IAEA inspectors. If Khan had offered the P-2 to South Africa in 1988, why wouldn't he have tried to sell the same machine to the Iranians at the same time? He was certainly dealing with Tehran then, though he was believed to have sold them the rudimentary P-1. The discovery in South Africa raised an unsettling possibility: Khan had sold P-2 designs to Iran in 1987 or 1988, and the Iranians had produced the more advanced centrifuges at a secret facility. This raised the possibility that Iran was producing enriched weapons-grade uranium at an undisclosed facility.

The teams from all three foreign countries and the IAEA spent Monday and Tuesday going over the documents and examining the system Meyer had called "the beast." On Wednesday morning, however, the Germans did not show up for the convoy from the hotel to Pelindaba. No one knew where they were and eventually the others went on without them. When the German delegation finally arrived at lunchtime, its lead investigator acknowledged that he and his colleagues had spent the morning at their embassy in Pretoria interviewing Johan Meyer about his dealings with Lerch. The South Africans were furious. Meyer was the key prosecution witness in the case the South Africans were building against Wisser and Geiges. The South Africans felt that the Germans had no business talking with Meyer, taking advantage of the hospitality to interfere with a witness. The episode sparked a sharp deterioration in the relationship between the prosecutors of the two countries, which would later undermine efforts to convict network players in Germany and South Africa.

FROM THE PERSPECTIVE OF THE IAEA, the South African trip was a rare bit of international cooperation. They were not faring as well with the Pakistanis, who continued to refuse to allow any outsiders to interview Khan in his well-appointed house arrest. Heinonen and his crew were also having trouble in their efforts to interview Tahir, who remained in custody in Kuala Lumpur. When the Malaysian authorities had released the summary of Tahir's confession a year earlier, they made a public issue of the necessity to investigate European involvement in Khan's network. But in the months that followed, the very agency that was leading that investigation was refused access to Tahir, who held the keys to many closed doors in the nuclear bazaar. The Malaysian authorities kept saying that the time was not right, that Tahir didn't want to talk, that it would be unsafe to expose him to outsiders. The day after the IAEA team returned from South Africa, the Malaysian ambassador to the IAEA telephoned Heinonen. He said the agency had been given permission to talk to Tahir. The next day, Heinonen, Edwards, and Yonemura were on a plane to Kuala Lumpur.

The interview took place at the headquarters of Malaysia's Secret Service, the country's domestic intelligence agency. Tahir was brought to the headquarters from the outlying prison where he was being held. Accompanying him were two police officers who sat down and pulled out notepads, clearly intending to stay.

"Does it disturb you that the police are here?" Heinonen asked Tahir.

"Don't worry about it," said Tahir. "It's okay."

Heinonen assumed the room was bugged anyway, so he did not try to insist that the police leave. For his part, Tahir seemed eager to talk.

He had been held for nearly a year at a remote prison, where he was not permitted visits from his wife or anyone else.

Heinonen was a scientist, but he had learned a little about interrogation techniques in recent months. He had not come to ask Tahir about his guilt or innocence. "The idea was not to crucify him, but to get him talking," Heinonen said later. "What is important for me is not finding someone's guilt, but understanding every aspect of the network and determining the identity of the other customers. For sure there were other customers. We just don't know who and we don't know how far along they might be."

The questioning started slowly, to build trust. Heinonen asked about the conditions of Tahir's imprisonment and whether he missed his family. He thanked him for agreeing to help, praising him as someone who could shed important light on the inner workings of Khan's operation. The strategy was to save the tough questions for another session.

Over several hours, Tahir provided intriguing glimpses inside the Khan network, describing the jealousies and rivalries among the participants and corroborating information from the Tinners about how Khan sought to maintain control over the operation by withholding details from its participants. At various points, he downplayed his own role. He said SMB Computers had been started by his late father and left to his uncle Farooq; Tahir said he was little more than a tea boy and junior partner. He claimed that he had tried to extricate himself from the network on several occasions, but he had always been drawn back by his friendship with Khan. He said the two men had traveled to Mecca together twice for hajj, the religious pilgrimage required of all good Muslims.

Tahir proved to have a remarkable memory when it came to aspects of the inquiry that did not implicate him. Yonemura had a record of all known accounts used by network participants at banks around the world. She had assembled them from a variety of sources, official and unofficial, and they covered thirty or forty banks in Europe, Asia, the Middle East, and Africa. As Yonemura read him the account numbers and banks, Tahir matched them with particular people involved in the network or specific transactions.

The information was tantalizing and Heinonen was looking forward to the next session, which the Malaysians had promised would take place within a month. At the end of the session, Yonemura handed a digital camera to one of the policemen and asked him to snap a photo of the group, promising to bring Tahir a copy on the next trip. The IAEA officials had no way of knowing this would be the last they saw of Tahir.

Edwards returned to Vienna, but Heinonen and Yonemura headed for Singapore. They had arranged to meet with Marco Tinner. The visit from Tinner's father had reopened the lines of communication with the family, and Heinonen was eager to see if he could learn more from Marco. At the time, Marco was living in Bangkok, where he had married a Thai woman. With his brother in a German prison and fearful that he would be the next person arrested, Marco had suggested meeting in a neutral place. The choice was Singapore. At the meeting, Marco seemed relieved to provide bits of information to the IAEA. He was worried, however, about the CIA discovering that he was going off the reservation by communicating directly with the IAEA and he suggested that they adopt a code to encrypt future communications.

As Heinonen and Yonemura had gotten deeper into the investigation of the Khan network, they had grown worried that the Americans were intercepting their conversations and monitoring their e-mails and text messages. Those fears seemed confirmed when the *Washington Post* published an article describing how the Bush administration had been intercepting the telephone calls of Mohamed ElBaradei; in fact, within the IAEA headquarters in Vienna, senior officials had begun to assume that their conversations were being monitored by the vast American eavesdropping network.

When Tinner raised the issue of encrypting their exchanges, Heinonen said that technicians back in Vienna had installed a commercial encryption service, called "Pretty Good Privacy," on their computers, which afforded a high degree of security. Tinner did not think PGP would stop the CIA. Instead he proposed using an old-fashioned method that he said his family had employed for years. Over the next hour, he explained to Heinonen and Yonemura how to set up the encryption system known as a book cipher. The basics were fairly simple. Messages could be decoded only by referring to the exact page, line, and sentence in a book. Only parties that had identical editions of the same book could match the page, line, and sentence to decode the message. Heinonen found the system awkward, but he thought to himself, "If they like it, let it be." Marco said he had a book at home that he would use on his end, and he promised to send Heinonen a copy of the same edition.

Before Heinonen and Yonemura left, Marco asked them to meet soon with his Swiss lawyer. They agreed to talk to him.

On May 13, Marco's lawyer, Peter Volkart, arrived at IAEA headquarters to meet with Heinonen, Edwards, and Yonemura. Volkart had several motives for the trip. On the one hand, he wanted help from the IAEA's experts in understanding the intricacies of the export laws that he expected his client to be accused of violating. He also wanted to understand the significance of designs that Marco was suspected of passing to Libya and others. Most importantly, the lawyer wanted to see if he could extract exculpatory information from Heinonen and his associates.

From the start of the meeting, Heinonen made it clear that the IAEA was not involved in the criminal investigations of the Khan network in Switzerland or anywhere else. The agency's role, he said, was strictly to verify that nuclear technology was being used for peaceful purposes and not diverted to secret weapons programs. He acknowledged that he had met several times with the Tinners, and that their information had been helpful to the agency. But he said he could not interfere in any of the criminal investigations under way.

Opening his briefcase, Volkart withdrew a sheaf of engineering drawings and placed them on the conference table. He said he believed these were designs for centrifuge components that had been sabotaged during their manufacture at SCOPE. Edwards knew centrifuges better than anyone in the room, better than anyone at the IAEA. As he inspected the drawings, he realized that he was looking at two sets of identical drawings, one in black and white and one in color, of components for P-2 centrifuges. Comparing them with what he had seen in the past few months, Edwards calculated that some of them had been made in Malaysia. Others, however, appeared to be too sophisticated for the Malaysian operation. He thought it was more likely they had been produced at the Tinners' factory in Switzerland.

Volkart said he had come to Vienna in hopes of getting answers to two questions: Are these drawings for components that were subject to export control laws, and do they appear to have been modified in a way that would cause them to malfunction? The questions framed the defense he was developing for the Tinners in case the matter came to trial. He would argue that the brothers and their father had only produced components, without any clear knowledge that they were destined for a nuclear weapons plant anywhere. The Tinners, he would say, were honest businessmen. Once they learned from the CIA that the technology was destined for Libya, they tried to stop the proliferation by sabotaging the equipment. Volkart maintained that his clients had taken enormous risks by working covertly with the CIA for years, but he did not expect the Americans to corroborate his story or release any of the sabotaged components for a trial. So he was prepared to argue that the Tinners could not get a fair trial because key evidence was being withheld from the court. What the lawyer needed from the IAEA officials was confirmation that the Tinners had been working with the CIA long before the network collapsed.

Heinonen said export controls were the province of national governments, and Volkart would have to ask the Swiss whether the components depicted were subject to controls. As for the modifications, he said he could not venture an opinion on whether the drawings showed that components had been altered. The IAEA officials had listened several months earlier when Urs claimed that he had sabotaged components manufactured at SCOPE, but Heinonen was not about to discuss that with a Swiss lawyer. Instead he told Volkart that components manufactured to the specifications in his drawings had been found in Libya. He said they were being stored by the Americans at the national laboratory in Tennessee. Perhaps, he said, the lawyer should ask the Swiss government to request that the Americans send some of them to Europe so they could be tested to determine whether they worked.

Heinonen repeated what he had told Friedrich Tinner several months earlier: The cooperation between the Tinners and the IAEA did not begin until February 2004, after the collapse of the Khan network. Volkart left the meeting with little hope of getting any help. Before leaving, he said that he expected Urs to be extradited from Germany to Switzerland within the week.

Heinonen had a reputation with the IAEA for keeping information to himself, often not even sharing critical material with his closest colleagues. The joke at the agency was that if he were hit by a bus, the entire Khan investigation would be lost. In this case, he withheld a critical development from Volkart.

Several months earlier, Edwards had arranged for the Americans to ship sample centrifuge components from the stockpile of Libyan material to Urenco's plant in the Netherlands. There the components were run through a battery of diagnostics and tests to determine whether they had truly been sabotaged. The results indicated that Urs Tinner was either lying about what he had done or that his attempts at sabotage had not been effective. The Urenco scientists had reported back to the IAEA that the components functioned, though they might not last forever.

Beyond casting doubt on Tinner's claims, the verdict from Urenco appeared to undermine the CIA strategy of sabotaging equipment going to the nuclear programs of Iran and Libya. If the centrifuge components Tinner said he altered on instructions from the CIA still worked, the same might be true for the German-made vacuum pumps, the Turkish electricity regulators, and other pieces of equipment that supposedly had been sabotaged. While the Libyans lacked the technical skill to detect sabotage and had never gotten close to operating an enrichment plant anyway, the Iranians were another story. Many of the scientists and technicians involved in Iran's nuclear program had been trained at top universities in Europe and the United States. Some of them had long experience with their own country's nuclear research reactor in Tehran and other civilian installations. They possessed the expertise and background to detect the flaws and repair them; in cases like the supposedly sabotaged centrifuge components, even slight adjustments might be unnecessary. The Urenco tests surely represented a blow to the CIA sabotage program, but no one knew how serious a blow it was.

Volkart turned out to be right about Tinner's extradition. Before the end of the week, Urs was moved from Germany to a prison cell in Bern. He complained about his new quarters to his lawyer, Roman

Boegli. His cell was filthy and it smelled. The sheets on the iron bed were foul. When he complained to his jailers, Tinner was told they were only changed twice a year.

THE SWISS HAD NOT PARTICIPATED in the review at Pelindaba, but their investigation was progressing slowly under the direction of Peter Lehmann, a deputy attorney general. With Urs Tinner safely in a Swiss jail, Lehmann was working with the police to arrest his brother and father. The ambitious prosecutor knew that the Americans were determined to sidetrack his investigation, and he proceeded with care and discretion. In September, Lehmann convinced a judge to issue search warrants for the Tinners' homes and offices. He was allowed to take Marco into custody after portraying him as a flight risk because he was spending so much time in Thailand and was suspected of having assets hidden in overseas bank accounts. There was not yet enough evidence to detain Friedrich. In a peculiarity of Swiss law, the Tinner brothers were not charged with crimes. Rather, they were held in what was called preventive custody while the investigation proceeded.

The real prize was the fruits of the search warrants, which were executed over the course of two days at three locations—Marco's apartment in Jenins, the home of his parents in the village of Sax, of Haag, and the three-story building in the nearby village of Sax, which housed the joint offices of Phitec and Traco. The police seized eleven personal computers, one hundred and fifty computer disks, and six mobile telephones from the home of Friedrich and his wife, Hedwig. From Marco's house they removed six personal computers, more than sixty CDs, two flash drives, and four external Zip drives. At the Phitec and Traco offices, the police found more computers along with tens of thousands of pages of paper records. In the basement they discovered hundreds of pieces of equipment stacked in a large work area that contained various tool-and-die machines. The police officers did not recognize any of it. They simply packed everything into carefully numbered and labeled evidence boxes. Eventually the evidence from all the locations was loaded into police vans and driven to headquarters.

As Lehmann and senior police officials surveyed the amount of material, the first question was how to secure it. They didn't know yet what they had in their possession, but they suspected that it was extremely sensitive, perhaps even dangerous in terms of nuclear proliferation. It was essential that everything be protected. There wasn't enough space in the police evidence room, so they lugged everything to the jail in the basement of the police building. There the computers, mobile phones, the mysterious pieces of equipment, and the dozens of boxes were stacked inside two cells, lining the walls and reaching the ceilings.

In the days that followed, police computer technicians were brought in from the information technology center in Zurich to begin examining the electronics. After a preliminary look, the technicians estimated that the computers, disks, and storage devices contained about five hundred gigabytes of information, the equivalent of millions of pages of plain text. After a couple of days, the technicians met with Lehmann and Jean-Luc Vez. They explained that the volume was so huge that they needed to remove the hard drives from the computers and take them, along with the various flash drives and Zip drives, to the IT center in Zurich. The information would be safe from hackers, and the technicians and other experts could review the material in more comfortable surroundings. Even then, one of the technicians said, there was so much complex information that it would take months to review all of it unless they brought in an army of experts. Lehmann agreed to sending the material to Zurich, though he would keep the equipment from the factory.

Unlocking the secrets inside the computers would take some effort. Some of the files had been deleted multiple times, presumably a conscious attempt by the Tinners to erase potentially incriminating information. The technicians were confident that, once back at the IT center with their powerful computers, they could recover the deleted files, but it would add to the time. Then there was the matter of the e-mails. The family appeared to have used Hedwig Tinner's computer for most of their business communications. Nearly all of the 3,400 e-mail messages stored there were encrypted. Again, it would take more time to understand what they had recovered.

The hard drives and computer storage devices were taken to Zurich, where the contents were transferred to a secure server. As the technicians began to examine the material in more detail, they could see a jumble of almost incomprehensibly complicated engineering schematics in various forms and formats, extensive financial records dating back to the 1970s, correspondence between members of the network, and, from one of the computers, a large collection of pornographic photographs. Organizing the huge volume of material into evidence that could be explained thoroughly enough for a court to understand its significance would require time and outside assistance.

As the evidence grew, so did the anger of Lehmann and his counterparts in the police. For the first time they were getting a sense of the scope of the scheme to which the Swiss government had turned a blind eye for so many years. They also were beginning to understand how much the American government, and in particular the CIA, had been withholding from them. Switzerland had decided decades before not to pursue atomic weapons, so no one in the country had experience with nuclear technology. That meant Lehmann and the police had nowhere to turn within their own government for help in understanding the evidence that had been taken from the Tinners. But there was a growing concern that they might be sitting on highly sensitive material related to building nuclear weapons.

Even knowing that elements of the U.S. government were trying to stop their inquiry, the Swiss felt they had no choice but to turn to the Americans for help in understanding the scale and significance of what they found. They sent formal requests through the American embassy to Washington for information about the Tinners' role in the larger network. They asked for technical help in understanding the significance of the evidence obtained from the computers. Copies of the Swiss requests found their way to the CIA at Langley, where they renewed concerns about the possibility that the whole mess would become a public scandal. The intelligence agency made sure that no arm of the U.S. government would assist the Swiss. Better to let them grope around in the dark until they got discouraged and closed down their inquiry.

With Urs and Marco stuck in a Swiss jail, it was more important than ever from the CIA's perspective that the former spies remain silent. The agency didn't want them cutting a deal with prosecutors to testify about their relationship with the CIA in exchange for leniency. Solving the problem fell to Kinsman at a delicate time in his career. The earlier departures of Tenet, Kappes, and others had left him feeling isolated. He was approaching his twenty-fifth year at the agency and still planned to retire. He would be rehired as a contractor, which would allow him to keep an eye on the case, but he would no longer control the fate of the Tinners. Others within the Counter-Proliferation Division at Langley would wind down the investigation that Kinsman had started many years earlier. He would keep an ear to the ground. He would stay in touch with Urs Tinner through back channels that they had set up over the last five years. But the case would no longer belong to the man who had been head of the Khan task force at the CIA. Before leaving, Kinsman undertook one last mission: He would try to secure the long-term cooperation of his Swiss assets. So, with the approval of his superiors in the Directorate of Operations and Counter-Proliferation Division, Kinsman promised the Tinners that they would be well compensated for any time they spent in jail, as long as they kept quiet.

The CIA could not afford another international embarrassment. In June an Italian judge had issued arrest warrants charging thirteen CIA officers with illegally abducting a Muslim cleric from the streets of Milan and sending him on a private jet to Egypt. The practice, known euphemistically as "extraordinary rendition," involved capturing a terrorist suspect and flying him to a country where he was likely to be tortured. In most cases, suspects were arrested by local authorities and turned over to the CIA, technically absolving them of any charges of kidnapping. In the case of the cleric Hassan Moustafa Osama Nasr, known as Abu Omar, he was snatched without the knowledge of the Milan police in 2003 and was not heard from for another year. After he resurfaced in his native country of Egypt, he accused the CIA of kidnapping him and sending him there to be tortured.

The Italian charges were highly unusual, particularly coming from a country whose prime minister, Silvio Berlusconi, was one of the few European leaders who supported the American invasion of Iraq. As details surfaced in the weeks that followed, it became clear that a team of more than twenty CIA agents had been involved in the abduction and that they had bungled the operation, leaving a trail of unencrypted telephone records and credit card bills at luxury hotels in Milan. Before the case was over, twenty-three Americans, including the chief of the CIA base in Milan, would be convicted in absentia of kidnapping. The Milan accusations marked the first time a judge in an allied country had ordered CIA agents brought to trial.

Kinsman and his colleagues had broken Swiss law by recruiting the Tinners and breaking into Marco's house. They didn't want to be targets of a second case brought by a foreign government. Along with buying the silence of the Tinners, the CIA persuaded the rest of the U.S. government to stonewall the Swiss prosecutor who was trying to build a case against them.

Lehmann's requests for assistance were ignored. By the time his third letter had met with complete silence, the Swiss prosecutor knew that he needed to get help somewhere else. The logical solution was the International Atomic Energy Agency. Lehmann had been corresponding with Heinonen, occasionally sending him updates on information related to the Tinners. He knew that the IAEA had the experts who could decipher the designs and documents. Plus, the prosecutor knew enough about the agency's investigation of the Khan network to believe that he would find an ally in Heinonen.

CHAPTER FIFTEEN

BERN

On the morning of November 21, Trevor Edwards and Miharu Yonemura arrived at Zurich airport after a short flight from Vienna. Chasing A. Q. Khan had taken the two IAEA officials to exotic locations, following a labyrinthine trail of the far-flung crime ring that had led from Dubai to Kuala Lumpur, from Tehran to Tripoli. They were getting closer and closer to a danger they still did not understand. Now the chase was headed to Switzerland, the place where much of the network's nuclear technology originated and where they hoped to find the answers that had so far eluded their global investigation.

Faced with American silence in the face of his requests for assistance, Peter Lehmann had called the IAEA. He explained that he had recovered a cache of drawings and equipment from the homes, offices, and factory of the Tinner family. Lehmann told Heinonen that the volume of the material was enormous, and that he needed help to evaluate its significance. An unmarked police car was at the airport to take Edwards and Yonemura the sixty miles to Bern, where Lehmann was waiting for them in his office overlooking the River Aare.

Coffee was served as Lehmann told his guests that he had turned to them because the Swiss government did not have anyone with the expertise to understand the Tinner material and the Americans had failed to respond to his letters. Thanking Edwards and Yonemura for coming, he spread the first package of drawings on the table, describing them as a fraction of what had been seized at various locations associated with the Tinners.

Before allowing the IAEA officials to dig in, however, Lehmann said his investigators had come across some unusual, coded e-mails on one of the computers seized from Marco Tinner.

"What do you know about codes and how you can use codes to communicate?" he asked.

Edwards said he didn't know anything about coded messages. But Yonemura flushed and acknowledged that she knew what Lehmann was talking about. Prodded by Lehmann, Yonemura explained the basics of a book-based cipher system. With some hesitation, she described how two people with identical copies of a book could use page numbers, line numbers, and even specific word numbers to encrypt and decode messages. For example, she said, a string of numbers in an e-mail would designate the page to turn to in the book, the line to select, and the exact word in that line that you wanted to use.

"I am glad you told me, Miharu," said Lehmann.

The prosecutor handed Yonemura a printout of a coded e-mail that she had sent to Marco months before. His investigators had found the e-mail on Marco's computer. He handed her a second sheet of paper, which contained a decoded version of her e-mail. The contents were innocuous, but Yonemura was surprised that the Swiss had broken the book cipher.

Lehmann said the Tinners were cooperating, at least to some extent. After the searches and arrest of Marco, he and Urs had begun to fill in some of the gaps in what the Swiss knew about their proliferation activities. As they had with the IAEA, they were trying to protect themselves and put the best face on what they had done. But the Tinners had not told the Swiss how to break the code. When he was asked by Lehmann about the encrypted e-mails found on his mother's computer, Marco had laughed and said he didn't know what the prosecutor was talking about.

Chief Inspector Kurt Senn, the senior officer on the case and the head of national security for the Swiss federal police, has a reputation for single-minded determination. The secret code was one of the most unusual elements of the investigation he was leading. The first clue to the mysterious code was a receipt from FedEx obtained in the raids. It showed Marco sending what was described on the customs form as a book to Heinonen. The idea that Tinner was communicating with the

IAEA had caught Senn's attention at the time. That Tinner would be sending Heinonen a book seemed odd. Then he remembered hearing something, somewhere about a book cipher.

The key was uncovering the exact book on which the code was based. Going over the coded e-mails again and again, Senn spotted what he suspected were clues. Initials at the start of each message seemed to correspond to book titles. For instance, one of the e-mails started with "TKOTJG." The last two initials, JG, turned up in other e-mails. It seemed possible that the pattern might represent the author. Turning to his own computer, Senn entered "JG" into a search for book titles. The name John Grisham popped up quickly. A search of books written by the massively popular American writer turned up *The King of Torts*. Senn had his first hit. By conducting thousands of searches over a number of days, Senn had assembled a list of books that he suspected the Tinners had used. It was an eclectic list, right out of an airport bookstore. There was another Grisham, *The Last Juror; Pompeii* by Robert Harris; *The Little Prince* by Antoine de Saint-Exupéry; *Dude, Where's My Country* by Michael Moore; and, most appropriately, *The Da Vinci Code* by Dan Brown. Senn persuaded Lehmann to get another search warrant, this time for any books found in any of the Tinner residences and businesses. The search turned up copies of all of the ones on the detective's list.

By the time Yonemura acknowledged her correspondence with Marco, several hundred e-mails had been decoded. Lehmann told the IAEA expert that there was still work to be done. Then he spread his hands about six inches apart and said, "We have a stack of printouts like this."

Lehmann wasn't quite done with his demonstration. He pulled out another printout and read from one of the decoded e-mails. Marco had sent it to Urs in July 2003. In it, Marco had instructed his brother to press A. Q. Khan for information about the network's suspected fourth customer. Someone referred to only as "Jim" was insisting on the information. Yonemura and Edwards recognized the name immediately.

What concerned the IAEA officials was the discovery that the CIA had been pressuring the Tinners to find out more about the network's elusive fourth customer. The IAEA had been worried for months that there was at least one other buyer. They had taken some solace in the idea that the Americans probably knew at least something about the identity of the other customer. The idea that the CIA was as much in the dark as the IAEA was an unwelcome development.

THE REVELATIONS KEPT COMING. LEHMANN said his technicians had decoded another series of e-mails that he initially thought might be connected to an unknown customer. They said the e-mails showed that the Tinners had sold two P-2 rotors to a customer in a transaction that they had kept secret from Khan and Tahir. The e-mails reflected a dispute over the price of the rotors. The Tinners were demanding a million dollars for the pair, but the buyers argued that the price was too high for something that Urs had essentially stolen from the factory in Malaysia and a storage facility in Dubai. In the end, the buyers had agreed to pay a half million, and Urs had turned them over. When questioned about the deal, however, the brothers said the buyer was the CIA and that the transaction was part of their work for the American intelligence agency. Indeed, cooperating with the CIA was central to the defense the Tinners were trying to build, and they were providing the Swiss with glimpses into the relationship. So far, however, they had refused to provide the real names of the CIA agents, assuming they even knew them. Lehmann suspected that "Jim" was their CIA handler.

These were undoubtedly the same rotors that Urs had told the IAEA eighteen months earlier he had thrown into the Persian Gulf when Khan's empire began to crumble. That supposition was confirmed when Lehmann showed the IAEA officials an e-mail exchange between Urs and his CIA handler from the week before the Tinners met with the IAEA for the first time in Vienna. Swiss authorities had found the e-mail on one of the Tinner computers and, using Senn's code-cracking abilities, had decoded it. Mentioning the upcoming meeting, Urs had asked how he should respond if the issue of rotors arose. He was told, "Tell Heinonen and Edwards that you threw the two rotors in the sea."

The e-mails seemed to prove that the rotors had not ended up in the hands of another customer. The question was, why had the Americans, who had arranged the debriefing with the Tinners and even sat in on the questioning, instructed Urs to lie? No one was naïve enough to imagine that the Americans were sharing everything with the IAEA, or that the Tinners had told the whole truth. But the discovery of the lie raised another question: What else were the CIA and the Tinners hiding?

Finally, Lehmann set aside the stack of e-mails and pointed to the first of the drawings. It showed the floor plan for some kind of huge hall, with places marked for fifteen long lines of machines. The IAEA officials immediately recognized the layout for a uranium enrichment facility, with fifteen cascades of 164 centrifuges each. A quick calculation determined that 2,460 centrifuges specified for the hall could probably produce enough highly enriched uranium (HEU) for one bomb a year, depending on the type of machine and the efficiency with which they operated. If the cascades contained P-1 centrifuges, they would probably fall short of enough HEU for a bomb a year; if they were P-2, they would likely exceed the amount required. A second drawing showed the piping system that would be used to connect the cascades. Lehmann said he believed the system had been designed and built by Marco Tinner.

At that point, it was the IAEA's turn to share. Edwards reached into his briefcase and showed Lehmann a photograph of the exact system, which he said had been discovered in Libya and later taken by the Americans to Oak Ridge. The plans that Lehmann had were for a small version of the larger system that had been built in South Africa. For Lehmann, the match seemed to connect the Tinners directly to the Libyan nuclear project. It was just the type of evidence he would need to prosecute them. But he would need official confirmation from the Americans that the piping system in the drawings matched the actual system that had been found in Libya.

Lehmann continued to push documents in front of Edwards and Yonemura, covering components manufactured by the Tinners and shipped to various elements of the network. There were also mountains of photographs, invoices, and financial records that appeared to show the Tinners at the very center of the network, buying and shipping equipment around the world for the SCOPE factory in Malaysia and Libya. This was familiar territory for the IAEA: They had seen bits and pieces of this puzzle in many locations.

But there were some surprises. The IAEA, as well as most of the world, was well aware that Khan had stolen plans from Urenco to build two different types of centrifuges, the P-1 and P-2. The packet of documents, however, contained designs for a centrifuge system with four separate rotors; the work appeared to be based on a German design called the G-4, which had been under development at Urenco in the 1970s. Khan had apparently copied those designs, too, but it had escaped notice for three decades.

Another folder of letters and documents mystified the two IAEA officials. Invoices showed that Phitec had shipped large numbers of packages on two occasions to a company called Deramo Systems in Chicago. The first shipment, which occurred on January 16, 2004, contained thirty-two packages of valves valued at $1.5 million; a second shipment of ninety-four boxes of machined parts had been sent four days later. Each was accompanied by a standard customs letter signed by Friedrich's daughter. Why, asked Lehmann, would the Tinners be shipping what appeared to be valuable nuclear technology to the United States?

The IAEA checked the address later and found that it was an empty building. While some people wondered why the Tinners would be shipping anything to Deramo in Chicago, Heinonen speculated that it was a sham transaction, set up to cover a payment to the Tinners, perhaps from the Americans. "I would be surprised if a lot of equipment went to that address," he said later. "Maybe it was nothing but a way to give them some money."

The drawings in Lehmann's office were only the beginning of what the Swiss showed the IAEA team on its two-day visit. Later on the first day, they went to the federal police headquarters, where they were met by Markus Kellenberger, the head of counterproliferation. He took Edwards and Yonemura down a corridor and stopped at a locked door that bore the word ATOMOS and the trefoil sign of radiation danger. Inside, the only thing radioactive was more Tinner documents, which were locked in two large cabinets. Kellenberger said that a nearby room contained additional records, which had been culled from the files obtained from the Tinners. The records were neatly labeled, but Yonemura and Edwards had only two days in Bern and it was clear that a careful examination of the material would take much more time. Kellenberger offered to show them pieces of equipment and components removed from Phitec and Traco, which had been moved from the jail cell to a storage area in the same building. There they saw an array of high-tech pieces designed for centrifuges. Some of the pieces were finished; others were in the early stages of manufacture. Examining the equipment took the rest of the afternoon, and they agreed to meet the next day back in Lehmann's office.

The next morning, the prosecutor and a police technician spent several hours reviewing the contents of a hard drive from one of the computers at Marco's house with Edwards and Yonemura. The technician described how he and his colleagues in the police IT unit had been forced to recover the files because they had been deleted from the computers. The Tinner effort had fallen far short of cleaning the computer, so the technician said that they had been able to retrieve several hundred drawings from that hard drive alone. Work was continuing on additional drives. The drawings amplified the material from the previous day.

Back in Vienna the next day, Edwards and Yonemura provided Heinonen with a description of what they had seen in Bern. The Finn was surprised by the scope of the evidence and how deeply it implicated the Tinners in the Khan network. There also was a recognition of how much more work was involved in running every aspect of the network to ground. The e-mail showing that the Americans suspected there was a fourth customer but appeared to have made no more progress in identifying the country or group than the IAEA, was most alarming.

Well into the description of what had transpired in Bern, Edwards and Yonemura came to the part where they described the e-mails they had seen showing that the CIA had bought the P-2 rotors from Urs Tinner. Not only had the CIA bought the rotors, they said, but the messages indicated that the Americans had instructed Tinner to lie about it to the IAEA.

Heinonen erupted. Why had the Americans told Tinner to lie? Why had the IAEA wasted so much time and energy trying to find those two critical missing rotors when they were probably sitting in a storage room in Oak Ridge? Heinonen tried to figure out the American motive. The CIA knew that the IAEA had found invoices showing that seven rotors had been shipped from Khan's lab in Pakistan to Dubai. He had told them himself. Yet for some reason, the CIA didn't want them to know that the rotors were in the United States. One possibility was that the CIA recognized the significance of the rotors to any attempt to prosecute the Tinners in Switzerland. Keeping their location secret could hamper that effort. Or perhaps it was a simple case of industrial espionage. In the 1970s, the British, Dutch, and Germans had set up Urenco as a joint operation to provide enriched uranium for Europe's commercial nuclear reactors. At the time, the United States controlled the nuclear fuel supplies for the world's civilian reactors. In developing the P-2, the Europeans wanted to break what some considered an American stranglehold so they would be free to develop nuclear power on their own terms. There had been many advances in centrifuge technology since the late 1970s, when the P-2 was the most efficient machine available, but it was possible that the Americans still didn't want Urenco to find out that they had two of the rotors. "This was a big problem," Heinonen said later. "Urenco wouldn't like it that the U.S. had the rotors because the U.S. could learn, particularly with the P-2."

In Switzerland, the evidence was still being organized. Lehmann had asked Edwards and Yonemura to return to examine the rest. Heinonen agreed, authorizing them to make as many trips as necessary. "Go see them all," he said, referring to the documents. "Go see the Swiss and take a full inventory."

THE SWISS PROGRESS FRUSTRATED THE CIA and Kinsman. The case officer had retired in the fall of 2005 but remained at the agency on a contract, which allowed him to monitor Lehmann's ongoing investigation. The silence of the U.S. government had not been enough to derail the Swiss inquiry. And now the CIA was learning through its sources that the IAEA was helping the Swiss understand the dimensions of the case. The danger that the Tinners might be charged and wind up in court seemed to be increasing. At Langley, it was becoming clear that stopping the Swiss was going to require some bigger guns.

On January 19, 2006, Ambassador Willeford returned to the Justice Ministry in Bern to repeat her government's fears about the Swiss investigation of the Tinners and the potential damage to ongoing intelligence operations. The Americans were not sure that Christoph Blocher would come through for them, so Willeford invited the justice minister to meet the following week with Michael Chertoff, the U.S. secretary of homeland security, on the sidelines of the World Economic Forum in Davos, Switzerland. Blocher agreed.

Chertoff is an intense man with an impressive résumé, particularly when it comes to terrorism. He had been a federal prosecutor in New Jersey and he was the chief of the Justice Department's criminal division in the two years after the September 11 attacks, a job in which he had supervised the prosecution of the so-called "twentieth hijacker," Zacarias Moussaoui. In 2003, President Bush had nominated Chertoff to a prestigious judgeship on the United States Court of Appeals in Philadelphia. When Bush needed a new head of the Department of Homeland Security in early 2005, Chertoff had agreed to resign his lifetime appointment to the bench and return to the administrative branch of government. Since then, he had been a major player in the American antiterrorism effort, particularly on the domestic front. Where Blocher had little experience with international terrorism, Chertoff was steeped in it, which seemed to make him a good choice to explain where the Tinner case fit in the larger context of the fight against terrorism and to underscore the importance of making it disappear.

Davos is best known as the place where the stars of business, government, and entertainment meet to talk about serious topics. The invitation-only event transforms the tiny alpine village into the world's most extreme networking site, a place where billionaires and mere millionaires rub shoulders with the likes of former president Bill Clinton, Queen Rania of Jordan, and movie star Angelina Jolie. For 2006, there were more than 240 sessions packed into four and a half days, with events running from seven in the morning until past midnight. Topics ranged from the serious, "Could a nuclear bomb go off in your city?" to the frivolous, "All you ever wanted to know about relationships, but were afraid to ask." The Middle East dominated the political discussion, and seminars on economics focused on the rise of China and India. One of the most popular sessions was a discussion of the digital future between Microsoft founder Bill Gates, Google chief executive Eric Schmidt, and Skype inventor Niklas Zennström. The best party was thrown on Friday night by Google, which was held at the Kirschner Museum on Davos's main street and featured an A-list of the powerful and celebrated, topped only by a wine list that started with a 1990 Krug champagne, moved on to a 1989 Château Margaux, and finished with magnum bottles of Château Lynch-Bages, vintage 1955. Much of the business of Davos, however, takes place on the sidelines, in the cafeteria at the conference center and various hotel suites scattered around the village.

It was in one of those suites where Chertoff made his pitch to Blocher. Using his personal knowledge of terrorist threats, the American official tried to convince the justice minister to back off the Tinner investigation. Chertoff stressed the role the Tinners had played in helping bring down the Libyan nuclear program. He said they had knowledge of people involved in ongoing intelligence operations, both assets and targets.

Explaining that it was essential to protect the continued effort to roll up the rest of the Khan network and keep nuclear weapons from ever falling into the hands of terrorists, Chertoff asked for Blocher's help. Make sure that the relationship between the Tinners and American intelligence is not revealed and that no member of the family will ever testify in open court. They knew too many dangerous secrets.

Blocher understood the gravity of the situation, but he still faced a dilemma. Lehmann's investigation had turned up evidence that the Tinners had probably violated Swiss export laws for years. Shutting down the investigation now could violate the separation of powers under Swiss law. Blocher also did not want to be portrayed as bowing to American pressure if his actions ever became public. It could mean the end of his political career. He made clear to Chertoff that he understood the sensitivities, but he said he was not ready to interfere with the inquiry quite yet. Not until he understood more about what the Tinners had done, how they had done it, and how to protect the Swiss government.

Chertoff would report back to the White House that he wasn't certain he had convinced the Swiss justice minister to do the right thing. With Marco and Urs Tinner languishing in jail, the CIA wondered how much longer their Swiss spies would keep their mouths shut. And the upcoming trial of another network participant in Germany added to the nervousness that details of the intelligence operation were about to spill into the public arena.

A MONTH AFTER DAVOS, THE reason for Chertoff's concern was evident at a secret meeting in the interrogation rooms of the police headquarters in Bern. Urs Tinner had been in jail for more than a year, and he was desperate to get out. Kinsman had arranged for his family to receive hefty payments during the time they spent in jail but Urs was losing faith in the ability of the CIA to secure his freedom. After all, he couldn't spend any money locked away. In early February, he asked the prosecutors if he could talk to the IAEA. He hoped its officials would explain the extent of his cooperation. Lehmann agreed. On February 20, Olli Heinonen and Trevor Edwards arrived in Bern.

Lehmann met the IAEA officials in his office and led them down two flights of stairs to the interrogation rooms in the basement. In one of the windowless rooms, they found Tinner, his lawyer, Roman Boegli, and two senior Swiss federal police officials, Kellenberger from the counterproliferation office and Chief Inspector Kurt Senn. It was agreed that the meeting would be recorded, but Boegli insisted that Tinner would not sign a statement attesting to the truth of the information. He said he did not want it to be used against his client in the event of a trial. For his part, Heinonen repeated that he and his people were still abiding by the confidentiality requirement set up in the "rules of the game" two years earlier at the first meeting with the Tinners.

Though Heinonen had met with Friedrich Tinner and with Marco and his lawyer, this was the first time he had been face-to-face with Urs since Innsbruck in the fall of 2004. Tinner was paler and the months in jail had robbed him of his swagger. As he started his presentation, Tinner was clearly angry and frustrated about the way he had been treated, but he focused most of the blame on the CIA. He claimed that he had cooperated extensively with the Americans but that neither he nor his family had been able to contact the CIA since his arrest in Germany in October 2004. The assertion was not true, but no one in the room knew it. Tinner's defense strategy entailed some risks. Swiss law was serious about the country's neutrality, and cooperating with a foreign intelligence agency violated specification sections of the criminal code. But that crime was less serious than a conviction for helping a foreign country develop nuclear weapons. So Tinner took pains to claim he knew nothing of the ultimate destination of the parts he manufactured and the shipments he orchestrated.

Casting himself in a heroic role, Tinner said that he had only manufactured components in Malaysia, without knowing that they were destined for any nuclear program. Once he learned where the material was going, he described the precise steps he had taken to sabotage centrifuge components produced at SCOPE. This was old news to Heinonen and Edwards. The problem was that Tinner's supposedly sabotaged designs seemed to work quite well. Tinner was either lying about his sabotage or the alterations had not been enough to cause the centrifuges to malfunction.

Edwards told Tinner that Urenco had conducted tests on the designs from SCOPE and determined that they met the specs for centrifuges. In addition, he said, the IAEA had asked Urenco to build a few P-1 centrifuges using the actual parts produced from Tinner's designs. Edwards said Urenco had nearly finished the machines and it would soon be clear whether the sabotage had worked—or even occurred.

Flustered, Tinner reached for a life raft. He claimed that he had hidden a hard drive containing sensitive information and some documentation in the house he had rented in Kuala Lumpur. He described the precise spot beneath the floorboards where, so far as he knew, the material was still concealed.

Lehmann was comfortable making Urs Tinner available to the IAEA. He trusted Heinonin, and he desperately needed the expertise the agency had to offer. The same could not be said for the Americans. In recent weeks, some of the prosecutor's associates had come to believe that there was a leak in the investigation. The Americans seemed to have developed a source inside the Swiss government who was keeping them up to date on developments. The Americans seemed to know every move being made by the Swiss authorities, from the assistance they were receiving from the IAEA to plans under way to try to help the German prosecution of Lerch. They did not suspect the IAEA. The Americans appeared to be receiving far more information about the progress of the Swiss investigation than the IAEA possessed. Instead the concern was that the leak was coming from inside the Swiss government. Suspicion had fo-

cused on a senior Swiss intelligence official who had a long-standing relationship with the Central Intelligence Agency. Among the few officials
who knew about the Tinner affair, he was the one unashamed friend of
Washington's neoconservatives, and the most vocal evangelist for greater
cooperation with the American intelligence service. He shared the CIA's
determination to make the Tinner case disappear. Senior police officials
had suggested to Lehmann that the suspect should be prohibited from
attending future meetings at which sensitive aspects of the case were on
the agenda.

Other signs of outside interest in the case had popped up. The Swiss
police detected a spike in attempts to hack into their computer network.
The attacks seemed to be aimed at the IT center in Zurich, where the
Tinner documents were kept on a secure server. Police computer technicians tracked the attempts to a company in Iraq that had connections to
the Pentagon, but they could get no further.

The Swiss investigators were finally getting a sense of the scope of
what they had come to call "the Tinner affair." The Tinners had maintained that they had helped the CIA, something that the Americans had
acknowledged somewhat grudgingly. Investigators believed the Tinners
and the Americans were withholding information about the full extent
of the relationship. The searches had turned up the contract signed by
Marco with Big Black River Technologies. As they had with a dozen
other companies, the Swiss police followed up by trying to contact the
company. But this time they got only the answering machine in Washington.

During a trip to the U.S. capital, a Swiss police official had gone to
the address and found that there was no listing for the company. Then
there were the names on the contract. The police could find no trace
of W. James Kinsman and Sean D. Mahaffey. The names didn't appear
anywhere in databases and didn't mean much until the investigators read
the last will and testament that Marco had left in a lockbox at his Jenins
apartment. To assure that his wife received money owed to him, the will
mentioned a contact and listed a contact name and telephone number.
The name was Jim Kinsman and the phone number appeared to be
in Washington. No one answered the number. When the Swiss police
asked Marco about Kinsman, he told them a story that led to a new

determination among the police to get to the bottom of the CIA's role in the Tinner affair.

Up to this point in the interrogations, the Tinner brothers had provided few details of their dealings with the CIA. They were trying to protect themselves from being prosecuted for working for a foreign intelligence agency, and they were trying to protect the hush money coming from the CIA. Confronted with his own will, Marco finally shed some light on the arrangements. He acknowledged that he had signed the contract and that Kinsman had been the family's primary contact. Like his brother, Marco was critical of the Americans. He said the family had tried to help bring down the Khan network but that the Americans did not appreciate their efforts or trust them. To illustrate his point, he said that he had signed the contract with Big Black River the same day that six Americans had insisted on searching his apartment in Jenins and his office in Sax. During the searches, he said, he believed that they had copied all of the records on his computers. He even said that Kinsman had told him to claim that unknown people had broken into the apartment if the incident were ever discovered by the Swiss authorities.

This was the first the Swiss police had heard that the CIA had operated on Swiss soil. The idea that they had searched two locations, even with the coerced permission of Marco Tinner, elevated the anger. From the perspective of the Swiss authorities, recruiting Swiss citizens as spies was bad enough. Violating Swiss sovereignty made the CIA more than common criminals. Some factions within the police and governmental circles of the Swiss government had begun to talk about expanding the Tinner case by prosecuting the CIA for recruiting Swiss citizens for spying and conducting espionage on Swiss territory.

PART III

THE ENDGAME

CHAPTER SIXTEEN

MANNHEIM, GERMANY

Mannheim is a medium-size city in southwestern Germany best known for the large American military base on its outskirts. The city's courthouse was built in the 1960s, and the years have not treated it well. The exterior is poured concrete, with the second story covered by dull, rusty steel. Inside, the courtrooms, with their popcorn-stucco walls and yellowed ceilings, can be described most charitably as utilitarian. All in all, it was an inauspicious location for an event of historic importance. But at ten o'clock on the morning of March 17, 2006, the trial of a suspected member of A. Q. Khan's nuclear mafia started in courtroom two, which was the size of a high school gymnasium.

Sitting at the defense table that morning, arms folded across his chest and a binder open in front of him, was Gotthard Lerch. At sixty-three and about six feet tall, he looked fit and comfortable, particularly for someone facing the possibility of spending the rest of his life in prison. Perhaps Lerch appeared at ease because he was confident that the case against him had been fatally weakened. Infighting among the governments of several countries was threatening to deprive the prosecution of key witnesses against Lerch. Or perhaps Lerch wasn't showing any sign of worry because he had been through it all before: The German government had tried twice to prosecute him, once in the late 1980s and again in 1992. Each time, he had walked away a free man and resumed selling nuclear technology.

This third attempt was in trouble before the judge called the proceedings to order that Friday morning. For months the German prosecutors had been struggling to gather evidence against Lerch. The intelligence agencies that presumably knew the most about his role, the CIA and MI6, were providing no information. The prosecutors had even run into a stone wall with their own intelligence agency, which had been cooperating with its counterparts at the CIA and MI6 but was not inclined to share any information with colleagues in its own government. Requests for help from governments of Malaysia, South Africa, and the United States had fallen largely on deaf ears, too. Prosecutors had traveled to Malaysia and interviewed B. S. A. Tahir, who had repeated his accusations that Lerch had been involved intimately in procuring and shipping centrifuge technology to Libya for its nuclear weapons project. But the Malaysian government was refusing to send Tahir to Mannheim to testify. Instead they provided an affidavit confirming his statements, which was inadmissible because German law entitles a defendant to cross-examine his accusers. Similar problems arose when prosecutors tried to arrange for Gerhard Wisser and Daniel Geiges to come from South Africa to testify. Still smarting over the unilateral interview conducted by the Germans during the Pelindaba review, the South Africans were refusing to make either man available. They did offer, however, to have Wisser and Geiges respond to questions through a video linkup from a South African courtroom. The prosecutors were still negotiating with both governments, but prospects looked dim.

The prosecutors also faced problems related to the deal in which the Swiss had agreed to send Lerch back to Germany for trial in exchange for Urs Tinner. The Swiss had required the Germans to drop the treason charge because it was regarded as a political crime and the Swiss constitution prohibits extradition for political charges. Dropping the most serious charge against Lerch meant the case was transferred from the federal system to the local court in Mannheim, where prosecutors had less experience with complex international crimes. The Germans had also failed to obtain a guarantee from Switzerland that Tinner would be returned to testify against Lerch.

Tinner was expected to be the star witness. During his months in a German prison, he had been coddled by his jailers. The first time that

Roman Boegli, his lawyer, had gone to see Tinner in his German prison, they met in a restaurant reserved for police officers. His client was wearing jeans and a T-shirt. He seemed on friendly terms with the police. "He was a king in Germany," Boegli said. "They liked him there. I believe he was used by the German secret service. They never tried to accuse him of anything, but they got as much information from him as they could." The truth was, the Germans had been treating Tinner well because they needed him for their own prosecution of Lerch.

But now the star witness was looking like a no-show. Just as Tahir's affidavit was of limited value without his presence in the courtroom, Tinner's statements also would be almost useless if he were not on the stand to testify. For reasons that the Germans could not understand, the Swiss were refusing to send their prisoner to Mannheim.

The prosecution needed to lay out an understandable case that demonstrated that Lerch had knowingly helped the Libyan nuclear program through specific actions. The defense strategy, on the other hand, planned to exploit the mystery surrounding the case. They would argue that their client could not get a fair trial when the witnesses against him were hidden away in foreign countries. Further, the defense lawyers were contending that the intelligence agencies of the United States and Germany were conspiring to conceal the extent of their involvement in the Khan network and how they had manipulated evidence against their client. Without information from the CIA and other intelligence services, the lawyers maintained, the court could not understand how their client had been sucked into an operation concocted by intelligence agencies. Lerch, they contended, was a victim, not a perpetrator.

On March 17, most of the opening session was taken up by arguments from Lerch's lawyers that they had been denied full access to secret material used against their client. Even the small amounts of evidence disclosed to them was classified and they had been forbidden from copying or taking notes. The lawyers said they weren't sure what they could discuss with Lerch or what they could bring up in court.

"I don't know what I'm allowed to say," Gottfried Reims, the lead defense attorney and a man given to dramatic statements, complained to the presiding judge. "Help me."

The judge, Michael Seidling, said he had asked the German intelligence service how to handle the classified information, but that he had not yet received any instructions.

Reims's cocounsel was sitting at the defense table with a laptop computer and a portable printer, furiously typing away. Within minutes he produced a motion demanding that three of the six judges hearing the evidence be removed because they had refused the defense access to the secret material, claiming that it was classified and too sensitive to be disclosed to anyone without the proper security clearance. Seidling had no choice but to adjourn the trial until the matter could be resolved.

When the trial resumed near the end of April, Seidling was still on the bench and the chief prosecutor, Peter Lintz, was finally ready to lay out the case against Lerch. Unfortunately for the prosecution, the young attorney was no closer to having any of his key witnesses show up in court to supply the vital corroboration of his accusations. With broad strokes, he described how A. Q. Khan had agreed to provide Libya with the capacity to produce an arsenal of nuclear weapons, from enriching uranium to assembling warheads. "To produce and supply the goods needed by Libya, Khan used a circle of proven helpers who had already been of service to him for his own centrifuge program," Lintz said. Among the helpers he identified were Tahir, British businessman Peter Griffin, Urs Tinner, and Gotthard Lerch. "It was clear from the start to all those involved that the goods to be produced were for a gas centrifuge project for the purpose of highly enriching uranium in Libya," Lintz told the court.

The prosecutor argued that Lerch had played a central role in the Libyan project, organizing the training of Libyan technicians and arranging for a massive feed-and-withdrawal system to be constructed in South Africa for shipment to Libya. In exchange for his work, Lintz said, Lerch had been paid $34 million, about half of which was profit. His actions, said the prosecutor, "endangered peace between peoples, did considerable damage to Germany's foreign relations, and risked seriously threatening Germany's external security."

A conviction relied heavily on proving that Lerch attended specific meetings at which the Libyan project was discussed and took specific actions to supply designs and equipment. Lintz had paperwork that had been gathered by investigators, and he had the statements of people like

Tahir, Tinner, and Meyer. Live witnesses were needed to explain how the complicated scheme had worked and to link Lerch directly to the criminal activities. Even the delay until the end of April had not solved that problem for Lintz. So far, only one witness associated with the shipments had agreed to testify, and he would cause more damage than good.

In mid-May, Peter Griffin took the train to Mannheim from his home in Bordeaux, France. A British businessman who had retired to the south of France, Griffin had spent years denying accusations of involvement in illegal exports of nuclear technology to Pakistan and he had never been charged with a crime. Still, Griffin remained cautious. When the German prosecutor asked him to testify in Mannheim, he insisted that the court provide him with a letter promising that he would not be taken into custody by the Germans. "During the said period of time it is not permitted to apprehend or arrest the witness for a possible involvement in the charges specified in the above-mentioned indictment," said the letter.

Griffin arrived at court shortly after two o'clock on a Tuesday. The judge asked him to wait in the lobby until it was time for him to testify. As he sat on a bench with Steve Coll, the writer for the *New Yorker* who was covering the trial, the two men watched as a stream of spectators from two other courtrooms gathered in the lobby and chatted about their cases. One of those trials involved a prostitution ring and the other was a double murder arising from a love triangle. "This is nothing, then," Griffin said to Coll. "This is only the Apocalypse."

The businessman spent two hours on the stand, focused on proving his own innocence and saying little about Lerch. Griffin testified that he had been duped by Tahir, who had never told him that any of the shipments through his company were destined for Libya or any other nuclear program. At one point, he said that Tahir had forged invoices from his company, Gulf Technical Industries. Worse for the prosecution, Griffin said on the stand that Tahir's statements should be regarded as unreliable; the testimony brought a smile to Lerch's face. The case seemed to be slipping from the prosecution's grasp. It looked as if Lerch would walk free again.

Lerch's lawyers certainly seemed unconcerned. During breaks they often gathered in a corner of the hall outside the courtroom where they could smoke and banter. One afternoon not long after Griffin's testimony, Reims was talking loudly about articles he had read that described how George Tenet had boasted that the CIA's penetration of Khan's network was so thorough that agents had even searched the Pakistani's house.

"Let us presume that is true," Reims said to no one in particular, but loud enough for anyone to hear. "Then let Mr. Tenet tell us what he found out in his brave operations, in Khan's living room and at his company. What is the role of the CIA? What is the role of the other secret services? Are all these people we hear about here, whose payroll are they on?"

On July 27, Judge Seidling delivered the verdict. He announced that the judges had determined that Lerch should be freed. The lack of foreign cooperation and absence of key witnesses meant that the defendant could not receive a fair trial, said the judge. However, the court stopped short of exonerating Lerch. Instead they left open the possibility that the trial might resume after a fuller disclosure of evidence. Lerch's bail was set at $5 million. Given the difficulties surrounding his extradition from Switzerland, the court ordered Lerch to remain in Germany until a decision was made on whether to reopen the case against him. For a third time, Lerch walked away.

A SIMILAR DRAMA WAS PLAYING out in South Africa. Prosecutors there who were building the case against Wisser and Geiges were confronting difficulties getting cooperation from the American government. The South Africans had the hard evidence—eleven shipping containers of equipment that was intended for a uranium enrichment plant. They had the cooperation of a key witness, Johan Meyer, who was prepared to testify that he had built the feed-and-withdrawal system on instructions from Wisser and that they both knew it was destined for a Libyan nuclear plant. But the prosecution wanted to strengthen the case with testimony from American experts. They were the ones who could provide the context for the Libyan program and describe the scope and danger of the Khan network. But the Americans were threatening to withhold all help unless the South Africans agreed to conduct the entire Wisser and Geiges trial behind closed doors, which contradicted South African law.

The American attitude was confounding and contradictory, pulled in two distinct directions. "As a general rule, we wanted to see these individuals prosecuted," Robert Joseph, the Bush administration's undersecretary of state for arms control who was involved in negotiations with many countries over prosecutions of network participants, said later. "I have this old-fashioned notion that people ought to be punished for crimes, and we need to show the world that if you engage in this illicit but lucrative business, there will be a punishment. It would have to be something that demonstrates a deterrent effect. If there is no downside, why wouldn't you do this?"

But Joseph's old-fashioned notions of justice ran into opposition from the CIA and its advocates at the White House and elsewhere in the administration. Certainly there were genuine fears among the American officials that public trials could jeopardize continuing intelligence operations. For many people those risks outweighed the consequences of failing to prosecute network participants. They were more determined to protect the illusion that shutting down the Khan operation was a huge intelligence victory by keeping the Tinners out of a Swiss court, even if it meant allowing some nuclear traffickers to escape punishment.

By the end of 2006, three years after the seizure of the *BBC China*, only one person had been convicted in connection with the nuclear network. He was a minor figure, Henk Slebos, who had no direct role in supplying Iran or Libya.

Khan's nuclear mafia was widely acknowledged as the most dangerous private proliferation ring in history, helping Pakistan build its atomic arsenal and providing critical assistance to at least three other countries—Iran, Libya, and North Korea. But in trying to deal with crimes that threaten international security, prosecuting the criminals who sell nuclear technology and know-how requires a balancing act. On the one hand there's the goal of putting individuals in jail, and on the other hand is the goal of protecting the sources and methods at the heart of intelligence gathering. Too often, however, the CIA and other intelligence agencies claim to be protecting sources and methods when they are really protecting bad judgments and operational errors.

In Khan's case, the balance tipped to the intelligence side of the ledger from the start. As far back as 1975, he could have been stopped when the Dutch secret service first discovered that he was stealing centrifuge designs from Urenco. But the CIA intervened, pressuring the Dutch government to allow Khan to remain free so that his activities could be monitored. Initially the intelligence imperative allowed Khan to operate. The Americans and other intelligence agencies watched over the years as he played a central role in building his country's nuclear arsenal. But Khan's way was also smoothed by a succession of American leaders. They traded strict standards against nuclear proliferation for other goals, starting with the Carter administration's determination to ignore Pakistan's nuclear ambitions in order to maintain the country's assistance against the Soviets in Afghanistan in late 1979.

The same sort of permissiveness resurfaced in the Bush administration after Khan's confession in 2004. The United States never complained when the Pakistani government treated Khan with what Leonard Spector, a nonproliferation expert in Washington, referred to as "unseemly leniency." Instead of insisting on questioning Khan to get to the bottom of who received what technology from his nuclear network, the administration allowed Pakistani authorities to isolate Khan from any outside interrogation as the price of Islamabad's support in the fight against the insurgency in Afghanistan. And instead of providing the Americans or the International Atomic Energy Agency with a road map to undo the damage he caused, Khan was allowed to boast on a Karachi television show about the extensive assistance he provided to Iran's nuclear program and why he did it. "If Iran succeeds in acquiring nuclear technology, we will be a strong bloc in the region to counter international pressure," Khan said. "Iran's nuclear capability will neutralize Israel's power."

The same shortsighted strategy was behind the American government's refusal to cooperate fully in prosecuting the individual participants in the Khan network. Washington should have been providing all of the expert testimony and evidence available to go after every individual and company associated with a nuclear black market that had provided the world's most lethal technology to countries like Iran, North Korea, and Libya. Instead, the intelligence imperative was driving U.S. policy. Protecting the chess pieces in the game of espionage outranked punishing Khan and his associates and sending a powerful message of deterrence to future proliferators. The intelligence community, where information too often becomes the end goal, failed to act at critical junctures throughout the history of the Khan network. It failed to stop Khan in 1975, and it compounded that failure by not detecting the extent of his success in building Pakistan's atomic bomb. It also failed to detect the extent of the network's proliferation activities, both in terms of geography and technology. And, in what may turn out to be the biggest blunder in counterproliferation history, the CIA and other intelligence agencies missed Iran's acquisition of the hardware and know-how to make an atomic bomb. Even the best-intentioned policymakers had not been able to overcome a flawed intelligence strategy that spanned three decades.

The failure to convict Lerch in Germany and the difficulties confronting the prosecution of Wisser and Geiges in South Africa were stark evidence of the ongoing cost of the American position. But the most extreme example of this wrongheaded strategy was the widening campaign of the CIA and its backers to prevent the exposure of the Tinners in Switzerland. Senior administration officials were arguing that the risks to continuing intelligence operations were too high. No one was asking about the long-term costs of burying the truth about the damage done to world security by the Khan network generally and the Tinners specifically. Such costs extended beyond the growing threat posed by a nuclear Iran, because no country develops the atomic bomb in isolation. The ripples of Iran's success—a success that would have been impossible without the help of Khan and his associates—will be felt across the Middle East as its neighbors are forced to confront a new nuclear reality.

CHAPTER SEVENTEEN

WASHINGTON AND BERN

Alberto Gonzales was unyielding in his loyalty to George W. Bush. A Harvard-educated lawyer and partner in a big Houston law firm, Gonzales began working for Bush after he won his first election as governor of Texas in 1994. When Bush was elected president in 2000, Gonzales followed him to Washington as White House counsel. While veterans of the Texas years like Karl Rove and Karen Hughes stood out, Gonzales built a reputation as someone who operated quietly behind the scenes. His image was of someone whispering in the president's ear, not speaking into a microphone. His legal advice dovetailed neatly with the president's worldview, particularly when it came to the so-called "war on terrorism." Gonzales argued that the Geneva Conventions did not apply to prisoners taken in Afghanistan and Iraq. In a 2002 memo, he wrote that the threat of future terrorist attacks "renders obsolete Geneva's strict limitations on questioning of enemy prisoners." And he vigorously defended Bush's right to authorize the National Security Agency to monitor e-mails and telephone calls between the United States and overseas if one of the parties was suspected of having links to a terrorist organization, without obtaining the court order required by U.S. law. His defense of the program ran counter to twenty years of settled law, but Gonzales believed that some basic legal precedents had to be sacrificed in the fight against terrorism. He was rewarded for his loyalty by being appointed attorney general in 2005.

The Tinner affair dropped onto Gonzales's desk in the summer of

2006. By that point the CIA and the U.S. Embassy in Bern were filing disturbing reports that the Swiss federal police were continuing to make slow but steady progress in their investigation. The criminal cases in Germany and South Africa were adding to the nervousness. The concern at the CIA was that the Swiss, with two Tinners in jail already, might feel compelled to have their show trial, too, to demonstrate the country's commitment to nonproliferation. The Swiss constitution also represented a nuisance to the Americans. Under the constitution, the Justice Ministry did not have the authority to stop a preliminary investigation. Blocher could, however, use his authority to invoke Switzerland's "war articles" to derail an actual trial. But Swiss law required him to convince the other six members of the Federal Council to go along with the emergency measure. All in all, the situation in Switzerland was getting tricky.

A senior intelligence official involved in the operation described the CIA as "frantic" about making sure the Tinners were not charged and dragged into court, where they might tell everything they knew. Acknowledging that the CIA had broken Swiss law by recruiting its citizens, the intelligence official justified the action by arguing that the Swiss authorities had failed for decades to take steps against the Tinners and other nuclear traffickers within their borders. In addition, he said, the danger was that the mounting publicity surrounding Khan's operation and the pending trials might close down the intelligence operation too early.

"The network had not been totally dismantled," the intelligence official said. "When the Swiss finally decided to act, or were forced to act, it was the worst possible time. It could disrupt a major intelligence operation, which was one of the major intelligence successes of the post–World War II period."

Afraid to allow events to unfold on their own, the Americans had tried to intervene at lower levels. Sending the ambassador to talk to Blocher first had not raised the stakes much. Neither had the chat on the sidelines of Davos between Chertoff and the Swiss official. So the White House turned to Gonzales, as the nation's top law enforcement officer. He was asked to convince his Swiss counterpart to derail a criminal investigation and turn over the evidence to the United States. To increase his chance of success, the CIA provided Gonzales with some extra ammunition. He was briefed on portions of the most highly classified intelligence from the Tinner files and authorized to share it with Blocher if it became necessary to close the deal.

The opportunity came in July. Blocher arrived in Washington for discussions with the attorney general, FBI director Robert Mueller, and senior CIA officials to put the finishing touches on an agreement between the two countries to improve cooperation on a broad range of terrorism cases. The agreement would allow for joint investigations of terrorism and terrorism financing cases once prosecutions were started in both countries. The Swiss had been stung by accusations that some of their banks were used to transfer terrorist money around the world, so they were eager to showcase their commitment to going after Al Qaeda and any related extremist groups. If anyone noticed the irony of promising better collaboration at a time when the Americans were actively and unilaterally trying to subvert the Swiss justice system, they didn't say anything.

On the morning of July 12, Blocher and a small entourage of aides from the Swiss embassy walked down the hushed corridor on the fifth floor of the Justice Department building and stopped at the desk outside the room marked OFFICE OF THE ATTORNEY GENERAL. A secretary ushered them into the large conference room, where they waited only a short time before Gonzales and his team arrived. The details had been worked out and this was the ceremonial signing for the press. Blocher praised the new cooperation, saying that it "contributes to the security of our country and its people."

When the talks were over, Gonzales asked if he could speak to Blocher alone for a few minutes. The aides left the room. The attorney general explained that the White House had asked him to speak confidentially about the Tinner affair. He said that he and his colleagues in the intelligence community were extremely concerned that the continued investigation by the Swiss authorities threatened to upset a very volatile applecart. The Tinners, Gonzales said, had helped the Americans and the British shut down a great threat to world security. If they were hauled into court, they might divulge secrets that could jeopardize ongoing intelligence efforts to eradicate the rest of the Khan network. The worst scenario, he said, would be that sensitive information would be disclosed to the public during a criminal trial in which the defense lawyers would probably try to expose as much CIA involvement with the Tinners as possible in order to save their clients. The attorney general did not disclose anything about the operations that might be jeopardized by a trial. Essentially, he asked his Swiss counterpart to trust him.

Blocher had heard the pitch before, and he nodded. Yes, he said, he understood the dangers of a public trial. He said the Swiss investigators were proceeding with great caution and that no decision had been made on whether to bring formal charges against the Tinners. Blocher said that he, too, had security interests to worry about. If Swiss citizens had been involved in nuclear proliferation, his government had a responsibility to understand the full range of what had happened, he told the attorney general. The United States had an obligation to cooperate with the Swiss, not to obstruct its efforts.

Gonzales must have realized that the time had come to up the ante. He told Blocher that what he was going to say was highly classified and that the information had to stay in the room. When Blocher agreed, Gonzales told him that computer records seized by the Swiss police from the Tinners contained detailed designs for a nuclear warhead. These designs, he said, were not the rudimentary Chinese blueprints that had turned up in Libya at the end of 2003, which had been described in the press. Rather, the Tinners possessed plans for a more sophisticated, smaller warhead that had come directly from the weapons laboratories in Pakistan. In the wrong hands, these digitized designs would allow competent engineers to construct a warhead that would fit on an Iranian missile capable of reaching parts of Europe, the attorney general said. In fact, Gonzales said, the designs were so dangerous that the Swiss should not even possess them. Those records, and the other material taken from the Tinners, should be transferred to the United States for safekeeping, said Gonzales.

For the first time the U.S. government was telling a Swiss official the full extent of the damage done by the Tinners. Disclosing the existence of the warhead designs was a calculated risk. At this point Blocher knew from the interrogation of Marco Tinner a few months earlier that the CIA had conducted a search of Tinner's office and home. Now he had what sounded like confirmation that the Americans had copied the contents of his computers, too. It might have dawned on Blocher that his own investigators had no idea what was contained in the computers and other records that had been seized from the Tinners.

In fact, the Swiss police did not yet understand the significance of the evidence they had obtained. At the end of May, the federal police had prepared a report summarizing the potential case against the family based on their evidence. The summary and thirty-eight additional folders containing copies of what appeared to be the most critical evidence were turned over to Peter Lehmann, the prosecutor. Neither Lehmann nor the police grasped the significance or the danger of the material. Lehmann tucked the files away.

Blocher was shocked and embarrassed to learn from the American attorney general that his own police had such dangerous material in their possession. But Blocher did not promise to end the investigation, and he was even more resistant to turning over evidence to the Americans. All he could do was assure Gonzales that everything was secure and promise to review the situation as soon as he got back to Bern.

A senior Swiss official said later: "The fact is that Blocher was a bit lost. He was never totally briefed by his people because his people, well, they had not been doing anything about the Tinners for so long. They actually bore some responsibility for the mess we were in. They had problems in their cupboards." Blocher understood that he had not been getting the whole story. Back in Bern, he ordered the prosecutor and the police to develop a fuller inventory of everything seized from the Tinners and report back to him as soon as possible.

The prosecutor and police could not tell Blocher what they did not know. They had compiled what they suspected were key documents into thirty-eight folders, but they still didn't understand the full significance of what they had discovered in the search. Most importantly, the Swiss authorities did not yet know that they possessed designs for nuclear weapons. Blocher did not tell them what he had learned in Washington about the contents of those records. Lehmann knew only that he needed more help, so once again he turned to the IAEA.

Edwards and Yonemura had made a couple of trips to Bern since seeing the initial evidence the previous November. Because of Swiss reluctance, they had not been given access to what appeared to be the most sensitive of the seized computer records. In response to Blocher's orders, Lehmann contacted Heinonen and promised full access to his team if they returned to Switzerland as soon as possible. He couldn't tell Heinonen what they would be looking for. The American information was deemed too sensitive to share, even though it had been lying around in computers, briefcases, and flash drives for months. Lehmann did let Heinonen know that the American government was pressuring the Swiss to turn over all of the evidence to it, arguing that the material was too sensitive for Switzerland to keep.

The IAEA's own inquiry had stalled by the summer of 2006. Pakistan continued to refuse to permit the IAEA or any outsider to interview A. Q. Khan, who remained under house arrest. Evidence was stronger than ever that crucial equipment had gone missing. At Tahir's offices in Dubai, the IAEA had discovered a collection of photographs of sensitive technology. The Tinners had explained that the photos were used as proof of what had been shipped to Libya and Iran because export records and bills of lading were routinely falsified. "They didn't trust each other and they didn't have proper documentation, so they took pictures to prove what had been sent," an investigator said. Not everything in the photos could be found. "We are far from knowing everything," said a European diplomat monitoring the inquiry at the IAEA. "I'm frustrated by the lack of cooperation. We are losing time."

The IAEA officials were not the only ones losing time. Iran was moving forward with the installation of thousands of centrifuges at its underground enrichment plant near Natanz, but they were running into difficulties as they tested the cascades of machines. In April, Iran announced that it had used a cascade of 164 centrifuges to enrich its first uranium, progress later confirmed by IAEA inspectors. But the inspectors also discovered that the cascade had stopped working after a number of the linked centrifuges crashed. The Iranian scientists testing the centrifuges offered no explanation for the problems. The CIA, however, saw the crashes as the result of the sabotage that had introduced flawed components and other equipment into the Iranian program.

Edwards and Yonemura arrived in Zurich in late July in response to Lehmann's latest request. Instead of going to Bern, they were taken directly to the federal police information technology center, which was located in a separate building from the police headquarters in Zurich. There the Swiss had stored the computer data from the laptops, personal computers, and flash drives taken from the various Tinner locations on a secure server that was not connected to the outside world. The IAEA officials had been surprised at the extent of the material they had seen in Bern, but they were unprepared for the vast amount of information stored on the police computer. A rough inventory listed tens of thousands of files, ranging from normal business records to designs for centrifuges, cascades, and equipment that mystified the Swiss police and their experts. There was no way to search everything, but the most promising material seemed to be in several dozen files that had been on the laptop computer that the police believed belonged to Urs Tinner.

Edwards and Yonemura sat alongside a police technician who scrolled through the files for them. There were extensive blueprints for centrifuge components, designs for the huge halls to hold the cascades of centrifuges to enrich uranium, plans for the feeder system for uranium hexafluoride to fuel the machines and withdraw the enriched uranium. All of these they recognized and understood. In scanning through the files, they noticed a strange design that appeared unrelated to a centrifuge or any part of the enrichment process. Neither Edwards nor Yonemura is a nuclear weapons expert. Neither one had the level of security clearance that would allow them to even examine plans for an atomic bomb. But Edwards knows centrifuges from top to bottom and what they saw had nothing to do with any aspect of a centrifuge that he had ever encountered. The suspicions were strengthened by the initials on the drawing—"PAB."

A few months earlier, Heinonen had instructed his staff to review documents discovered in Iraq in the mid-1990s that showed Khan's aborted offer to build a nuclear weapons factory for Saddam Hussein. The records showed that Khan's offer had referred specifically to the bomb plans with the initials "AB," which seemed to stand for "atomic bomb." Sitting at the computer terminal in Zurich in July, Edwards asked the technician to type in "PAB" and scan all the files for anything with those initials. Files started popping onto the screen. Opening the first, the IAEA officials saw another drawing with the initials PAB. It was followed by two other files with the same initials—one was a list of mechanical components and the other was an inventory of electrical parts. Neither the components listed nor the two drawings had anything to do with centrifuges.

The files appeared potentially far more dangerous than anything the IAEA had uncovered in the past three years. If these were electronic copies of a nuclear implosion device fitted to a warhead, the network could have sent them to anyone. The Tinners had traveled extensively and carrying the plans was as easy as carrying a flash drive the size of a pack of gum. If the Americans convinced the Swiss to turn over all of the material to them, as Lehmann had mentioned, it would mean the full extent of the threat posed by the network could disappear into the closed world of the CIA or some other U.S. agency. Edwards needed to get the most sensitive records back to Vienna, where he could get a weapons expert to examine them. Kurt Senn gave permission to copy some of the files onto a computer disk so the material could be sent to Vienna for examination. After receiving the chief inspector's okay, the technician copied the PAB files onto a CD. Because of the extreme sensitivity of the material, arrangements were made to ship the disk to the IAEA through a diplomatic pouch. The disk clearly contained information beyond centrifuges, but it was still not clear that the designs were for a weapon. What was certain was that someone with the appropriate knowledge in Vienna should review them.

After several days of scouring the computer files, Edwards and Yonemura met with Lehmann and Markus Kellenberger, the police official in charge of export control regulations. They said they had scanned through about 10 percent of the computer files so far, and some designs were suspicious and appeared to be extremely sensitive. Other records contained the names and addresses of at least a dozen network participants in Europe and Asia who were previously unknown to the IAEA. They said they would analyze the information back in Vienna, and they agreed to return later to share their findings and begin looking through the rest of the files. Lehmann did not mention that the Americans had warned Blocher that the files contained weapons designs. He repeated, however, that the Americans were demanding that the entire cache be turned over to them for safekeeping. Lehmann said he expected the matter to come before the governing Federal Council in the near future, and he was worried that he would lose the evidence that he needed to charge and convict the Tinners. Edwards promised to analyze what they had seen and return as soon as possible. He, too, was worried that the records would disappear before he and his colleagues had the chance to explore the hundreds of gigabytes.

IT TOOK SEVERAL DAYS FOR the disk to find its way to the IAEA. When it did, Edwards spent three days organizing the information. Even to his untrained eye, the results appeared to be related to a bomb. The PAB designs seemed to be for an ignition system and hemispheres for a nuclear warhead. The parts lists also appeared to be related to a weapon. Some other files on the CD appeared to be Chinese in origin. Edwards printed out some of the designs, organized them into folders based on his interpretation of what they were for, and took them to Heinonen's office.

Heinonen studied the folders, shuffling through the papers faster and faster. As the meaning of the initials dawned on him, Heinonen was stunned. He didn't have the clearances required to see weapons plans, but he had been around long enough to recognize the danger they represented.

Edwards said that he did not know what he had when he discovered the designs in Switzerland. Heinonen was not mollified. Rising from the table, he ordered Edwards to go to his office, get all of the hard copies and the CD, and return immediately. He picked up his telephone and told his secretary to find Yonemura and tell her to come immediately to the office with one of the official canvas bags that the agency used to contain sensitive information. He also summoned Jacques Baute, a French nuclear weapons expert who had led the IAEA's investigation into Iraq's weapons program in the 1990s. Baute was one of the few people at the IAEA with the appropriate clearances to examine weapons designs.

Right after the Libyans opened the doors to their secret nuclear program, Baute had traveled to Tripoli with another agency official, the American weapons expert Bob Kelley. Together they had examined the

Chinese warhead plans that Khan had provided to the Libyans. Baute had been alarmed by the designs in Libya, but they were for an older, heavier warhead that would have been difficult to mount on a missile. The Libyans had claimed that they had not used the plans or copied them, and the Americans had eventually taken the whole lot back to the States. In Tripoli, Baute's biggest fear had been that the weapons designs had been digitized and that they could be anywhere there was a computer.

As he examined the printouts from Switzerland in Heinonen's office, the Frenchman realized that this worst-case scenario had come true. Some of the plans in front of him were from the Chinese design, and they had clearly been scanned into computer files. Much worse were the two designs and the parts lists marked "PAB." There appeared to be elements of two separate Pakistani warhead designs, though there were too few documents to reach a final conclusion. But this was more advanced than what Baute had seen in Libya. Where the Chinese design was dated and clumsy, these were for a modern, lighter warhead, and they were easier to follow. Baute's first thought was, "Oh shit."

Baute confirmed that the designs were for nuclear warheads. Heinonen wasted no time and asked for no opinions. He ordered Yonemura to put everything in the bag and seal it. He said the bag would be taken immediately to the U.S. mission to the IAEA, which was located in a skyscraper a few hundred yards away. Baute agreed with the decision to secure the designs. He recognized the risk they posed. But he insisted on going to Zurich to look at the entire cache himself. He needed to understand the full scope of this nightmare.

Chapter Eighteen

Vienna and Bern

Within days of seeing the two weapons designs and other material, Heinonen sent Edwards, Yonemura, and Baute back to Switzerland. He wanted a more thorough assessment of the threat posed by the Swiss cache of electronic files. Baute would be the key this time. He had spent the first part of his career as a nuclear weapons physicist, working for the French national program. Unlike his colleagues, Baute had the expertise to review the records and determine the extent of the weapons designs, as well as the security clearances to allow him to assess them. Heinonen instructed his team not to tell the Swiss exactly what they were searching for; that was a decision that would be made later, once they understood the threat. From the IAEA's perspective, the bigger the threat, the more the need to fully understand and expose the Khan network through a thorough investigation of the Tinners in Switzerland.

Heinonen's visit to Pelindaba in South Africa in early 2005 had made a lasting impression on him. Though the South Africans had abandoned their nuclear weapons program a decade earlier and destroyed the related design documents, they had retained a complete catalog of the documents, parts, and blueprints required for a nuclear weapon. More than a historical record, his review of the catalog had helped Heinonen understand the process of assembling the technology on the black market to build an atomic bomb. In the case of the Tinner records, he wanted a similar record of what the Khan network had sold to the world, as a means of assessing both the current threat and future vulnerabilities. "I was certain we would have to return someday to the topic," he said later.

Even with Baute's assistance, assembling this new catalog of horrors would be a daunting job. The Swiss had seized an electronic cache that exceeded a terabyte, the equivalent of five million pages of paper. In addition to the huge amount of material to digest, there was no order to the computers or the files on them. Each time a new computer was purchased, it appeared that the hard drive from the old one was dumped onto the new one. As a result, countless files were repeated, sometimes with variations that might be important.

Examining every single file would take at least two years, and the IAEA clearly did not have that kind of time. The obvious solution would be to search by key words, which could pull up records related to specific topics. Plugging in "PAB" would presumably uncover every document containing those initials. But there was no guarantee that all of the weapons designs were labeled "PAB," so other words and phrases would be necessary. They also wanted to throw in other search terms to reduce the risk of alerting the Swiss technicians that they were looking for weapons designs.

Searching only for key words could not be their sole approach, however; they would not be able to find what they did not know was there. As a remedy, Baute planned to employ what's known as "the Monte Carlo method" of random selection to scan everything. The term, first used by physicists developing the atomic bomb at Los Alamos in the 1940s, refers to a number of techniques that rely on repeated random samplings to examine a problem. The simplest type is called "hit-and-miss" integration, which employs random samples to reflect the system as a whole. In Baute's case, he would choose computer files at random, with a scientist's confidence that they would portray the larger whole.

YONEMURA AND EDWARDS COULD NOT show up unannounced at the police building in Zurich, so Edwards had telephoned ahead to his police contact and made an appointment. Peter Lehmann knew that Edwards and Yonemura were returning, but the prosecutor had not realized they were bringing someone else. So when he learned that a third IAEA official had arrived, he drove from Bern to Zurich immediately to find out what was going on.

"Why are you here?" he asked after being introduced to Baute.

The response that Lehmann got was not satisfactory. "We found something interesting the last time," he was told by Edwards. Lehmann couldn't be sure whether the IAEA had found clues to the weapons plans that the Americans said were in the files but he decided not to interfere with their search. Once the IAEA experts were done, he would insist on full disclosure. Then he would find out for himself if the Americans were telling the truth about the danger in the computers, or trying to frighten the Swiss into turning over the evidence that he needed to build his case against the Tinners.

When the technician was finally asked to search for documents bearing the initials "PAB," he turned up more than three hundred pages of designs. Examining the drawings as they popped onto the monitor, Baute understood that he was looking at blueprints for two separate nuclear weapons. Both were so-called implosion devices, more advanced and more powerful than the Chinese weapon. The initials certainly indicated that they were from Pakistan's nuclear arsenal, and the designs themselves reflected what Baute knew about Pakistan's development of such weapons.

There are two basic types of nuclear weapons. The simplest to build is the gun type, which crashes two hemispheres of weapons-grade uranium together to create the critical mass for an explosion. The second type, known as an implosion device, relies on high explosives arrayed in a sphere around the fissile material. The explosives must be timed to go off simultaneously to compress the fissile material and create the critical reaction that unleashes the nuclear blast. Implosion devices can use either highly enriched uranium or plutonium as the fissile material. While they are regarded as more difficult to construct because of the precision requirements, they also are more compact and pack more power.

The PAB drawings represented only part of the information necessary to build a weapon. The files also contained the extensive lists and precise specifications for mechanical and electrical items required for such a device. To an engineer, such lists provide a road map to building something, whether a bicycle or a nuclear bomb. The PAB search turned up dozens of separate files for mechanical parts and electrical components. There also were specifications for the electronic initiators to set off the high explosives simultaneously, and typed notes for the type and amount of explosives required to force a supercritical blast. The inventory was far more extensive that anything Baute had seen in Libya, and the device itself was far more lethal because it was smaller and more powerful.

When the search switched from key phrases to the Monte Carlo method of random selection, they found fewer nuclear-related documents. Sixty-seven files describing the Chinese warhead were retrieved, a more extensive collection than Baute had seen in Libya but not a complete package. The same appeared to be true with the PAB material: There were hundreds of drawings and an extensive shopping list of parts, many readily available on the open market to someone with the knowledge to ask for them. But in Baute's mind, what he saw in Zurich did not add up to a complete weapon design. "This information did not mean that a bunch of terrorists can assemble a weapon," he said. "There are still some technical issues to be resolved."

Despite the technical gaps, the drawings constituted a grave proliferation threat. What no one could understand was why Khan would have let these copies out of his personal control. They were the crown jewels, the most valuable item in the inventory he could offer potential customers and the item that would cause the biggest outrage among his countrymen should his theft of them be discovered. Yet the material already had been transferred to at least one computer in the Tinner enterprise. And no one knew how many electronic versions existed elsewhere.

"I am one hundred percent convinced there are more somewhere," Baute said later.

Baute could not know, however, exactly where.

While Baute was most concerned about the weapons plans, the files contained important information on aspects of the network's operations. There were business cards for suppliers around the world and endless invoices for shipments of sensitive technology to Pakistan, Dubai, Malaysia, Singapore, Libya, and many other countries, dating back to the late 1970s. For the IAEA and other investigators, this was uncharted territory. Many of the names had never come up before in connection with nuclear trafficking; many of the specific companies receiving or supplying equipment had never been on anyone's radar.

One of the most puzzling finds was a set of files describing Syria's attempted purchase of a type of remote manipulator devices for handling radioactive material, almost never used outside a plutonium reprocessing facility. Remote manipulators have many uses in the handling of dangerous materials. But the version sought by Syria had the unusually long reach required to handle highly radioactive material from behind a thick protective wall. Syria had been on the IAEA's list as the potential fourth customer. Khan had gone there in the 1990s and urged the Syrian military to develop its own nuclear arsenal. There were no indications that Damascus had taken up Khan's offer, but the discovery was sure to increase Heinonen's concern when his team returned to Vienna with the news.

DESPITE HIS REPUTATION FOR HOARDING sensitive information, Heinonen was not about to keep revelations of this magnitude from Mohamed ElBaradei, particularly since the director general of the IAEA was scheduled to give a major speech on counterproliferation efforts in a few days.

On October 14, Heinonen had sat in the director general's twenty-eighth-floor office in Vienna and delivered a rundown on the weapons plans and other records found on the Tinners' computers in Switzerland. He explained how the agency had obtained a handful of designs from Switzerland that appeared to be related to nuclear weapons. Heinonen said he had ordered them sealed and transferred to the U.S. mission immediately. But he said he had sent Baute back to Zurich in order to get an expert's assessment of the drawings. He told ElBaradei that the Frenchman had returned convinced that the designs were for two Pakistani warheads that were more advanced than the Chinese version discovered earlier in Libya. Heinonen said that he had not yet informed the Swiss prosecutor or police about the dangerous records in their possession. When ElBaradei asked about the security of the documents, Heinonen explained how the Swiss were storing them on an isolated server in a police building.

But Heinonen could not reassure ElBaradei that others might not have copies of the designs. In the worst news he could possibly have delivered to his boss, the Finn cautioned ElBaradei that the IAEA's own investigation had found that electronic copies of sensitive designs were already in wide circulation among the participants in the Khan network.

"What is alarming is that we have found these sorts of records on several computers in several places," he said. "These guys had been copying information and collecting it everywhere they went. These weapons components, we found less of them, practically all of them were in one place, Switzerland. But the P-1 and P-2 designs were all over. Practically every computer had those. That's the way these guys worked, in their hotel rooms and homes. When they left in a hurry, they didn't clean up, so electronic information was left behind."

ElBaradei's reaction reflected his training as a lawyer and diplomat. He told Heinonen that the Swiss government would have to be informed quickly about the nature of the material it possessed so officials there could take the proper steps to secure the information. Even before that step was taken, ElBaradei said he believed that the agency's mandate required informing the five permanent members of the United Nations Security Council—the United States, Britain, France, Russia, and China, all nuclear powers themselves—that Switzerland, a nonnuclear nation, possessed plans to manufacture atomic weapons. The Americans, and probably the British, were well aware of the cache of material in Switzerland. The French, Russians, and Chinese, on the other hand, got an unwelcome surprise.

On October 16, 2006, two days after his startling conversation with Heinonen, the television cameras were on their stands and more than a dozen international reporters were waiting when ElBaradei opened a conference on tightening controls on nuclear proliferation. The weapons plans in Switzerland were not the only item weighing on his mind. The previous week, North Korea had conducted its first detonation of a nuclear device. Iran was continuing to defy demands by the Security Council that it suspend its enrichment activities. There were fears in capitals around the world that international controls might prove too weak to prevent a new arms race in both Asia and the Middle East.

"Unfortunately the political environment is not a very secure one," he told the audience. "So it's becoming very fashionable, if you like, for countries to look into the possibilities of protecting themselves through nuclear weapons." He warned that twenty to thirty countries "have the capacity to develop nuclear weapons in a very short time span. We are dealing with almost, as I call them, virtual nuclear weapons states."

ElBaradei did not single out any particular country, though he was clearly alluding to North Korea and Iran. Other countries, however, had recently announced that they were considering developing enrichment programs, the first step down a road that could lead to weapons. Among them were Australia, Argentina, Brazil, and South Africa. Countries like Germany and Japan already had the means to produce weapons-grade uranium if they chose to do so. While none of those countries had indicated any desire to develop a nuclear weapon, ElBaradei's point was that they and many others had the technology to go nuclear almost overnight.

"The knowledge is out, both for peaceful purposes and unfortunately also for not peaceful purposes," he said.

Few people in the room that day knew the full scope of his warning about the spread of nuclear knowledge.

On October 25, nine days after the speech and once the notification of the nuclear powers concerning the Swiss weapons designs was completed, ElBaradei summoned the Swiss ambassador to his office. There he provided a bare-bones description of what his team had found in the Tinner records. The Swiss police have in their possession highly sensitive, proliferation-related drawings and other material that must be held under the tightest security, ElBaradei said. The five nuclear powers had been notified already, but he said it was now up to the Swiss to guarantee that the information did not fall into the wrong hands. The IAEA review of the documents so far had been informal. ElBaradei asked that the Swiss government, as a signatory of the Non-Proliferation Treaty and member of the IAEA, allow the agency to conduct a more thorough official inspection of the evidence. The ambassador promised to contact the Foreign Ministry in Bern immediately.

- - - - - -

THE NEWS FROM THE IAEA reverberated through the Foreign Ministry. Up until now, the concerns about the contents of the Tinner files had been shared only among a select number of officials within the Justice Ministry, the federal police, and the prosecutor's office. The foreign minister, Micheline Calmy-Rey, telephoned Blocher at the Justice Ministry and demanded a full explanation. He promised to get back to her as soon as possible.

Two days after the meeting between ElBaradei and the Swiss ambassador in Vienna, Swiss police conducted another series of surprise raids on the offices and homes of the Tinners. Even though Urs and Marco were still in jail, their residences were searched again, too. Blocher had ordered the second round of searches to make certain that nothing had been missed the first time around. At the same time, the paper records and equipment that was being stored in jail cells were moved to a more secure location.

Blocher recognized that he could no longer keep a lid on the Tinner case, despite the pressure from the Americans to make the whole matter disappear somehow. There was a real risk that word of the nuclear weapons plans in Swiss custody could leak, either from the Swiss government or the IAEA, resulting in a wave of bad publicity. After the raids and securing the material, his next move was to spread the responsibility to his fellow members of the Federal Council.

On November 1, Blocher presented the council with a written statement describing the existence of nuclear weapons plans in the Tinner files. It was accompanied by the request from the IAEA for formal access to the material in order to determine the extent of the proliferation risk. Blocher acknowledged that he and others on his staff had met several times with their American counterparts in recent months to discuss the Swiss investigation of the Tinners. The Americans were arguing, he said, that the documents were so explosive in nature that they should be turned over to the United States for safekeeping. Blocher recommended providing the IAEA with access to the records, writing that the international agency had the expertise and authority to evaluate them. He did not recommend turning over any material to the Americans at this point. The full council accepted the justice minister's recommendations.

The Swiss police involved in the investigation were outraged when the IAEA confirmed that its people had found weapons plans on the Tinner computers. The Americans knew the plans had been there all along; in fact, they had made copies of the records for themselves in June 2003, if Marco Tinner was to be believed. For some of the police team, the discovery of the weapons plans put the American pressure to destroy the documents in a completely new light. If the Americans were truly determined to stop the spread of nuclear knowledge, they would not have left the material on unprotected computers. For more than three years, the CIA had allowed the most sensitive material possible to remain in the hands of some of the worst traffickers in history, people with a track record of helping Libya and perhaps some other country or group. Only now did the Americans want everything destroyed, said one of the investigators, "to hide their own stupidity. They are responsible for the spread of this dangerous technology. You cannot stop it now. The Tinners were free. They were computer freaks, traveling, living in different countries, and duplicating all those files."

On top of the anger that such sensitive files had been left on the Tinner computers, the Swiss investigators were growing increasingly suspicious that someone inside their intelligence circle was providing confidential information to the Americans. The latest example involved Blocher's presentation to the Federal Council, which was supposed to be secret. But the next day, U.S. secretary of state Condoleezza Rice wrote a letter to the justice minister, suggesting that the United States take control of the Tinner documents to ensure their security. Rice said that Swiss prosecutors would be allowed access to the records for any criminal investigation. The next month, the CIA station chief in Switzerland and other U.S. officials met with Blocher. The Americans knew that the IAEA had discovered the weapons plans. They repeated the offer to take them for safekeeping. They also asked Blocher again to make certain that the Tinners' collaboration with the CIA would not be revealed or pursued in criminal proceedings.

CHAPTER NINETEEN

WASHINGTON AND BERN

On March 24, 2007, the United Nations Security Council voted unanimously to ban all Iranian arms exports and freeze the financial assets of twenty-eight Iranians linked to the country's nuclear and military programs. The fifteen-to-zero vote came a day after the Iranian president, Mahmoud Ahmadinejad, had canceled a planned trip to New York City to confront the Security Council. The resolution was the third set of sanctions imposed on Iran over its refusal to suspend its uranium-enrichment-related activities until the IAEA could verify that it was not secretly pursuing a nuclear weapon. Even as the latest sanctions were being approved, the consensus among experts was that they would be ineffective in persuading Iran to stop enriching uranium or open its facilities fully to IAEA inspectors. Although previous sanctions had taken a toll on the Iranian economy, they had not persuaded the country's leaders to back away from what they contended was their right to enrich uranium for what they said was a civilian energy program. Instead, Iran continued to make strides in its enrichment program.

In February, diplomats at the IAEA had reported that Iran had moved nine tons of uranium hexafluoride, the feedstock for centrifuges, to the underground enrichment plant at Natanz. The amount was enough to make at least one atom bomb if the Khan-supplied centrifuges enriched it to a weapons-grade level. The report caused new concern in Israel, which viewed the prospect of a nuclear-armed Iran as an existential threat. The Israelis stepped up their surveillance of Iran and began to push the Americans quietly for a green light to launch air strikes on the Iranian enrichment plant at Natanz and other nuclear installations.

The U.S. government had developed its own contingency plans to bomb Iran's nuclear facilities as early as 2003, but knew that the prospect was fraught with dangers. Secretary of Defense Robert Gates made clear to his Israeli counterparts that, while a military strike was feasible, the repercussions would be impossible to control. Iran could increase its efforts to destabilize the fragile government in Iraq and provide new help for insurgents attacking U.S. troops in Afghanistan. Retaliation against Israel could involve missile strikes on major cities, and Tehran would most certainly provide more weapons and encouragement to its anti-Israeli proxies, Hezbollah in Lebanon and Hamas in Gaza.

In early 2007, Bush said publicly that he did not support military strikes against Iran. "I think it's absolutely absurd that people suspect I am trying to find a pretext to attack Iran," he told a group of White House reporters.

Against such a volatile mix of foreign policy woes, the problem of persuading the Swiss government to cooperate in covering up the role of three of its citizens in helping bring down the Khan network may have seemed small. But the Swiss saw events through a different lens. The CIA and its illegally recruited Swiss agents contributed to the most serious proliferation violations in the history of nuclear science. The CIA and its Swiss spies may have helped enable Iran to develop a nuclear weapons capacity, and they were so cavalier that the same technology was probably on hard drives and the far reaches of the Internet, which put them within reach of international terrorists and rogue regimes. In the spring of 2007, U.S. patience with the Swiss was wearing thin, too. The decision was made to take a more aggressive approach.

The Americans had long believed that Blocher was inclined to cooperate in closing down the Tinner case. The criminal investigation of the Tinner family for export violations was clearly within the Justice Ministry's portfolio. But Gonzales and other administration officials recognized how difficult it would be for Blocher to turn over the documents and eviscerate the espionage case against both the Tinners and the CIA agents who had searched Marco's places in 2003. A decision of that magnitude would require the backing of the Swiss Federal Council, which acted by consensus on major issues. Even then there was a constitutional question about whether the council had the legal right to intervene in a criminal investigation under the separation of powers in Switzerland. So the sense in Washington was that Blocher had not made the final decision on how to raise the issue with the six other members of the Federal Council.

The Americans developed a new strategy. They would take their argument beyond Blocher to two other ministries, Defense and Foreign Affairs. Both agencies had responsibility for aspects of the Tinner affair and perhaps together they could sway the rest of the council. If turning over the records to the United States offended Swiss neutrality, the Americans would suggest that they could be destroyed. The effect would be the same—the cases against the Tinners and the CIA agents who had searched Marco's properties would disappear. And the Americans already had their own copies of everything.

THE CAMPAIGN BEGAN IN APRIL. Samuel Schmid, the Swiss defense minister, arrived in Washington for three days of talks on bilateral defense issues and Afghanistan. Like Blocher, Schmid was a member of the right-wing Swiss People's Party, but he was regarded as a moderate counterweight to the hard-line attitudes of the justice minister. Before entering politics, Schmid had been a lawyer in Bern, and he retained a lawyer's disciplined and cautious outlook. Since taking over as defense minister in 2000, his primary mission had been to reform the Swiss military.

In Washington, Schmid met with Gates and the deputy defense secretary, Gordon England. Gates had just returned from Quebec, where he had made a plea to NATO allies to increase their troop commitment in Afghanistan in anticipation of a spring offensive by the Taliban. Switzerland is not a NATO member, and the country had only two advisers assigned to the international forces in Afghanistan. Schmid resisted efforts by Gates to provide a symbolic increase in troops, arguing that the Swiss were more comfortable at peacekeeping missions.

The Swiss official was more receptive when Gates and other administration officials raised the issue of the Tinner case. Along with the defense secretary, Schmid met with Chertoff, the administration's top terrorism official, and Charlie Allen, who was running the new intelligence office that Chertoff had set up at the Department of Homeland Security. All three U.S. officials made the same basic argument to Schmid. Putting the Tinners on trial would jeopardize critical intelligence operations aimed at eradicating the rest of Khan's nuclear network. The highly sensitive nuclear weapons plans would be safer in American hands. If Swiss law would not allow them to hand over the records, they suggested that the Swiss could destroy them.

Allen argued with the most authority. Before joining Homeland Security two years earlier, he had spent his career in the CIA. As a young analyst in 1962, he had worked on a team that planned to set up a new Cuban government in the wake of the Bay of Pigs invasion. He had achieved a measure of fame in the 1980s when he was identified as the CIA analyst who blew the whistle on the Reagan administration's illegal efforts to finance antigovernment rebels in Nicaragua, leading to the Iran-Contra scandal. As a veteran of the antiterrorism world who was now in his early seventies, Allen's views carried particular weight with the Swiss minister.

On the last morning of his trip, Schmid flew to Houston to visit the NASA space center and two military bases. While he was there, he paid a visit to former president George H. W. Bush. The unusual meeting had been arranged by the White House. Schmid was accompanied to Houston by Urs Ziswiler, the Swiss ambassador to Washington. The topics for the session with the former president hardly seemed earthshattering: Schmid and Bush were to talk about a host of international issues, ranging from relations with Russia to the troubling Iranian nuclear program. Near the end of the meeting, Ziswiler was asked to step out of Bush's office, leaving Schmid and the former president alone. The ambassador later told associates that he believed Bush raised the Tinner issue, urging Schmid to go along with American requests to exercise caution in handling the case. "Maybe he was involved because some of this happened while he was president," Ziswiler said. "Maybe his son asked for his help."

Schmid returned to Washington and talked with Swiss reporters about his trip. He said he had ruled out sending more Swiss troops to Afghanistan. He also spoke glowingly about Bush, describing the former president as "very switched on, very interested and very up to date on the topics." There was no mention of the Tinner case, but the Americans were confident the defense minister was firmly in their corner. The next target was the Swiss foreign minister, Micheline Calmy-Rey, and of course, they would reinforce earlier conversations with Blocher. At this time Calmy-Rey also held the rotating post of Swiss president.

THE AMERICANS HAD MISREAD BLOCHER slightly. The blustery justice minister had not decided to rein in his investigators. He remained torn about whether to try to shut down the entire Tinner mess. The nationalist in him wanted to prosecute the Tinners and the CIA. The politician in him worried that trials could lead to embarrassing disclosures about how little the Swiss had done to stop proliferation in previous years. Embarrassment could turn to scandal if the Americans claimed to the world that the Swiss trials were jeopardizing ongoing intelligence operations. Also, he did not want to do anything that would create obstacles in the fight against nuclear proliferation.

On July 2, Blocher wrote a letter to Schmid and Calmy-Rey seeking their opinions on how to proceed with the investigations of the Tinners and what Blocher referred to as a "suspected foreign intelligence service." Police investigators had found that six CIA agents had searched Marco Tinner's house when they recruited him as a spy in 2003, he wrote. The search compounded the violation of Swiss law by the CIA, leading Blocher to write that he thought there was sufficient evidence to prosecute the specific agents for espionage. As for the Tinners, Blocher wrote that there was no doubt that their cooperation with the CIA broke Swiss law, too. He believed the legal conditions for the criminal prosecution of the Tinners and the CIA agents for espionage had been met. But the letter was not a recommendation for going forward. It was more a search for political cover within the Federal Council if the decision were made to abandon the investigation and turn over or destroy the records, as the Americans were demanding.

Schmid already agreed with the Americans, but Calmy-Rey knew little about the Tinner case beyond a couple of earlier statements that Blocher had submitted to the council. She assigned a member of her staff to research the history of the Tinners, sending him deep into the government archives. There he found a trail of official notifications from the United States and Britain about suspected nuclear trafficking by a host of Swiss individuals and companies. Among those singled out by the Americans was Friedrich Tinner, the patriarch of the very family that the CIA would later recruit. The warnings from the late 1970s focused on Friedrich Tinner's sales to Pakistan. The Swiss had never taken the American and British notifications seriously. The findings could be used to justify the Americans' actions, suggesting that they had acted unilaterally because the Swiss had failed to take action against possible proliferation activities within their country. The staffer concluded in a written report to Calmy-Rey that the foreign minister should oppose opening criminal proceedings against the Tinners or the CIA. Accepting the logic required a leap of faith that no one would ever uncover the degree to which the Swiss had buckled to American pressure. It would soon prove to be an unfortunate leap for the Swiss government.

Calmy-Rey, the foreign minister, was a veteran politician who had worked her way up through the Social Democratic Party, which was the most left-leaning of the major parties. In 2002 she had been elected to the Federal Council and in January 2007 she had taken the one-year post of Swiss president. The position is more ceremonial than influential. As first among equals, the president presides over the council meetings and carries out the formal functions of a head of state. As president, Calmy-Rey could act on behalf of the entire council only in an emergency.

After more than two decades in Swiss politics, she recognized the potential dangers outlined in the report. The Swiss could find themselves held up to international ridicule for ignoring serious export violations and then obstructing the American efforts to clean up their mess. On the other side of the coin, killing a criminal investigation and destroying evidence carried its own potential for scandal. One Swiss official compared the dilemma to "a train coming, about to hit us full face." In July, she set up a series of discreet lunches with some of her colleagues on the council to brief them on the situation and search for a way to escape the locomotive heading down the tracks at Switzerland. Calmy-Rey told her colleagues that she was inclined to grant the requests of the Americans. She said she favored destroying the documents instead of giving them to another country.

Toward the end of July, the justice minister traveled to Washington again. The public purpose was further discussions with Alberto Gonzales on cooperation in prosecuting terrorists. The undisclosed agenda was the Tinners, and the key meeting was with Michael McConnell, the director of the Office of National Intelligence.

McConnell was sixty-five years old, about the same age as Blocher. He had served in the navy during the Vietnam War, patrolling the Mekong Delta in search of Vietcong fighters. Later he was director of the National Security Agency, the biggest of the intelligence agencies and charged with responsibility for monitoring worldwide communications to protect the United States. He had retired from government service a decade earlier and earned a fortune helping big corporations protect their computers from intrusion. Bush had enticed McConnell back into government to head the new Office of National Intelligence, which was established after the September 11 attacks to coordinate the activities of one hundred thousand people spread over sixteen government intelligence agencies. On paper at least, McConnell oversaw the CIA. In reality, his office and the older intelligence agency were sometimes bitter rivals.

But on July 27, when he met with Blocher, McConnell was fully on the side of the CIA. He tried to impress upon the Swiss justice minister that essential intelligence operations would be jeopardized unless the Swiss agreed not to prosecute the Tinners or the CIA agents. The arguments were the same ones Blocher had been hearing for the past year from his American interlocutors. This time, however, he provided the answer that the Americans had been eager to hear. The Federal Council would soon be asked to rule on formal requests to institute legal action against the Tinners and the CIA, he said. Blocher said that he had consulted the defense minister and the foreign minister. He told McConnell that he expected those two ministers to join him in recommending that the request be refused.

Finally the U.S. intelligence community and the Bush administration could imagine an end to the Tinner affair. All that was left was executing the third leg of the strategy by ensuring that Calmy-Rey was firmly in the American camp.

AT THE BEGINNING OF HIS second term in 2005, President Bush named Condoleeza Rice his secretary of state. Even after the failure to find weapons of mass destruction in Iraq and systematically marginalizing and weakening the State Department, Rice was a major star and the chief architect of the administration's morally fervent foreign policy. *Forbes* ranked her as the most powerful woman in the world, and *Time* listed her three times as one of the world's most influential people. Rice was a natural to put an end to the difficulties with Switzerland by making sure her counterpart in Bern was on board.

On August 9, Rice telephoned Calmy-Rey in Bern. After discussing some general foreign policy matters, Rice said she was happy to hear that the situation involving the Tinners appeared to be on the verge of resolution. In case the Swiss foreign minister did not understand the stakes, Rice provided a quick synopsis. The Swiss government had known for years about the nuclear trafficking of the Tinners and had failed to act. This failure, she said, had come despite years of official and unofficial warnings from the United States about the dangers of Swiss involvement in nuclear proliferation. Now, Rice warned, initiating legal proceedings against the CIA agents and the Tinners risked exposing intelligence that would give the international community the impression that the Swiss were once again obstructing international efforts to prevent proliferation. The mere publicity from the trial, according to Rice, would inhibit further efforts by the United States and the IAEA to dismantle the remainder of the Khan network. Rice also suggested that the Swiss government would jeopardize its relations with the United States if it proceeded with a case that would embarrass the Bush administration. The conversation was conducted in the polite language of international diplomacy, but the meaning was clear: If the Swiss didn't dispose of the cases against the Tinners and the CIA, the United States would portray them as a hindrance to worldwide counterproliferation efforts and roll out the years of warnings that went unheeded by Swiss officials.

Stripped of its niceties, the conversation was extortion. The Swiss had the option of caving in to the U.S. plan or being made to look like collaborators in the spread of nuclear weapons. Instead of challenging Rice, Calmy-Rey repeated what she had already told her own colleagues. She understood the dangers of proceeding against the Tinners and the CIA. And she was certainly not willing to risk rupturing relations with the United States. She assured Rice that she would oppose any step that would damage international efforts to stop the spread of nuclear weapons or embarrass her allies in Washington. Neither Calmy-Rey nor anyone else in authority in the Swiss government was prepared to make the obvious counterargument: that it was the Americans who watched and waited over the years and decades as Khan and his accomplices sold nuclear technology, even advanced bomb designs, to some of the most dangerous regimes on the planet.

On August 27, Blocher submitted a formal proposal to the Federal Council asking that the attorney general be denied authorization to institute legal proceedings against the Tinners or the CIA agents who had searched their properties. He said that "current indications led to the suspicion of illegal intervention of the United States on Swiss territory," but he also argued that the American actions "played an important role in interrupting the program aimed at granting nuclear arms to Libya." As part of his proposal, Blocher also asked the council to authorize the destruction of all of the material seized from the Tinner family that could contribute in any way to nuclear proliferation.

Such blatant interference in a criminal investigation was deeply troubling for some of Blocher's colleagues on the Swiss Federal Council. The Swiss system of government provided a clear separation of power between the executive branch, which was represented by the council, and the judiciary, which was represented by the attorney general's office and the police. Stopping an ongoing case, and destroying the documentary evidence on which it was based, had never occurred before in Swiss history.

Blocher and his staff had, however, developed a rationale that they thought might carry the day. The war articles in the constitution, the justice minister informed his colleagues, granted authority to the council over national security matters such as espionage. The articles were designed to give the Federal Council unusual powers in time of war. But they had been applied broadly in the past to foreign affairs, such as freezing the assets of dictators in Swiss banks. Still, invoking the war articles in an espionage case did not have a legal precedent.

The council seemed to be on solid constitutional ground when it came to deciding not to pursue the espionage cases against the Tinners or the CIA; most of them thought it was not too big a stretch to determine that those investigations could be covered by the war articles. More troubling, however, was the effect that destroying the documents would have on the investigation into the export violations by the Tinners. Those potential crimes were not covered by the war articles, yet the destruction of the evidence in the espionage case could make it impossible to prosecute the export violations.

And some council members were angered by what they viewed as Blocher's high-handedness in monopolizing negotiations with the Americans until recent weeks. They also resented the American pressure, seeing it as an intrusion on Swiss neutrality. But two days after Blocher's presentation, the council unanimously ordered the attorney general to halt legal proceedings against the CIA officers and the Tinners in connection with espionage.

The issue of whether to destroy the documents lingered for nearly three months. Finally, in November, Blocher pushed for a final debate and a decision. He told the other six ministers that the Americans had pledged to make the documents available to Swiss prosecutors if they proceeded with the case against the Tinners for export violations. No one believed the Americans would relinquish the documents once they gained custody, so there was no support for turning them over to Washington. In addition, such an act would constitute a major and politically indefensible breach of Swiss sovereignty in the face of U.S. pressure.

Despite their reservations, particularly when it came to interfering with the judicial process, on November 12 the council members voted unanimously to destroy all of the documents that were related to nuclear proliferation and the Tinners. The destruction would take place as soon as the police and prosecutors could identify which among the tens of thousands of blueprints, plans, and documents constituted a nuclear threat.

ON DECEMBER 4, THREE OFFICIALS from the IAEA arrived in Bern. Jacques Baute, the French nuclear weapons expert, led the delegation. He was accompanied by Trevor Edwards and a Swiss national who worked at the IAEA. They had come to review the Tinner records to determine what should be destroyed immediately and what might be held a little longer for review to help the IAEA understand the inner workings of the Khan network.

As the group gathered in Lehmann's office overlooking the River Aare, the tone was frosty. The Swiss police were bristling over the order to destroy the records. They saw three years of investigation about to disappear, and they worried that it would be impossible to prosecute the Tinners once the evidence was gone. They blamed international pressure for forcing the Federal Council to acquiesce and suspected that the IAEA had supplied some of that pressure.

When one of the Swiss police officials hinted that they blamed the IAEA, the IAEA group was surprised. They said the Swiss misunderstood their position. Months before, the IAEA and the Swiss had discussed the agency taking possession of all the documents. In the end, concerns about the ability to maintain the security of the proliferation-related records stopped the deal. The IAEA had then suggested that the Swiss could retain everything under secure conditions until the conclusion of the criminal prosecution; they could turn the material over to one of the five approved nuclear powers; or the documents related directly to nuclear weapons could be destroyed. IAEA officials had made it clear that they preferred the first two options. It was the Americans who had given the Swiss the ultimatum to either turn over everything to them or destroy it. When the IAEA was told that the Federal Council had ordered the destruction, the team had been dispatched to try to help identify what did not pose a proliferation danger and could therefore be safely retained for review.

That morning Baute said that he hoped to identify nonsensitive documents that would help the agency understand the scale and method of operation of clandestine networks like Khan's. This was not a fishing expedition. The IAEA knew that the material contained extensive information about elements of the Khan network that had not yet been exposed or investigated. There were records pointing to a prominent Belgian businessman who appeared to have sold nuclear-related technology to the network. A Bulgarian company had shipped nine tons of special metals to Dubai on behalf of the network. A company in Singapore had provided three hundred tons of high-strength aluminum alloy to the factory in Malaysia. A company in Zug, Switzerland, appeared to have shipped material to a Russian firm with connections to the Tinners. Then there was the mystery of the fourth customer, which constituted the biggest security risk of all. Destroying the material would make it far more difficult, and maybe impossible, to track down these sorts of leads.

Baute wanted to come up with a plan that would allow the agency to obtain copies of e-mails and faxes between these and other network members, their suppliers, and customers. He wanted copies of shipping and financial transactions, and the hundreds of business cards from potential suppliers found in the Tinner offices. There also were photographs of buildings, equipment, and network members that he wanted to salvage. None of the material would help anyone build a bomb, he explained, but it would provide a road map to identify undisclosed elements of the network and to understand how it operated. Even with Khan under house arrest and presumably retired from the black market, the network could not be reconstituted unless every aspect of it was identified.

"The problem is that we see everything in terms of Khan," Baute said later. "The boss is gone, so therefore the problem is gone. I don't think so. The Khan network was simply a bunch of people benefiting their bank accounts. These guys could come together another time in a way that would not be labeled Khan." The IAEA was given two days to review the records and come up with a list of what should be destroyed as soon as possible and what could be examined and possibly copied later. It was a ridiculously short amount of time, but the IAEA officials were already familiar with much of the material.

The computers, much of the written material, and some sample components had been transferred to three storerooms just down the hill at the federal police headquarters after the Swiss realized how sensitive the records were. Lehmann had removed some of the material that he was using to build his case against the Tinners and he kept it in a safe in his office. Before the IAEA began its review, the police said additional documents were being kept at another secure site.

For the remainder of that day and the following day, the three IAEA experts reviewed the records in Bern under the supervision of the police. At the end of the process, the two groups reconvened in Lehmann's office. Baute said that they had not discovered "a scoop" among the documents or the computer records. But he said that new information was found that could be helpful to future investigations of the network. Baute agreed that it was desirable to destroy some of the equipment and the designs related to building a weapon as soon as possible. He asked, however, that the destruction of information useful to understanding the network be delayed until he could report his findings to Olli Heinonen in Vienna. He promised to provide a list as soon as possible.

The meeting continued into the evening. Before the IAEA team left to catch the last plane to Vienna, the discussion turned to whether copies of these records existed elsewhere. Lehmann said that he believed six or seven copies of the information from Tinner's hard drive existed elsewhere. He suspected that one copy remained in Malaysia; Tinner had told IAEA investigators and the Swiss police that he had left it under the floorboards of his house when he had to leave on short notice in 2003. IAEA officials had taken Tinner seriously enough that they traveled to Kuala Lumpur in search of the cache. They needed help from the Malaysian authorities to get access to Tinner's former house, and they were made to wait several days while the police said they were securing a search warrant. When the IAEA officials finally got to the house and pried up the floorboards, they found nothing. Perhaps Tinner had been lying and there was never anything hidden there. Perhaps, and this theory seemed most plausible to the IAEA, the Malaysian police had used the extra time in which they claimed to be getting the warrant to search the house and discovered the records themselves.

Another set of drawings was in the custody of the police in Thailand. Marco had been living in Bangkok with his Thai wife for several months. But in September 2005 he had returned to Switzerland to visit his father and mother and he was arrested. The Swiss police had asked the Thais to search his home in Bangkok. A few days later, the Swiss learned that the Thais had retrieved a computer containing twenty-two thousand files, which they copied onto a CD and sent to Switzerland. The police in Bangkok, however, had retained the computer, and the files were presumably still on it.

Still another set of the records had been in the possession of Johan Meyer, the South African engineer. When he started cooperating with the South African authorities, he had turned over his copy, which he said had originated with Gotthard Lerch.

Then there was the inadvertent proliferation by the Swiss prosecutor himself. Lehmann had passed some of the same information to the German prosecutors for use in the failed case against Lerch. He also had provided copies to Marco's lawyer, Peter Volkart.

No one knew whether other copies existed, either hidden by the Tinners or sold to other customers. But those in Swiss hands were destined for destruction.

CHAPTER TWENTY

BERN

The sheer mass was staggering. Sitting inside a large room at the federal police headquarters in Bern was the accumulation of a lifetime of nuclear trafficking by the Tinners. The room was protected by an electronic lock on a metal door; several burly policemen stood guard outside. Inside, stacked along one wall, were 360 thick files, each bulging with thousands of pages of financial records, blueprints for centrifuges, and all manner of other technology necessary to enrich uranium to produce an atomic bomb. A large table along one wall was covered by the small, rectangular hard drives that had been removed from ninety computers. Alongside them were three laptop computers and more than a dozen flash drives, each of which held gigabytes of information. Elsewhere in the hall were bins containing more than six thousand CDs and DVDs, all of which had been seized from the various Tinner businesses and homes in eastern Switzerland. Pieces of centrifuges, from the six-foot cylinders to flanges, were in packing crates. In the center of the room stood several industrial-strength paper shredders and a couple of power drills with large bits capable of penetrating metal. In total, there was 1.9 tons of paper and 1.3 terabytes of digital information. Everything was waiting to be shredded, drilled, hammered, and incinerated into oblivion.

On February 25, 2008, eleven senior officials gathered in the office of Peter Lehmann, which was just up the hill from the police headquarters. They were there to carry out the final orders of the Federal Council. The records would not be turned over to the United States. They would not be preserved for possible prosecution of the Tinners. Only some of the records stood a chance of being spared a few more weeks, long enough for the IAEA to sort through them for additional clues about the Khan network.

Some of those present that morning were pleased to see what they thought was the end of the line for an investigation that had meant nothing but trouble from the start. Others worried that they were obstructing justice and participating in a cover-up that would damage Swiss democracy and derail international efforts to use the law as part of the battle against nuclear proliferation.

The Swiss were represented by the senior officials who had been involved in the Tinner investigation over the past four years. They were led by Michael Leupold, the deputy justice minister. Only months earlier, Leupold had prepared a legal brief arguing that the Federal Council lacked the authority to destroy the records. But once the decision was made to destroy them, Blocher had put Leupold in charge of overseeing the destruction protocol. Kurt Senn, the senior police official who had led the Swiss investigation and cracked the book code, was there. From the start he had been outraged at the pressure applied by the U.S. government and the actions of the CIA officers who he was convinced had violated Swiss law and Swiss territory. Accompanying him was Jean-Luc Vez, the director of the federal police. Trevor Edwards was there, along with another observer from the IAEA. The Americans had sent a man named Tom. Official records listed him as a counselor at the U.S. mission. Everyone in the room knew that he was the senior CIA officer in the country, the station chief for the agency that had pushed the hardest for this day. Joining Tom was Jon Kreykes, an American nuclear weapons expert from the national laboratory in Oak Ridge.

Edwards had arrived in Bern a week before the February 25 meeting. He had spent four days going over the records. In keeping with the deal struck back in December, he identified the material that the IAEA wanted to retain, singling out twenty-five folders and marking each with a red dot. The Swiss agreed not destroy those folders until the end of May, to give the IAEA time to analyze the contents and take notes.

The actual destruction was a monumental task, which spanned two days. At times it nearly seemed like a comedy. Police in plain clothes were feeding the papers into the industrial shredder as fast as possible. The shredding increased the volume of the paper about threefold, and as the process continued, the paper began to fill the room at police headquarters. Boxes were brought in and packed with the shredded documents, which were then taken under guard to a loading dock on the ground floor of the building, where they were loaded into three unmarked vans. For security the vans were driven in a convoy to a commercial incinerator, where the shredded material was tossed into the fire.

The shredded material produced by hundreds of thousands of pages of paper records filled so many boxes that the convoy required more than a dozen trips. The police were not in uniform, but the operators of the incineration plant had been notified to give them special treatment and not ask questions. So, each time the convoy arrived, the vans were motioned to the front of the line. Bern's regular trash haulers were mystified by the sight. The Swiss banking giant UBS was enmeshed in a growing scandal with the U.S. Internal Revenue Service over hidden bank accounts at the time, and one of the trash haulers was overheard telling another, "They must be bankers."

The process was equally thorough when it came to the hard drives and computer disks. Each one was drilled individually, then put in a crushing machine and smashed. The flash drives, which were much smaller, were broken in half and tossed into the crusher. The pieces of equipment were reduced to tiny pieces of twisted metal in the largest of the crushing machines.

Two days later, on February 27, everything except the folders with the red dots had been consigned to the dustbins and incinerators. The group returned to the attorney general's office. There was an air of satisfaction among most of the people in the room. Leupold praised the cooperation and stressed the need to maintain the strictest security about what had just transpired, telling those around the table that they should only share the information with their immediate supervisor. Tom said that he would inform his colleagues orally only, but he wanted to send a letter to the Swiss Ministry of Justice praising its handling of the case.

The celebratory mood was too much for Senn, who had become convinced that the destruction constituted political interference in his investigation. Senn reflected the position of a faction within the Swiss government that deeply resented the interference of the U.S. government.

"I am speaking for myself and not for my colleagues at the table," he said, gesturing to the other senior police officials seated alongside him. "This is a very sad day for me today. I thought I lived in a democracy. Yet in a real democracy, the political decisions are kept away from the police investigations. This Switzerland is a banana republic now."

Senn went on for about five minutes, castigating those who had succumbed to American pressure and damaged the chances of prosecuting the Tinners. After he had had his say, the Swiss inspector turned to the IAEA representative and said, "I'm sure that Mr. Edwards from the agency agrees."

Edwards hesitated. The IAEA respects protocols and consensus above all else. But he was angry, too, both at the loss of material that he believed would help fight future proliferation networks and at the smugness of the other participants. "I am upset and I am sad," he said finally. "It appears that because they changed sides for the last four or five years and worked for the CIA, we forgot what the Tinners did before, what they did for the last three decades."

DESPITE THE SECRECY, WORD HAD leaked to the press that something was afoot even before the material was destroyed. On February 7, the largest-selling Swiss newspaper, *Blick*, published an article hinting that the Federal Council had decided to destroy documents in the Tinner case. By then there had been numerous press reports about the family's involvement in the Khan network. There had also been a handful of indications that Urs Tinner had worked for the CIA and that the Americans might be trying to protect him by pressuring the Swiss government to destroy the evidence. But the extent of the Tinners' involvement with the CIA and the massive amount of evidence seized from them remained unknown outside a handful of government officials.

Still, the newspaper article attracted the attention of Senator Claude Janiak, the head of parliament's oversight commission. The day after the article was published, Janiak contacted the Justice Ministry and asked if it was accurate. In December, Blocher had been replaced as justice minister by Eveline Widmer-Schlumpf, a more moderate politician.

Widmer-Schlumpf had not been involved in the decision to destroy the documents, but she told Janiak that the council had tentatively decided last November to get rid of most of the material. Her understanding was that the council had acted on the recommendation of the IAEA.

Janiak, a lawyer and member of the liberal Social Democratic Party, suspected that the council had overstepped its constitutional authority and interfered with the independence of the judiciary and police. After consulting with other lawyers and officials at the IAEA, Janiak came to a different understanding of the advice that the IAEA had provided to the Federal Council. Instead of recommending destruction of the records, he believed the international agency had suggested that the Swiss keep the documents secure until they were no longer needed for criminal investigations. Destruction was seen as a last resort. Janiak believed that the Federal Council was wrongly trying to shift the blame from itself to the IAEA. He was too late to stop the destruction, but in early March, Janiak opened a formal parliamentary investigation into the episode. And his investigation put pressure on the government to disclose its actions, forcing the secret out in the open.

On May 23, 2008, Pascal Couchepin, the interior minister serving his rotation as the Swiss president, stepped to a podium in Bern to announce that the government had ordered the destruction of records in the Tinner case. By then, even the twenty-five "red-dot" folders had been destroyed. "The information contained in these papers presented a considerable risk to the security of Switzerland and the international community as a whole," he said. "There were detailed construction plans for nuclear weapons, for gas ultra-centrifuges to enrich weapons-grade uranium as well as for guided missile delivery systems."

Couchepin emphasized that the action had been taken under the supervision of the IAEA and that it was necessary to fulfill Switzerland's obligations under the Nuclear Non-Proliferation Treaty. Couchepin also acknowledged that the Federal Council had blocked a request by the attorney general to investigate whether Urs Tinner had broken Swiss law by working for a foreign intelligence agency. At that time, only Urs had surfaced in the press as a possible CIA spy. The Swiss president made no mention of the spying by Urs's father and brother, and he did not say a word about the pressure applied by the U.S. government or its involvement in the destruction of the documents. In another bit of subterfuge, he downplayed the quantity of material involved, suggesting that about thirty thousand records were destroyed. As the reporters called out questions, Couchepin walked off the stage without answering.

As politicians have learned over the decades, stonewalling rarely solves a problem. Couchepin's limited statement, and his refusal to answer questions, inflamed the controversy, which the Swiss press quickly dubbed "Operation Shredder." The mention of a foreign intelligence agency seemed to confirm suspicions that the CIA's cloak-and-dagger tactics had ended up interfering in a sensitive Swiss domestic matter. "There are more questions about this affair than there are answers," Ken Egli, an editor at the International Relations and Security Network at the Swiss Federal Institute of Technology, told a reporter from *Time* magazine.

The public disclosure in Switzerland put the IAEA in an uncomfortable spot. The agency's spokeswoman, after consulting with Heinonen, told reporters in Vienna that she would not comment on any possible IAEA involvement in the episode. Agency officials had no desire to get in the middle of a Swiss political spat. Nor did they want to cross the Americans by explaining that the IAEA's first proposal to the Swiss government had been for them to keep the records for any criminal trials, not destroy the material. In fact, some senior IAEA officials believed the U.S. government had unwisely elevated the issue by using high-ranking officials like Alberto Gonzales and Condoleezza Rice to lobby the Swiss government. They also believed that the Swiss president's announcement that crucial nuclear documents had been destroyed probably had the effect of causing everyone in the market for a nuclear weapon to start scrambling for their own copies.

In the end, there was a split among the handful of senior people who knew what had happened. Heinonen is a pragmatist, and he was satisfied that the agency had seen as much material as its mandate required. He believes the IAEA is responsible for understanding proliferation patterns and stopping the diversion of nuclear material to weapons programs, not prosecuting individuals. Others were deeply disappointed that evidence that could have contributed to prosecutions of major figures in the Khan network and to the discovery of other participants was now gone forever. People in both camps, however, agreed that the manner in which both the Americans and the Swiss had handled the material contributed to the danger of nuclear proliferation in a world where electronic information is spread so easily.

A. Q. KHAN HAD BEEN largely absent from the international scene since he was placed under house arrest in Islamabad in early 2004. But the destruction of the evidence offered him a blank slate on which to rewrite history. He quickly claimed that the material would have proven his innocence by showing that the information and equipment he had confessed to supplying to Iran, North Korea, and Libya was easily available on world markets.

A few days after the Swiss president's announcement, a family friend smuggled out Khan's written response to questions from Japan's Kyodo News. "The documents revealed that all the information which I am accused of proliferating was available with the suppliers," he wrote. "It proved that the Western suppliers from Switzerland, Germany, and South Africa all had complete details on nuclear weapons. They provided this technology to all who were willing to pay."

Khan's assertion was false on its face; much of the material destroyed by the Swiss had originated with Khan himself. But his argument served a larger purpose. A quiet campaign was under way in Pakistan to rehabilitate the disgraced scientist and eventually restore his freedom.

THE DESTRUCTION OF THE EVIDENCE by the Swiss did not attract much attention in the United States. In the midst of two wars, the beginnings of an economic recession, and a presidential campaign, the newspapers and airwaves were filled with other news. On August 25, however, David E. Sanger and William J. Broad, reporters for *The New*

York Times who had been writing incisively about the Khan network for years, produced an article exploring what they described as "the compromises that governments make in the name of national security." The piece disclosed that the U.S. government had urged the Swiss government to destroy the Tinner files, but unidentified sources told the reporters that the goal was less to thwart terrorists than to conceal evidence of the CIA's relationship with the Swiss family. The article said that the CIA had paid the Tinners as much as $10 million in exchange for a flow of secret information that helped reveal aspects of Iran's nuclear program, end Libya's bomb program, and bring down the Khan network.

At the CIA, there was a strong sense that they had won a victory in terms of keeping the Tinners out of court and therefore protecting its secrets. The destruction of the Tinner material had no impact on the agency; its team had copied everything of relevance in 2003. "We didn't want any of this stuff aired in public, though once the arrest [of Urs] happened, it was inevitable that some of it would come out," said a former senior CIA official who was involved in aspects of the investigation for several years. "The agency never wants anything to get into the public or political sphere. Agency to agency, we can handle that and any fallout. But when the politicians get involved, things get sticky."

The former official had closely monitored the machinations behind the scenes in Switzerland and he was convinced that the Federal Council was on board with the destruction from the start. "When they talk about being upset about destroying the documents, that is not what they are really upset about," said the former official, who spent a considerable part of his career working in Europe. "The thing they are most upset about is, I think, that this could somehow embarrass them or bring down a government."

There is ample reason to criticize the lax manner in which Switzerland and other European countries have treated nuclear proliferation in recent years. In cases from Pakistan and Iraq to Iran and Libya, many countries have turned a blind eye to the sales of dual-use technology. Among those that have shared technology with dictators is the United States itself. The administrations of Ronald Reagan and George H. W. Bush allowed the transfer of dual-use technology to Saddam Hussein in the 1980s when Iraq was fighting a bloody war with Iran. Sharing nuclear-related technology for profit or policy is a dangerous game, which assumes that no country or terrorist organization will ever actually detonate a nuclear device. Unfortunately, it is a game that only needs to be lost once to change the world.

But the position of those in the U.S. government who argued for destroying the documents to protect intelligence operations and avoid embarrassing the CIA was at least equally shortsighted. The loss of the evidence meant it was likely the Tinners would never be prosecuted. Instead the time that Urs and Marco spent in jail could be seen as a cost of doing business. Not only that, but other network participants would see that illegal actions do not result in serious consequences. Fights between countries like Germany and South Africa over access to evidence and witnesses damaged some cases. Political considerations derailed tough action in Pakistan, Malaysia, and Dubai. Even those who were convicted faced little or no time in custody.

In September 2007, Gerhard Wisser pleaded guilty in South Africa to attempting to export centrifuge equipment to Libya and transferring other sensitive equipment to Pakistan; he was given an eighteen-year prison sentence, which the court reduced to only three years of house arrest. A few months later, his accomplice, Daniel Geiges, pleaded guilty to manufacturing and exporting equipment to Libya and Pakistan; he was given a thirteen-year suspended sentence. Johan Meyer, whose company built the feed system for Libya, was granted complete immunity in exchange for helping prosecutors in the Wisser and Geiges cases. B. S. A. Tahir was released from custody in Malaysia in June 2008 without ever being formally charged. In October 2008, after three earlier failures, the Germans finally convicted Gotthard Lerch for shipping uranium enrichment equipment to Libya between 1999 and 2003. He was sentenced to time he had served in pretrial detention, which meant he was released immediately.

On December 22, a Swiss court released Urs Tinner from custody on bail of $9,300. After four and a half years in prisons in Germany and Switzerland without being charged, he emerged angry and bitter. After his release, he said he had spent at least two years in isolation. When Tinner asked why he was not allowed out of his cell to exercise along with other prisoners, his jailers told him that he was the only man on the women's side of the prison and it was against regulations to allow him outside at the same time as the women. They claimed that the men's section was full. "That was their way of keeping me alone," he said later.

Once Tinner was freed, his lawyer, Roman Boegli, asserted that the destruction of the documents meant his client could never get a fair trial. Boegli said he would never be able to show that Tinner had worked for the CIA and sabotaged equipment destined for Libya. The lawyer also complained about the length of time Tinner had spent in jail without being charged, calling it a record for detention without being charged in Switzerland. In fact, a month before Tinner's release, Boegli had filed a case with the European Court of Human Rights arguing that the detention and destruction of evidence violated his client's rights. Tinner's incarceration, he said, was "worthy of Guantanamo."

Marco remained in prison after his brother was freed. Prosecutors argued that Marco still had access to nuclear secrets stored on computers around the world. A month later, however, he was freed after posting bail of ninety-three thousand dollars and was allowed to move back to Thailand.

PETER LEHMANN'S ESPIONAGE CASE AGAINST the Tinners and CIA agents was stopped by order of the Federal Council, and his efforts to build a case involving export violations had disappeared with the evidence. But he remained determined that some kind of justice would prevail. In January 2008, two months after the Federal Council ordered the destruction of the documents, Lehmann had tried to save part of his case by handing over the portion that dealt with export violations to an investigative magistrate in Bern, Andreas Mueller. Unlike Lehmann, Mueller did not report to the Justice Ministry. His independence provided an opportunity to preserve at least the part of the case that involved possible violations of Swiss export laws.

Mueller's first step was to review the files that the attorney general's office had sent over to him. Each file was recorded on a master index, something akin to the docket sheet in an American case file. The index listed seventy files, each of which should have contained a massive amount of written material that could be used to build the case. But the files were empty; every piece of paper that should have been in them was gone. "I could tell that tons of material was gone," Mueller said later.

He did not find out what had happened to the evidence until May 2008, several months after he took the case, when Couchepin announced that the material had been destroyed. Since then, Mueller had been trying to collect evidence from other sources to reconstruct the case as much as possible. A determined and inventive lawyer, he set about trying to recover portions of the records from Germany and other countries where the Khan network had been active. It was slow going, and in the spring of 2009 his inquiry was about to take a bizarre turn.

A FEW DAYS BEFORE URS Tinner was released from prison in December 2008, a new cache of evidence was discovered gathering dust in the archives of the attorney general's office. Hundreds of pages of blueprints, shipping invoices, and weapons designs were arranged neatly in thirty-eight large folders, each of which was dedicated to a different aspect of the original investigation of the Tinner family. A thirty-ninth folder contained a summary of the evidence and an outline of the plans to prosecute them for espionage and export violations. Somehow the damning compilation had escaped the destruction ordered by the Federal Council.

There are conflicting stories about how the folders were discovered. One version was that a custodian cleaning the document storage area stumbled across the folders. In a second scenario, a secretary had set aside the material and forgotten about it until some unknown event or conversation jogged her memory. Neither is convincing. And both beg the central question: Was the material really forgotten, or was it hidden in hopes of keeping the investigation alive? The only certainty was that the resurrected material put the Swiss government in another embarrassing bind.

Peter Lehmann immediately alerted the Justice Ministry. Trying to explain how the files had eluded destruction, Lehmann said they were copies of material prepared by the federal police in May 2006 as part of their investigation. He said his office had asked for the copies as a courtesy, but because of storage constraints the files had been transferred to the archives. When the order was issued in November 2007 to destroy all of the evidence, Lehmann said no one remembered the archived files.

Lehmann had a real problem. Inadvertently or not, he now possessed material that the government had ordered destroyed months earlier. Michael Leupold, the deputy justice minister who had overseen the destruction, was livid. He and others in the ministry debated firing Lehmann. The public sacking of a senior prosecutor would attract more attention and controversy, however, so Lehmann kept his job while the powers above him tried to figure out how to handle the newest bombshell in a case that refused to go away.

The timing of the discovery could hardly have been worse. Senator Janiak's parliamentary oversight commission had ended its investigation and was scheduled to release its report at the end of January. The report was expected to be highly critical of the decision by the Federal Council to destroy the material. Christoph Blocher had pushed for the destruction and would probably take most of the blame, but he had already been voted out of office. It was up to his successor, Eveline Widmer-Schlumpf, to find an acceptable path for mitigating the potential new scandal. After several days of quiet discussions with some of her colleagues, they decided to withhold a formal report of the discovery from the full Federal Council until after the release of the parliamentary report. Delaying the formal acknowledgment allowed the government to avoid informing the Janiak commission until after its report was issued. This meant that the report would not include the explosive new information.

On January 22, the commission released its findings. As expected by the government, the commission faulted the Federal Council for destroying the evidence in the Tinner case and compromising the ongoing criminal investigation. The commission determined that the Federal Council had overstepped its constitutional authority by invoking articles of the constitution reserved for emergencies in time of war. The report rejected the council's rationale that it was acting to protect Swiss security in destroying the material. It also declared that the council's assertion that it had relied on recommendations from the IAEA was unconvincing.

At a press conference, Janiak said cryptically that the Swiss government had "acted under pressure." The report laid out a precise timeline showing that the council had acted in response to extraordinary pressure from senior officials of the Bush administration. The report listed contacts between Swiss officials and various American intelligence officers and senior Bush administration figures dating back to 2004. The parliamentary investigation concluded that American pressure, not security concerns, had driven the premature destruction of the records. "The commission could not prevent itself from thinking that, relative to the Tinner case, it was the pressure exerted by the United States more than the risk of proliferation that preoccupied the department in charge of the files and the Federal Council," said the report. "The destruction of all the means of proof in the Tinner file was a method that permitted them to rapidly yield to pressure exerted by Washington."

The findings were an indictment of both the Swiss and American governments, but the mainstream press in both countries ignored the details about of U.S. pressure. The Swiss press treated the release more like a political document than an investigative report. Articles focused on the behavior of Federal Council, describing the destruction of the records as an overreaction because the evidence was not a threat to Swiss national security. Some commentators argued that the council had not only compromised the criminal inquiry, but had also sacrificed Switzerland's cherished neutrality by bowing to American pressure.

In many ways, however, the report's release was overshadowed by a documentary that aired the same night on Swiss national television. The hour-long film, which was produced by documentary producer Hansjuerg Zumstein, explored the Swiss connections to the Khan network. The big news came when Urs Tinner appeared on camera for the first time. He described sabotaging parts bound for Libya and alerting the Americans to the cargo that was on the *BBC China* in the summer of 2003. "I had identified the last delivery of the *BBC China,* the biggest cargo," he said. "I said to myself, 'We must prevent this material from reaching its destination.'" Tinner went on to describe how he had made a copy of the shipping records by pressing the wrong button on the fax machine, which copy was eventually passed on to his CIA control officer. Tinner had offered only a tiny piece of the story, but it grabbed headlines around the world for a day. Then he retreated into silence.

THE SWISS GOVERNMENT REMAINED UNAPOLOGETIC despite the findings of the Janiak commission. The problem of what do with the remaining records, however, had not gone away. On February 11, Widmer-Schlumpf finally sent the official notification to the Federal Council that thirty-nine files had been discovered. The justice minister proposed that the files be preserved and made available to prosecutors in the event of a criminal case, but only after material considered "proliferation sensitive" was removed and destroyed. The council accepted the recommendation, and the IAEA was asked to send someone back to Bern to cull through the folders once again.

The decision to retain some of the documents contradicted the actions of the council back in November 2007, when the material was deemed so dangerous that all of it had to be destroyed. The council offered no reasoning for its inconsistency. But there was a significant difference in how this decision was reached: This time the Americans were not involved because they knew nothing of the discovery back in December. The council, which had been stung by the criticism that they had bowed to American pressure the first time, was determined to keep it that way. The American government would not be told of the existence of the files. As part of the effort to keep it secret, the federal police ordered that the Swiss intelligence official suspected of leaking to the CIA in the past not be told anything about what was under way.

On March 18, Trevor Edwards returned to the federal police headquarters in Bern to start the process of evaluating the few remaining documents. Vez, the head of the police, explained to Edwards that the new files were in the same room where Edwards had examined some of the previous files. He asked that Edwards identify documents that he believed the Swiss were prohibited from maintaining by the Nuclear Non-Proliferation Treaty (NPT) so they could be destroyed. The remaining records, Vez said, would be available to prosecutors and defense attorneys in the event of a criminal case against the Tinners for export violations.

Edwards was concerned. He had not seen the thirty-nine files, but he feared that eliminating "NPT-related" documents would not go far enough. Since his first exposure to the Tinner files in late 2005, Edwards had learned enough about the architecture of a nuclear weapon to be deeply worried about the contents of the files. So he proposed also destroying an equally dangerous class of records that might not be covered by the nuclear treaty. He described those records as "proliferation sensitive." The documents that he proposed sparing would be those that dealt with the export case that the Swiss magistrate was trying to develop and those that had value to the IAEA because they exposed the inner workings of the Khan network. Lehmann objected to the expanded definition, arguing that records relevant to the possible prosecution of the Tinners would be lost a second time.

Vez agreed to postpone the final decision on what would be destroyed. For now, Edwards would mark documents that he declared NPT-related with a green tab; those that were proliferation sensitive would get a red tab; and those that were both would be marked with a tab of each color. With the structure in place, Edwards began reading the files.

Edwards spent the better part of that day and the next going through the files, which contained about a thousand pages. The federal police had compiled a good sampling of the most damaging material seized from the Tinners. A few files held weapons drawings marked "PAB." Another held a single page of a report on how to manufacture the hemispheres of a nuclear device. Edwards decided that these records were covered by the treaty, and he affixed green tabs to the files. He determined that the records had been compiled by the Swiss police during the interrogation of witnesses.

Other files contained information from the police searches of Marco's business and apartment. Among them were designs for manufacturing centrifuges, and their possession was not strictly prohibited by the NPT. Centrifuges, after all, have civilian uses, too. Still, Edwards felt they should be destroyed, so he affixed red tabs identifying them as proliferation sensitive.

Only three files were judged so sensitive that they got both red and green tags. Those folders contained specifications for enriching uranium to the 90 percent level, which is optimal for nuclear weapons, and designs for a six-thousand-centrifuge production plant to turn out the highly enriched uranium. The files Edwards proposed sparing held shipping records, invoices, and supplier lists memorializing years worth of involvement in nuclear trafficking by the Tinners. They also contained transcripts of interviews with potential witnesses.

The outlier among the thirty-nine folders was No. 10. The file contained some detailed drawings of the P-2 centrifuge. It also held extensive written records of interrogations by the Swiss police in which the Tinners recounted the meetings that they had held with the IAEA in Vienna and Innsbruck, all under the supervision of the Central Intelligence Agency. The Tinners had been expansive in describing their contacts with the CIA and the IAEA because they had believed the Swiss government would back away from prosecuting them. As a result, the folder held evidence that proved what everyone was running away from as fast as possible—that the CIA and the Tinners had broken Swiss espionage laws. The originals of these reports were what Tom, the CIA station chief, had convinced the Swiss to destroy back in February 2008. This time, Edwards tagged the P-2 drawings red for proliferation sensitive, but he saw no proliferation danger in the interrogation transcripts, so he left them untagged. It would prove the most troublesome of all down the road.

When the Swiss returned to the storage room on March 20, they found the files arranged in four separate stacks. No single sheet of paper or drawing constituted a proliferation threat. Taken together, however, the material represented some of the most dangerous design material available outside the weapons laboratories of the world's nine nuclear powers. Michael Leupold, the deputy from the Justice Ministry, joined the small group. As he looked through the stacks, Leupold asked Edwards if the IAEA would consider taking possession of all of the material. Such a decision was above Edwards's pay grade. He said he would ask his superiors as soon as he returned to Vienna. In the meantime, all of the documents would remain locked in the room.

After Edwards's departure, the Swiss officials faced a decision on whether to disclose the existence of the thirty-nine folders. They were worried that word would leak, and they decided it would be better to release the news on their own terms. On March 31, Couchepin and Widmer-Schlumpf met with Senator Janiak to tell him about the rediscovered documents. The justice minister explained that steps had been taken to secure the records while the IAEA determined whether it could take possession of them. Janiak asked for a pledge that the material would not be destroyed before a decision was made on whether to prosecute the Tinners. He also recommended that the Justice Ministry tell the public that about the discovery of the records before it leaked.

ANDREAS MUELLER SAT IN HIS office in the modern, mid-rise building that also houses the attorney general's headquarters on the morning of April 1. Mueller is a slim man in his forties, about five foot ten, with a close-cropped beard and a soft voice. He has a low-key manner and a reputation for being particularly meticulous, even for a Swiss lawyer. Despite his diligence, after a year of investigating the Tinners, he had little to show for his effort and he was mildly frustrated.

Leafing through his internal mail that morning, he came across a press release freshly issued by the Justice Ministry. He read the heading, and then looked more closely. It was April Fool's Day and he could not believe what he saw. Only after reading the full document did Mueller realize it was no joke. The Justice Ministry press release said the authorities had discovered thirty-nine folders containing evidence against the Tinners. Material central to his inquiry had escaped destruction or detection, and Mueller was learning about it in a press release.

In a normal investigation, Mueller would have been notified weeks earlier about the discovery of the documents, which were vital to his case. But since he had been handed the Tinner file, the magistrate had learned there was nothing normal about the investigation. At every juncture he had run into a stone wall. He had discovered that the Federal Council had ordered the destruction of the evidence against the Tinners only when he read about Couchepin's press conference in May 2008. The federal police, who would normally work as the magistrate's investigators, had been ordered by senior police officials not to cooperate with Mueller. Instead the magistrate had to rely on the cantonal police, who had less experience with complex national security investigations. Requests had been sent to seventeen countries that he believed had evidence that would help him rebuild the Tinner case. Most countries had cooperated to some extent. But the United States, which held the most critical material, had maintained complete silence in response to requests for assistance that dated back to Lehmann's review.

"There is only one word that applies to this case," Mueller said later. "It is weird, just weird."

Now the newly discovered files promised a major break. Mueller had been handed only a few files in March when he started his inquiry, and he had immediately recognized that there were extensive gaps in the material. The press release made it likely that some of those gaps might be filled, but the magistrate did not ask to see them immediately. He observed strict independence from the Justice Ministry, so he thought it better to wait, assuming someone from the ministry would come and explain that new evidence had been discovered. But Mueller underestimated how weird and politically charged the Tinner case had become. After several days of silence from the ministry and speculation in the press about the newly discovered material, Mueller made some telephone calls. He got nowhere. He ordered the attorney general's office to turn over the thirty-nine files to him, but the prosecutor referred him to the federal police. He sent an order to the federal police, demanding the files, and he was told that the police did not have them. The police referred him back to the attorney general's office. The press release said the records were "open for inspection," but apparently not by the magistrate with the legal authority to review them.

Mueller did not see any of the evidence until May, when the Justice Ministry allowed him to inspect about half the files. He was limited to those that did not contain information that had been identified as "proliferation sensitive" or "NPT-related." One of the files Mueller examined was No. 10. As he read through the interrogations in which the Tinners recounted their cooperation with the CIA, the magistrate recognized that the evidence would play a major role in any prosecution. "The Tinners' cooperation with a foreign secret service could lead to a justification of their action, at least from a certain time onward, and could also have an impact on the sentencing by the court," he said later. "From this perspective, the issue of cooperation is relevant to our work."

Based on what he found in those files, the magistrate realized that he would have to inspect all of the files before he could reach a conclusion on whether to recommend prosecution of the Tinners. There was always a chance the other files contained exculpatory material. What he did not yet understand was that he would need the help of armed police officers to fulfill his responsibilities.

On June 10, the legal director of the IAEA, Johan Rautenbach, sent an e-mail to the Swiss federal police in which he said the agency was refusing to take possession of any of the records in the thirty-nine files. The IAEA had debated for nearly three months over how to handle the Tinner records. The delay reflected the unprecedented nature of the situation, as well as the general caution that pervaded the IAEA. Some officials had argued that the material should be transferred to the agency for safekeeping and use in ongoing investigations. Others had contended that the IAEA had neither the legal mandate nor the security procedures to take possession of weapons-related material. In the end the ball was tossed back into the Swiss court. The decision on what to do with the documents under the NPT, wrote Rautenbach, rested solely with Switzerland. In careful language, the e-mail suggested that the documents could be retained for use in any prosecutions so long as they were maintained in a secure environment. "Access should be on a strictly need-to-know basis and once the purpose for which it was obtained had been served, no further access would be justifiable," wrote Rautenbach. "Unfortunately, the IAEA is not in a position to take custody of any nuclear weapons related or other sensitive documentation."

This was not the answer that the Federal Council wanted. The IAEA had not recommended that the Swiss destroy the plans, even those that dealt with nuclear weapons. Instead the agency suggested that the material be kept under lock and key until the criminal proceedings were finished. At that point, the Swiss should destroy everything. The three-paragraph e-mail had buried the hopes of the Federal Council that it could transfer responsibility to the international agency. As a result the council faced a tough political decision: It could order everything destroyed, which would be consistent with its action in November 2007, or it could maintain some or all of the records for what could be a lengthy criminal investigation and possible trial.

Criticism of the secret decision to destroy the original documents had died down, but the controversy had never gone away completely. All seven ministers were, at heart, politicians and they understood the dangers of being perceived as kowtowing to American pressure. The council had justified its order to destroy the records in 2007 by citing its emergency powers under the war articles in the constitution. But it would be harder to justify this as an emergency, given the months that had passed. After several days of debate, the council decided to take a half-step. It ordered the destruction of 103 pages of the records that were judged the most dangerous—the PAB weapons designs and specific instructions for enriching uranium to weapons-grade levels and constructing the hemispheres for a nuclear device. The fate of the remainder of the files, including No. 10, would be decided later.

The decision was announced on June 24. Citing security concerns, the Federal Council said that a hundred pages dealing with atomic weapons designs would be destroyed shortly to keep them out of "the wrong hands." Less sensitive documents, such as those dealing with uranium enrichment, would be kept under high security at the Justice Ministry, the government said. Investigators, prosecutors, courts, and the Tinner family's lawyers could view the remaining records under tight restrictions. The council press statement added that the remaining records would be destroyed at the end of the legal proceedings.

Janiak and other members of the parliamentary commission objected to destroying any of the documents until the criminal proceedings were completed. Surely, the senators argued, the government could maintain sufficient security to protect a mere hundred pages. "There is no international obligation to destroy the documents," said Hansruedi Stadler, a senator on the commission. The council agreed to postpone the destruction. Instead the pages deemed most dangerous were removed from the files and put in a more secure location. The missing pages were replaced by sheets summarizing their contents.

Andreas Mueller watched the debate with rising concern. He had seen enough of the records to know that they were essential to his investigation. The files contained evidence that the Tinners had shipped centrifuge components and other material for the Libyan project without obtaining the proper licenses. If he were denied access to the files, it would be far more difficult to prove his case or to show that the Tinners were innocent. Now, as the argument between the council and the parliament grew louder, Mueller worried that history was going to repeat itself. He feared the council would order the destruction of everything. He began to formulate a plan to rescue the evidence. For Mueller, the action he was contemplating would be totally out of character, but he believed firmly that his responsibilities as a magistrate required him to do anything within the law to obtain the evidence.

CHAPTER TWENTY-ONE

BERN AND WASHINGTON

O n the morning of July 9, Mueller gathered seven cantonal police officers in his conference room. As instructed, the officers were armed and in uniform. Based on his partial inspection, Mueller knew precisely where the material was being kept inside the police headquarters a few hundred yards from his own office. That morning, he explained to the officers that they were going to accompany him to the federal police headquarters, where he would demand access to the Tinner files. Their presence was purely symbolic. Mueller told the assembled officers: "We are not going to make this into *High Noon*. But if I go there alone, they will ignore me."

The contingent walked out of Mueller's offices and down a passageway that connected to the police headquarters. There they encountered several surprised police officers. The scene was more kabuki theater than Western standoff. The cantonal police knew their federal counterparts well; some of them were friends. The police summoned Kurt Senn, the chief of the national security division of the police. Senn and Mueller were well acquainted, and the senior police officer was sympathetic to the magistrate's determination to get the evidence. But when Mueller presented him with a warrant authorizing access to the files, Senn replied that the police were under orders not to allow anyone into the locked room where the documents were held in a safe. The orders, he explained, had come from the top of the Justice Ministry.

Mueller expected the response, and he had a contingency plan. He told Senn to turn over the lockbox that contained the key to the room where the documents were stored. No one had ordered Senn to maintain possession of the lockbox, especially when the police official was confronted by a legal search warrant. So he handed Mueller the box and the magistrate and his team left with it. While Mueller did not get the actual records, he thought his bold step might have prevented their destruction.

Word of what Mueller had done leaked to the press within hours. Some of the language was hyperbolic, with accounts describing cantonal police storming the federal police offices and seizing the keys to the room to stop anyone from destroying the evidence. One account suggested that Switzerland had become "the 51st State," arguing that the Federal Council was more concerned with protecting American interests than prosecuting wrongdoers. The following day, the Federal Council responded with its own press statement, saying that there were other keys to the room and that it still had access to the records. Mueller returned the box to Senn.

Mueller's confrontation and the resulting criticism of the council forced the Swiss government to make a final decision on the fate of the records. At the request of the federal police, Trevor Edwards returned to Bern to explain once again the significance of the evidence and discuss the options for dealing with it. The police began the meeting by outlining for Edwards the dispute between the Federal Council and parliament over how to handle the material. Once Edwards understood the political terrain, he and the police were joined by Justice Minister Eveline Widmer-Schlumpf and Senator Janiak in the storage room where the documents were kept.

The two senior Swiss officials, the chief antagonists in the dispute, asked Edwards to explain the difference between the various categories of documents he had identified by the colored tabs back in March. Picking up one of the files, he said the most dangerous folders were those that contained the nuclear designs that originated in Pakistan. Using a sliding scale of threat level, he reviewed the other files and tried to explain their relevance to a potential prosecution of the Tinners and the risk they posed if they became public through a trial.

"If you have only two or three drawings, what can you learn from that? Can you make a bomb?" asked Widmer-Schlumpf.

"You can't make a bomb with just a few drawings," Edwards said.

"What would be wrong with having them in an open courtroom?" she asked.

"Let's put it like this: I am cleared in the United Kingdom for certain nuclear information, but I was never cleared to see nuclear weapons designs," he said. "Just because I'm from a nuclear weapons state, it doesn't mean that I have open access. For example, I have never seen drawings showing a hemisphere. It looks just a like a football."

"Then could you make a bomb?" asked the justice minister.

"No, but you could learn an awful lot," he said. "You can see how many detonators it takes to cause an implosion. I had never known that before. Knowledge is cumulative."

Finally, Widmer-Schlumpf seemed to understand. The tons of material seized from the Tinners did not contain a magic formula for a nuclear weapon. Over the years, however, the family's involvement with the Khan network and its own considerable expertise in manufacturing nuclear-related components had led to the creation of a trove of designs, specifications, blueprints, and instructions. Taken as a whole, the material constituted a library in which a competent researcher could find the answers to many, if not most, of the technological problems that have to be solved to build the most destructive weapon in history. Within that context, a few pages could make a difference in the quest to develop a nuclear weapon. The Swiss government had a responsibility to protect all of the records. But for people like Kurt Senn and Andreas Mueller, there was an equal responsibility to prosecute those who profited from trafficking in these sorts of dangerous designs.

Edwards and the IAEA, however, had the responsibility of understanding attempts by countries, companies, and individuals to traffic in prohibited nuclear technology. A balance had to be struck. Even the most sensitive records could be protected and access restricted for the length of time required to determine whether to prosecute the Tinners. Then the records could be destroyed.

Securing and sparing the remaining records long enough to determine whether to prosecute the Tinners would have represented a balance between legitimate concerns. But the chance to reach a solution that gave equal weight to prosecuting the guilty and stopping proliferation had been wrecked by the interference of the CIA and senior officials of the Bush administration.

AT CIA HEADQUARTERS, THE ATTITUDE was that the battle with the Swiss had been fought and won. With the help of powerful figures in the Bush administration, the agency had succeeded in derailing the prosecution of its spies, the Tinners. It had also avoided the potential embarrassment of seeing six of its officers facing Swiss charges of espionage and breaking into Marco Tinner's office and apartment. And the CIA had kept the world from learning how its decisions over three decades had allowed Khan and his network to disseminate far more dangerous nuclear secrets than any outsider knew. The charade that shutting down the network and forcing Libya to relinquish its nuclear ambitions was a major intelligence victory would be preserved.

Since retiring, the CIA case officer who went by the name Jim Kinsman had continued his no-profile existence. He did some work for the agency, and he gave lectures and training seminars on counterproliferation and espionage techniques to people at the CIA and other government agencies. He must have felt vindicated—and relieved—when the Swiss destroyed the originals in 2007. In the months that followed, Kinsman had no reason to expect the Tinners would ever come to trial. He might even have found some satisfaction in reports trickling out of Iran that its technicians were having trouble getting centrifuges to enrich uranium at optimal efficiency. Perhaps the sabotage efforts were paying off, too.

Not everyone wished Kinsman a peaceful retirement. Back in Bern, Inspector Kurt Senn of the Swiss federal police was still angry about the six CIA operatives who had violated Swiss sovereignty. The government may have forbidden him from pursuing them, but the dogged officer was still on the lookout for a chance to exact some retribution. In the months after the destruction of the Tinner records, Senn had pulled the files on a number of American visitors over the last several years in the hopes of identifying some or all of the CIA people. He knew enough from the interrogations of the Tinners and conversations with his own intelligence officers to single out half a dozen suspects. He told the Swiss border authorities to notify him if any of them entered the country.

After resigning in anger in 2004, Stephen Kappes had returned to the CIA two years later as deputy director, the highest post ever achieved by someone from the operations side of the agency. He received a standing ovation the day he returned to Langley. One of the primary justifications for his return and elevation was his role in cracking the Khan network and persuading Libya to relinquish its nuclear ambitions. When President Barack Obama appointed former congressman Leon Panetta as his new CIA director in 2009, Panetta retained Kappes and gave him wide latitude in running the agency. Kappes still harbored ambitions of becoming director of the CIA, and he had powerful patrons on Capitol Hill. Chief among them was Dianne Feinstein, the head of the Senate Select Committee on Intelligence. There was widespread speculation that, after Panetta spent a few months in the job, Kappes would take over as director of central intelligence. So he would have had no desire to revisit any aspect of the Khan case or resurrect the Tinner affair.

But Kappes had other problems that could not be contained. After Obama's election, the new administration's intelligence transition team had interviewed Kappes. He and other CIA officials pushed to retain the option of building more secret prisons and resuming the use of torture techniques, euphemistically referred to as "enhanced interrogation." David Boren, the moderate Oklahoma Democrat who had once chaired the Senate Intelligence Committee was the head of the transition team. He was shocked that Kappes and others would continue to advocate using fear to justify policies and practices that violated American values. "It was one of the most deeply disturbing experiences I have had," Boren later told the *Washington Post*. "I wanted to take a bath when I heard it."

Kappes weathered Boren's outrage, but he was besieged by other difficulties. There was the inability to capture Osama bin Laden and the conflicting accounts of how videotapes of torture sessions of Al Qaeda suspects had come to be destroyed. The agency's Directorate of Operations, which Kappes had headed, had been deeply embarrassed in late 2009 when a judge in Italy convicted a base chief for the CIA and twenty-two other Americans, almost all of them CIA operatives, of kidnapping a Muslim cleric in Milan in 2003.

A tougher and more personal blow occurred on December 30, 2009. In one of the deadliest attacks in CIA history, an Al Qaeda double agent blew himself up in the midst of a CIA base in Afghanistan, killing seven Americans. Among the dead was a forty-five-year-old mother of three who was the agency's base chief at Camp Chapman, the outpost in eastern Afghanistan. The attack sparked enormous criticism of the agency's operational security and raised questions about whether the CIA had abandoned the in-depth training that had been mandatory for agents sent into the field.

No one blamed Kappes personally, but the deaths in Afghanistan and the embarrassment in Italy cast a dark shadow across the portion of the CIA that he was supposed to have mastered. Rumors began to circulate at Langley that the agency's No. 2 was on his way out because it was clear that he would never be elevated to the director's job. In April, the agency released a brief statement saying that Kappes was resigning. No reason was given, but Panetta praised Kappes for his "skill, loyalty, dedication and discipline, integrity and candor."

CHAPTER TWENTY-TWO

BUCHS, SWITZERLAND, ISLAMABAD, AND WASHINGTON

I n the spring of 2010, Urs Tinner was sitting in a noisy bar next to the
Hotel Buchserhof, a modest stucco building in the village of Buchs in
eastern Switzerland. He cradled a glass of Coca-Cola in his hands, which
were nicked from his constant work with tools and machinery. His face
was thinner and more lined than the passport photograph that had been
published on the Internet when the Khan ring came crashing down in
early 2004. Today, the man who had once been involved with that no-
torious nuclear black market, who had spied for the CIA in the Middle
East and Asia, who had spent more than four years in prison, was working as a mechanic near his hometown, repairing tractors and other farm
machinery. But old habits die hard. In an effort to keep his conversation
with a visitor from being overheard, Tinner had chosen a table directly
beneath one of the speakers blaring rock 'n' roll.

Tinner was reluctant to talk about the last few years of his life. Instead he wanted to focus on what he regarded as his mistreatment in
Swiss prison and the lawsuit he had filed against the Swiss government
in the European Court of Human Rights for being held so long without
charges. He said he was halfway finished writing a memoir, not about
his days as a spy for the CIA, but about how he survived the years of
isolation in prison. Pulling out his cell phone, he displayed photographs
of intricate nature scenes and tiny model airplanes. These, he said, were

how his remarkable technical skills had helped him keep his sanity. After his jailers had refused to provide him with drawing supplies, Tinner said he invented his own. He cooked the jelly that came with his breakfast until it formed a charred black paste, a rudimentary sort of ink. Using a Q-tip for a pen, he had drawn birds and other wildlife on pieces of paper. In another innovation, he collected the ends of candles given to each prisoner at Christmas and shaped the wax into small models of airplanes. The propellers were fashioned from pieces of tin; the aircraft's trim was crafted from bits of foil rescued from chocolate-bar wrappers. When he left prison, he took his mementos with him.

Tinner's skill with his hands was one of the reasons his father had sent him to Dubai to work with Khan in the first place. It was certainly a skill that Khan found useful. "I would always know a way to do something, even without the right tools," he said. "Maybe that is why Khan was interested in me. Sometimes he would be surprised that I could do things. Maybe that is why he trusted me. Maybe more than he should have trusted me."

There was no hint of bitterness toward Khan, though Tinner claims that he did not realize until it was too late that the parts he was manufacturing were for a nuclear weapons project in Libya. "I know Khan as a normal person," he said. "He's an old man. He was always friendly to me. I went to his home and he said, 'Oh, can you help me make all those pictures hang right?' Do you know what I was discussing with Khan so many times? How to make electricity out of windmills. He had so many projects."

Tinner was less forthcoming about his father, saying only, "For me, my father was always my hero. He was an engineer and very clever in whatever he did." Yet Roman Boegli, Urs's lawyer, blamed Friedrich Tinner for involving his unwitting son in the Libyan project. "He trusted his father," said Boegli.

His work for the CIA was off-limits in the conversation, Tinner said. He acknowledged that he had expected the family enterprise to attract the attention of an intelligence service, but he said he thought the first contact would have come from the British. "I had not planned on the CIA," he said. "I was waiting for somebody else." Yes, he said, he had met the man he knew as Jim, but he would say nothing about the specifics of their dealings or any money that the American might have given him for services rendered. He acknowledged tampering with equipment bound for Libya, and he admitted that he had been worried about being discovered by Tahir or someone else associated with the project. He ignored questions about specific meetings with the Americans or what happened to the money he and his family had received from the CIA. "Let's not talk about the CIA," he said. "It's too early."

In his mid-forties and with little formal education, Tinner said he did not know what his future holds. The Swiss police investigation was still open, but given the lack of access to the evidence, few people expected any of the Tinners to be charged. His brother Marco's passport was returned soon after he was released in 2009, allowing him to move back to Bangkok, where he was living with his wife and young daughter.

Over several years, the CIA had paid the Tinners a substantial amount of money for their services. The total remains a secret; it was certainly several million dollars, with estimates ranging as high as $10 million. As part of the criminal proceedings, the Swiss government froze what it could find of the Tinners' assets, which left Urs back where he was in 1999 when he moved to Dubai in search of a better future. But tax evasion is not a crime in Switzerland and it is unclear how long the government can hold onto the money.

For now, Tinner said he was trying to save enough money to restart the aquarium-building business he had been pursuing a decade earlier when he left for Dubai. He was no longer anonymous—he had been on Swiss television, and thousands of articles had been published about him around the world. But the notoriety was beginning to fade. Television crews and photographers were no longer camped on the street in front of his parents' home in Haag. Tinner remained wary of outsiders, and he was angry at what he viewed as ill-founded accusations about him and his family. Most of all, he was trying to slip a little further from public view. A local shop in Buchs took in his mail because he didn't want anyone to know where he was living. Tinner wanted to disappear into history.

A. Q. KHAN HAD NO intention of fading away. In August 2008, his nemesis, General Pervez Musharraf, was forced to resign as president of

Pakistan. Musharraf's political support in the country had plummeted after he imposed martial law and removed the chief of justice of Pakistan's highest court. The resignation sparked intense wrangling among rival political parties. In the ensuing political turbulence, Khan and his supporters mounted a sustained public relations and legal campaign to refurbish his image and release him from house arrest.

The legal aspect of Khan's rehabilitation had its ups and downs. Throughout 2009 and into 2010, his lawyers petitioned various courts to remove the restrictions on Khan's movements and ability to communicate with the world outside his estate overlooking the Margalla Hills on the edge of Islamabad. Each time a court ruled in favor of Khan, the government took steps to try to restrain him. Some of the motivation was pressure from the United States, which was pouring billions in military and civilian assistance into Pakistan, and objected to allowing him to go free. At one point a bipartisan group of members of Congress introduced legislation aimed at cutting off military aid to Pakistan unless U.S. officials could question Khan; the bill never went anywhere and the scientist remained outside the reach of American intelligence. Slowly the house arrest was eased, though Pakistani troops still stood guard outside his estate and he was prohibited from traveling outside the country without permission.

While he was off-limits to the IAEA and Americans, the seventy-three-year-old scientist was playing the starring role in his own PR campaign. In the summer of 2009, he started writing a column for the *News,* one of the country's leading newspapers. He wrote about a wide range of topics, though he seemed most determined to rewrite his own role in Pakistan's nuclear history. His career as a columnist ran into trouble when he was accused of plagiarizing large sections from the websites of three British universities, including Cambridge, in one of his articles on computer science. The episode raised the old image of Khan as a thief.

He also began granting telephone interviews with select reporters, claiming that Musharraf had coerced him into confessing to proliferation crimes in 2004 and asserting that he had always acted with the knowledge and approval of Pakistani government and military leaders. Khan's most outspoken comments were reserved for the country's Urdu press, where his word reached the vast majority of Pakistan's

170 million people. In an extensive interview with an Urdu-language Pakistani television network, Khan provided a lengthy description of how his network operated and acknowledged its role in sending nuclear equipment to Iran, North Korea, and Libya—the very actions to which he had supposedly been forced to confess five years earlier. Accusations that he stole designs and lists of suppliers from the Netherlands, Khan said, were "rubbish." He said he had gotten to know the suppliers while working at Urenco and that he turned to the people and companies that he knew could provide the equipment Pakistan lacked. In a sense he provided a tutorial on how to avoid export regulations, including how he exploited the decision by the U.S. government to ease restrictions on Pakistan's fledgling nuclear program to secure the country's support after the Soviet invasion of Afghanistan in late 1979.

"You had admitted in an interview that the Afghan war provided you an opportunity to develop and enhance the nuclear program," the interviewer, Nadeem Malik, said.

"Yes, I maintain that the war had provided us with space to enhance our nuclear capability," Khan replied. "The credit goes to me and my team, because it was a very difficult task, which was next to impossible. But given the U.S. and European pressure on our program it is true that had the Afghan war not taken place at that time, we would not have been able to make the bomb as early as we did."

Khan went on to describe how he purchased equipment from the same suppliers who had worked with Urenco. When his procurement efforts occasionally ran into trouble with export regulators, he said that he shifted the destinations to countries like the United Arab Emirates. He also recounted developing a network of suppliers who later provided technology and expertise for Iran and Libya. "They could not outmaneuver us, as we remained a step ahead always," he said.

For the first time, Khan offered a public explanation for using his network to sell nuclear technology to Iran, describing the strategic role envisioned for a nuclear alliance between Iran and Pakistan that would counter Israel's nuclear advantage. "Iran was interested in acquiring nuclear technology," he said. "Since Iran was an important Muslim country, we wished Iran to acquire this technology. Western countries pressured us unfairly. If Iran succeeds in acquiring nuclear technology, we will be a strong bloc in the region to counter international pressure. Iran's nuclear capability will neutralize Israel's power."

Khan's comments were designed to appeal directly to Islamic hardliners in Pakistan and elsewhere as part of the campaign to rehabilitate him. His defense of nuclear weapons for Muslim countries coincided with Pakistan's own work to scale up its atomic arsenal by increasing its production of enriched uranium and designing more powerful bombs. Bruce Riedel, a former CIA official, said in May 2010 that Pakistan has "the fastest-growing nuclear arsenal in the world."

American concerns about Pakistan's eighty to one hundred nuclear weapons have increased steadily in the decade since the attacks of September 11, 2001. The fears focused primarily on the security surrounding the country's arsenal. As security conditions deteriorated in Afghanistan and the threat of instability spilled across the border into neighboring Pakistan, American worries increased. The threat posed by radical militant groups inside Pakistan, some of them aided by sympathizers in Pakistan's military, led the Obama administration to develop secret contingency plans for using U.S. troops to take control of Pakistan's nuclear arsenal if the government collapsed.

IN WASHINGTON, NATIONAL SECURITY OFFICIALS were more focused on the dangers posed by the Iranian nuclear program to which Khan and his network had provided critical technology and expertise over the years. After eight years of verbal warnings from the Bush administration to Iran, President Obama had come into office with a new strategy based on diplomatic engagement with Tehran. But the change in American strategy did not lead to a change in Iranian behavior, leaving the new administration with little to show for its policy. Instead of negotiating with Iran, Washington found itself trying to build support from Europe, Russia, and China for yet another round of sanctions against Iran by the United Nations. And all the while, Iran pressed ahead with its uranium enrichment.

Iran's progress raised worries, particularly in Israel and the United

States, that Tehran was closing in on the ability to produce enough highly enriched uranium for its first nuclear weapon. But no outsiders had a clear view inside Iran's nuclear operations, and the two allies were at odds over how far along the Iranians were. The biggest dispute centered on whether Iran had stopped work on designing a nuclear warhead in 2003, as American intelligence had concluded in November 2007, or whether the work had proceeded, as the Israelis and some European intelligence agencies believed. Estimates of when the Iranians might be able to build their first bomb ranged from a year to three or five years, though the consensus was that the country's leaders had not yet made the political decision to complete the process. Like other countries before it, including Israel, India, and Pakistan, Iran was clinging to the charade of a civilian nuclear program. There was no reason for its leaders to abandon that position until they were ready to show the world that they possessed the capacity to complete a nuclear weapon.

In an appearance on the NBC-TV program *Meet the Press* in April 2010, Secretary of Defense Robert Gates confronted the inability of U.S. intelligence to determine exactly where Iran was in its quest for an atomic bomb. "If their policy is to go to the threshold but not assemble a nuclear weapon, how do you tell that they have not assembled?" he said. Cautioning that Iran had run into difficulties at its main enrichment plant at Natanz, Gates said, "It's going slow—slower than they anticipated—but they are moving in that direction."

At various points in recent years, Iranian nuclear officials acknowledged publicly that they were running into problems with centrifuges and other equipment at the vast underground enrichment plant they had built near Natanz, in the central part of the country. Some of Iran's difficulties were predictable. Within American intelligence circles, there was a small sense of satisfaction; some of the sabotage efforts appeared to be paying off when centrifuges spun out of control or regulators controlling the flow of electricity to the machines malfunctioned. Still, the Iranian technicians had recovered from each setback and resumed the enrichment process that would lead them to the edge of possessing the bomb and changing the balance of power in the Middle East.

On May 31, the IAEA issued another in its long series of reports documenting Iran's nuclear progress and the failure of the international community to stop that progress. The agency's inspectors concluded that Iran was enriching uranium to the 3 to 4 percent level required for civilian reactors, at a steady pace. Since February 2007, the report said, Iran's stockpile of enriched material had reached 5,300 pounds, enough for two nuclear weapons if it were processed to weapons-grade levels of 90 percent. The plant at Natanz relied on P-1 centrifuges produced from the designs that Khan had sold to Iran in 1987. At the pilot plant next door to the main facility, however, Iran was testing the more efficient P-2 centrifuges and a third generation that the Iranians called the IR-4. The IAEA report did not discuss the origins of the IR-4, but the centrifuges were based on the third set of designs that Khan had stolen from Urenco decades before. The more advanced design was based on a German machine called the G-4 or M-4, which incorporated four rotors in a single centrifuge. Khan's theft had not been discovered until IAEA officials examined the documents seized from the Tinners in the fall of 2005. Yet at some point along the way, Khan had provided the G-4 design to the Iranians, and they were now testing it at the pilot enrichment plant. The disclosure raised new questions about whether the CIA missed even more technology that Khan had supplied to Tehran—and possibly other customers.

The IAEA was having no more luck understanding the full extent of Iran's nuclear program than were the U.S. government and its intelligence agencies. From the start of its inspections, the international agency had raised questions about whether aspects of Iran's nuclear program were intertwined with its military. Some of the research was carried out on military bases and defense officials had been involved in the procurement of nuclear technology, including meetings with Khan in the mid-1990s. In August 2008, Iran stopped answering questions from the IAEA about the possible military dimensions of its nuclear program, claiming that the United States and Israel had fabricated evidence. But the fears ratcheted up in September 2009 when it was disclosed that Iran was building a secret enrichment plant in a tunnel on a military installation near the holy city of Qom. The May 2010 report highlighted the suspicions of the IAEA, and the paucity of hard proof about Iran's intentions. "Based on an overall analysis undertaken by the Agency of all the information available to it, the Agency remains concerned about the possible existence in Iran of past or current undisclosed nuclear-related activities, involving military-related organizations, including activities related to the development of a nuclear payload for a missile," said the report.

IRAN WAS NOT THE ONLY threat. A report earlier in 2010 by Rolf Mowatt-Larssen, a former senior CIA and Energy Department official, warned that Osama bin Laden and Al Qaeda had not abandoned their goal of attacking the United States with nuclear, chemical, or biological weapons. Drawing on his experience hunting for weapons of mass destruction for the CIA, Mowatt-Larssen said that Al Qaeda's leaders were determined and patient in their pursuit of unconventional weapons. In the report, which was published by the Belfer Center for Science and International Affairs at Harvard's Kennedy School of Government, the former intelligence official said bin Laden's threat to attack the West with weapons of mass destruction was a strategic goal, not an empty threat.

President Obama was well aware of the stakes involved in keeping nuclear weapons out of the hands of Al Qaeda and like-minded terrorist organizations. "If there was ever a detonation in New York City or London or Johannesburg, the ramifications economically, politically, and from a security perspective would be devastating," Obama said on the eve of a summit meeting of world leaders in Washington to discuss ways to safeguard bomb-making material. "And we know that organizations like Al Qaeda are in the process of trying to secure a nuclear weapon, a weapon of mass destruction that they have no compunction at using."

The connection between the Khan network and Al Qaeda was never direct, but that does not mean it was not a concern. In August 2001, bin Laden spent several days talking with two Pakistani nuclear scientists about his desire for nuclear weapons at a camp outside the southern Afghan city of Kandahar. The scientists were later arrested in Pakistan. No evidence has surfaced that Khan, despite his oft-expressed anger toward the United States and Israel, ever dealt with bin Laden or anyone associated with his network. Still, a former senior U.S. intelligence officer said that the failure to completely eradicate the Khan network left open the possibility that one of its members could still be open for business. "You could have someone in the Khan network who is really disgruntled now and out of work," he said. "Someone who still has lots of important stuff on disks that he can sell the Iranians or another customer."

It is simplistic to blame Iran's nuclear advances or Al Qaeda's quest for the ultimate terrorist weapon on the failures of American intelligence and U.S. policymakers. The omnipotent CIA of spy novels and movies does not exist. But the outcome of the last thirty years could have been very different if the agency had seen the world as it was, not as its case officers and spymasters wanted it to be. In 1975, the CIA persuaded the Dutch to let Khan go. The CIA never imagined that he could help usher a backward country like Pakistan into the elite club of nuclear weapons states. Similarly, U.S. intelligence underestimated Khan and his network in the late 1980s when evidence first suggested that they were helping Iran. A decade later, when the CIA and MI6 penetrated the network through Urs Tinner and other means, no one foresaw how quickly and easily some of the most dangerous designs in the nuclear world could be spread to computers and customers around the world.

Even after the analysts at Langley and the smartest scientists from the national weapons laboratories saw the threat posed by the designs on the Tinner computers, the CIA left the material in the hands of known traffickers. They could have cooperated with the Swiss in investigating and prosecuting the Tinners. They could have worked with Germany, South Africa, and other countries to make sure that every aspect of the network was rooted out, its participants identified and brought to justice. The CIA had the evidence to turn all of these cases into a potent deterrent for future proliferaters. Instead they went into cover-up mode. The CIA and other U.S. officials interfered with the criminal process of an allied nation, creating a ripple effect that derailed prosecutions not only in Switzerland but in many other countries. Instead of promoting the toughest possible legal approach to stopping proliferation, the message was that national interests once again trumped the greater necessity of international cooperation to thwart the catastrophic danger of a nuclear attack.

Nuclear terrorism has become the ultimate threat to the United States and the rest of the world, but it does not get the attention it demands. The opportunity to forge an aggressive and effective response to nuclear proliferation was defeated in places like Bern, Johannesburg, Tehran, and Tripoli. And Washington.

Acknowledgments

As with our first book on the nuclear black market, much of the credit for this work belongs to the scores of people who shared their information and insights with us. Many of them sat for multiple interviews, and some took risks to help us understand the complexities and nuances of a story that powerful people would have preferred remain concealed in the shadows. Anytime you write about intelligence operations, there is a danger that you won't get enough information to make sense of the story. With the help of people named and unnamed in the book and in these acknowledgments, we believe that we have unlocked enough secrets to provide an accurate portrait of how what appears to be operational success can still result in policy failure.

Many of the people who spoke with us did so on the condition of anonymity. Many people criticize the use of anonymous sources, but this sort of deep examination of an ongoing policy failure, rooted in the intelligence world, would not have been possible without the willingness of many involved to discuss these sensitive matters on a confidential basis. They trusted us to handle their information with care and discretion, and we have done our best to honor that trust.

Among those who openly helped us were the staff of the International Atomic Energy Agency in Vienna. We want to thank Olli Heinonen, the former deputy director general for safeguards, for his guidance. We also want to thank Mohamed ElBaradei, the former director general. Jacques Baute and Matti Tarvainen, both dedicated professionals, provided critical insights. So did Elizabeth Dobie-Sarsam and Ayhan Evrensel, from the IAEA communications team. And we owe a special debt of gratitude to Peter Rickwood for his help and friendship.

Switzerland is regarded, and rightfully so, as a difficult place for an outsider to find information. We were fortunate enough to locate some able guides there. First and foremost, we want to thank Andreas Mueller, the magistrate in charge of the Tinner case, and his assistant, Stefanie Heinrich, for their patience in helping us get the facts straight. We also want to thank Othmar Wyss for explaining the past and interpreting the future, and Ivo Kreiliger, who led us through the Swiss parliamentary commission's report and related material. We also benefited from the work and help of two Swiss journalists, Hansjuerg Zumstein and Christopher Eggenberger.

Many excellent journalists and writers have tackled the Khan network and its vast offshoots over the years. Few have done it better than David Sanger and William Broad of *The New York Times*, and we are grateful to them for staying after this story. Steve Coll of *The New Yorker* has brought his brilliance to bear on this subject in many ways over the years, and we benefited greatly from his work. Jim Risen of *The New York Times* is both a highly skilled investigative reporter who has uncovered many dark secrets and a personal friend; we owe him thanks on both those fronts.

Fulton Armstrong and Bob Baer, two former senior CIA officers, translated the arcane world of the intelligence community for us. Cath Conneely, a skilled researcher, played a vital role in making key interviews happen, and Janey and Bob Wallace served as important sounding boards.

Dominick Anfuso at the Free Press is the rare editor with the courage to take on tough topics and give his authors the freedom to follow the facts wherever they lead. We want to express our deep thanks to him and to his highly professional team for bringing this book to fruition. Dominick's assistant, Leah Miller, kept us on track; Tom Pitoniak copyedited the manuscript with a thorough yet light touch. Thanks also to Martha Levin, Carisa Hays, Nicole Kalian, and Maura O'Brien. Our respect for the professionalism of our agent, Kathy Robbins, and her team, especially David Halpern, Rachelle Bergstein, Mike Gillespie, is boundless. We are lucky enough to also count Kathy and her husband, Richard Cohen, as friends and advisers.

NOTES

The primary sources of material for this book were hundreds of hours of interviews with people who had firsthand knowledge of the subject matter. Many of these people spoke with us several times over the course of our research; some of them had provided information for our previous book on this topic. Most of them spoke on the condition of anonymity. Some insisted on not being identified because of restrictions imposed by their governments or employers. Others insisted on anonymity because they feared reprisals by governments or employers. Without exception, we corroborated the information provided by these anonymous sources.

The interviews were augmented by previously unpublished documents as well as thousands of pages of public records. The confidential records were extensive and, in most cases, highly detailed. They included notes taken during meetings at critical junctures in the dismantling of the A. Q. Khan network and the aftermath. There were also official inventories of designs and equipment seized from the Tinner family by Swiss authorities and lists of meetings between the Tinners and their contacts in the Central Intelligence Agency.

While interviews with direct participants were vital in reconstructing events, the documents proved invaluable. They have the advantage over interviews because they were written contemporaneously, before memories faded, and because they were highly detailed and technically precise.

No document used in this book was classified by any government. Many of them, however, contain sensitive information and were provided to us on condition that we not quote directly from them. In several instances, we have withheld the real names of CIA officers and operatives as well as the front companies used by the intelligence agency identified in the documents.

The book was written in a narrative style, with events and conversations reconstructed from interviews with participants, people who were briefed on the episodes, and written minutes and other post-conversation summaries prepared by participants.

1. JENINS, SWITZERLAND

PAGE

3   *Six people—five men and a woman:* The description of the break-in at Marco Tinner's apartment originated with our questions about a reference to a "search" contained in the Swiss parliamentary commission report of January 2009. Three officials with two separate governmental agencies provided consistent accounts of the circumstances that led to the break-in and details of the episode itself. The description of the tradecraft involved—the electronics that would have been used, the assembly of the B&E team—came from interviews with former CIA officers who were not involved directly in the episode.

5   *A few months earlier, two CIA counterterrorism officers:* The episode was described by one of the counterterrorism officers involved.

6   *Khan had first appeared on the CIA's radar:* Much of the background on A. Q. Khan and his network is drawn from our earlier book, Douglas Frantz and Catherine Collins, *The Nuclear Jihadist* (New York: Twelve, 2007). We will refer to this work as our first book in these notes.

11   *One of the keys to understanding:* The recruitment of Urs Tinner by Mad Dog was disclosed in our first book. The story was fleshed out here through interviews with Tinner and other people involved in the intelligence operation, several confidential documents that memorialized conversations between Tinner and various government officials, and an excellent documentary on SF-TV in Switzerland, *The Spy from the Rhine Valley,* by Hansjuerg Zumstein, which aired on January 22, 2009. The documentary was the first time Tinner confirmed working for the CIA.

12   *Mad Dog, who was using a cover name:* The meetings between the CIA and the Tinners were listed in a government document, which included dates, times, places, participants, and, in many cases, topics for the ses-

sions. We were able to corroborate some of the information through interviews and other records.

13   *Kinsman and a second CIA operative:* The role of Big Black River Technologies and the cover names for Kinsman and Sean Mahaffey were first revealed by William J. Broad and David E. Sanger, "In Nuclear Net's Undoing, a Web of Shadowy Deals," *New York Times*, August 24, 2008. Over several years, Sanger and Broad broke numerous important stories about the Khan network and their work was a valuable resource for this book.

2. Washington and Paris

PAGE

16   *The CIA was created as the successor:* Many histories of the CIA were useful in preparing this book, but none more so than Tim Weiner, *Legacy of Ashes: The History of the CIA* (New York: Anchor, 2008).

18   *One of the division's early recruits:* Valerie Plame Wilson, *Fair Game: My Life as a Spy, My Betrayal by the White House* (New York: Simon & Schuster, 2007), pp. 59–66. We also interviewed two former officers from the CIA Counter-Proliferation Division, both of whom requested anonymity.

19   *Early one morning in the summer of 1989:* We first heard the story of how Kinsman got his nickname from one of his former colleagues at the CIA. In an interview, Kinsman corrected some errors and expanded on the story. But he refused to discuss any aspect of his work for the CIA or the Khan case. Aside from the story about the dog bite, absolutely no other information in this book came from Kinsman.

20   *As a teenager, he had read* Hiroshima: George Tenet, *At the Center of the Storm: My Years at the CIA* (New York: HarperCollins, 2007), p. 283. We learned separately that Tenet was referring to Kinsman.

3. Dubai

PAGE

23   *In October 1990, two months after the Iraqi:* Khan's offer of nuclear technology to the Iraqis was recounted in our first book and several other places. New details of that plan were contained in confidential documents provided for this book.

28 *Unknown to the participants, they were under surveillance:* The origins of Khan's deal with the Libyans were described in our first book. However, the surveillance of the 1998 meeting is detailed here for the first time. It was described to us by a former government official who had access to the transcript of the meetings in Casablanca monitored by MI6.

29 *The CIA had its own window:* The CIA asset inside the Tinner operation was described in one of the confidential documents and corroborated by two people familiar with the operation. We have withheld the name of the operative and his company.

4. DUBAI

31 *No one ever paid much attention:* Tinner's background and the description of his early days in Dubai came primarily from an extended interview with him in 2010 and from *The Spy from the Rhine Valley.* Tinner refused to discuss his recruitment or dealings with the CIA in the interview.

33 *The law requires the CIA to apply:* Frederick P. Hitz, "Unleashing the Rogue Elephant: September 11 and Letting the CIA Be the CIA," *Harvard Journal of Law and Public Policy* 25 (Spring 2002).

34 *Amid the pictures of birds and flowers:* Tinner interview.

35 *In May 1999, a shipment of specialty aluminum:* The incident involving the British customs inspector was described in several newspapers and most thoroughly in David Armstrong and Joseph Trento, *America and the Islamic Bomb: The Deadly Compromise* (Hanover, N.H.: Steerforth, 2007), pp. 178–84.

37 *Not long after Amin was sent packing:* The details surrounding the recruitment of Tinner remain sketchy because of the nature of the event. The fact that Tinner was recruited is not in dispute; he acknowledged that in his Swiss TV interview and various confidential documents, and people with knowledge of the investigation confirmed his involvement. Tinner would not speak on the record about the incident; two former CIA officers provided information about what happened, based on their reading of documents and their conversations with people involved directly. We have reconstructed this episode as accurately as possible.

39   *"Once they have signed on":* Interview with a former CIA case officer.

40   *Tinner set up the training operation:* Tinner interview.

42   *The chance to get into the black cases:* Interview with a person with direct knowledge of the episode, confirmed by a former government official involved in the investigation.

5. Dubai and Kuala Lumpur

PAGE

45   *The drive from Urs Tinner's small house:* Tinner interview.

48   *A few people within the intelligence community:* James Risen, *State of War: The Secret History of the CIA and the Bush Administration* (New York: Free Press, 2006), pp. 194–207.

50   *About the time the Russian defector was turning:* The episode involving the altered vacuum pumps was first disclosed in Juergen Dahlkamp, Georg Mascolo, and Holger Stark, "Network of Death on Trial," *Der Spiegel,* March 13, 2006. Interviews with former CIA and International Atomic Energy Agency officials provided additional details of the sabotage effort. We also viewed, but could not copy, a document containing the serial numbers and price of the pumps.

52   *One of the other efforts involved tampering:* This sabotage effort was first mentioned in a confidential document and later described by two officials with the IAEA.

52   *When Urs Tinner told Kinsman:* Tinner described his sabotage efforts in debriefings with the IAEA, in *The Spy from the Rhine Valley,* and in the interview. The sabotage was also described in a confidential document.

55   *"When they held that press conference":* Interview with John Bolton.

58   *In March 2003, a few days after:* Tenet, *At the Center of the Storm,* pp. 288–89.

58   *In June, Kinsman summoned the Tinners:* Confidential document listing CIA meetings with Tinners, times, places, participants, and topics.

6. Vaduz, Liechtenstein

PAGE

60   *A million dollars was wired to Traco Group:* Broad and Sanger, "In Nuclear Net's Undoing, a Web of Shadowy Deals," and confidential documents.

60   *Recruited by the agency straight out:* Wilson, *Fair Game,* p. 309; David Corn, "What Valerie Plame Really Did at the CIA," *Nation,* September 6, 2006.

64   *But the analysts were surprised to find:* Confidential document and interview with former government official.

65   *Some of the files contained invoices:* The contents of the Tinner computers were described in confidential documents and inventories obtained by the authors. The contents and significance of the material were confirmed in multiple interviews with European officials and international diplomats who had access to the material or were briefed on the contents.

71   *"Tahir would say, what are you doing":* Tinner interview.

72   *The method is simple and effective:* The existence of the code was first revealed to us by IAEA officials. We later confirmed its use with Swiss officials.

72   *"I had identified the last delivery":* The Spy from the Rhine Valley.

74   *"There would be no signal":* Tinner interview.

75   *The CIA officer sent Urs a message:* Confidential document and interview with source describing the message.

75   *"Mr. President," Kinsman said:* Tenet, *At the Center of the Storm,* p. 284.

7. SINGAPORE AND KUALA LUMPUR

PAGE

77   *The meeting was in Khan's suite:* Interviews with Tinner and confidential source.

80   *Lerch's involvement wasn't a secret:* Confidential document.

81   *When Wisser returned home:* Information about Wisser's involvement in the network was from records filed with the South African court in Pretoria. It was supplemented with newspaper articles and interviews with South African officials.

82   *"A. Q. Khan is betraying your country":* Tenet, *At the Center of the Storm,* pp. 285–87.

87   *"Why were they looking for those five":* Tinner interview.

88   *Later, he would boast to investigators:* Interviews with IAEA investigators involved in the Tinner case.

88   *On the night of October 27, Tinner:* Interviews with IAEA investigators involved in the Tinner case.

8. VIENNA AND TRIPOLI

PAGE

95   *On the morning of Saturday, December 20:* Most of the information about the IAEA and Libya was contained in our first book.

9. WASHINGTON

PAGE

104   *The next day, Tenet delivered his speech:* Speech of CIA director George Tenet, February 5, 2004, Georgetown University, http://www.americanprogressorg/issues/kfiles/b27744.html.

107   *On January 16, Friedrich's daughter:* Confidential documents and interview with former senior IAEA official involved in the investigation.

110   *Back in Kuala Lumpur, the president's speech:* Interview with Malaysian diplomat and Malaysian police report, http://www.iranwatch.org/government/Malaysia/malaysia-police-libyareport-022004.htm.

10. VIENNA

PAGE

111   *On February 18, 2004, a week after:* The section on the debriefing of the Tinners by the IAEA and surrounding events is based in part on our first book and on later interviews with former IAEA officials involved in the investigation who provided new details. The description of the sabotage was confirmed by Tinner in his interview.

11. BERN

PAGE

118   *On the morning of February 21, 2004:* Interview with Othmar Wyss.

121   *The first step would be persuading Swiss intelligence:* The outline of U.S. interactions with Swiss officials as part of the effort to cover up the involvement of the Tinners with the CIA is contained in the report by the Swiss parliamentary commission. The report and related documents are available at http://www.parlament.ch/e/organe-mitglieder/delegationen/geschaeftspruefungsdelegation/fall-tinner/pages/default.aspx. The information from the reports was expanded upon considerably in interviews with Swiss government, police, and intelligence officials as

well as confidential documents that described many of the meetings in detail.

123 *"We were speaking the same language":* The Swiss official spoke on background because he was not authorized to speak to journalists or writers.

123 *Not every Swiss official would be so understanding:* Interview with Senator Claude Janiak.

12. Innsbruck, Austria

PAGE

132 *Without Khan's help, Heinonen's first step:* Interview with Olli Heinonen.

132 *Saudi Arabia was at the top of the list:* Information on Saudi Arabia's nuclear ambitions is contained in numerous publications, including Bruce Riedel, "Saudi Arabia: Nervously Watching Pakistan," *Brookings,* April 5, 2010; Thomas W. Lippman, "Nuclear Weapons and Saudi Strategy," *Middle East Institute Policy Brief,* January 2008; and most notably several works by Richard L. Russell, including *Weapons Proliferation and War in the Greater Middle East* (New York and London: Routledge, 2005), and "A Saudi Nuclear Option?" *Survival* 43, no. 2 (Summer 2001). We also interviewed Russell.

133 *In 1987, the CIA established:* Interview with former CIA case officer who worked in the Middle East.

134 *On May 10, 1987, Mubarak sent the prince:* A source provided us with a copy of the outline and Mubarak's accompanying letter to the prince.

134 *Muhammad Al-Massari was a young physicist:* Interview with Muhammad Al-Massari.

135 *Over the years, there have been hints:* Interview with Robert Baer.

135 *The existence of a Saudi nuclear weapons program:* "Pakistan Rejects Report on Secret Nuclear Help to Saudi Arabia," Agence France-Presse, March 29, 2006; "Pakistan Terms German Magazine's Report on N-Help to S Arabia 'Fabricated,'" *News,* March 30, 2006; UPI Intelligence Watch, March 31, 2006.

137 *In September, Heinonen and Edwards:* Interviews with Heinonen and another participant in the meeting.

141 *During the suspension, the inspectors had found:* Interview with person familiar with the episode.

13. JOHANNESBURG, FRANKFURT, BERN, AND WASHINGTON

PAGE

142 *When the South Africans asked for proof:* Interview with a senior South African counterproliferation official.

143 *As he was leaving the country on August 25:* Transcript of Wisser interview with German police.

144 *On the morning of September 1:* Court documents in Pretoria in the case against Wisser, Daniel Geiges, and Johan Meyer.

147 *The American ambassador to Switzerland:* Swiss parliamentary commission report and related records.

148 *Tinner also blamed Olli Heinonen:* Heinonen interview.

14. JOHANNESBURG AND BERN

PAGE

153 *Early on the morning of January 17, 2005:* Confidential records and interviews with two participants in the episodes at Pelindaba.

154 *The documents at Pelindaba shed new light:* Interview with IAEA official who reviewed the documents.

156 *The interview took place at the headquarters:* The interview was described in our first book and augmented with later interviews with IAEA officials.

159 *On May 13, Marco's lawyer, Peter Volkart:* Confidential records and interview with Heinonen and a second IAEA official.

161 *Several months earlier, Edwards had arranged:* The testing of the components and the results were described in interviews with IAEA officials and referenced in confidential documents.

162 *The real prize was the fruits of the search warrants:* The results of the search warrants were described in a confidential inventory of material provided to the authors and in interviews with Swiss and IAEA officials with firsthand knowledge of the situation.

15. BERN

PAGE

167 *On the morning of November 21:* Confidential documents, including minutes of the meetings, were provided to the authors. Participants were also interviewed to provide a complete picture of a critical moment in the inquiry.

168   *Chief Inspector Kurt Senn, the senior officer:* Interviews with two people involved in the Swiss police investigation.

170   *He was told, "Tell Heinonen and Edwards":* The comment was described by two participants in the debriefing of Tinner. In the interview, Tinner acknowledged lying about the fate of the rotors, but he said he told the lie to B. S. A. Tahir, not the IAEA.

172   *Another folder of letters and documents mystified:* The Deramo shipment was described in confidential records and confirmed by two people in interviews.

173   *Back in Vienna the next day:* Interview with Heinonen and a second IAEA official.

174   *On January 19, 2006, Ambassador Willeford:* The meetings between Blocher and Willeford and Blocher and Chertoff were outlined in the Swiss parliamentary commission report.

177   *Lehmann met the IAEA officials in his office:* Confidential documents include minutes of the meeting and a list of participants.

178   *In recent weeks some of the prosecutor's associates:* The concerns about a potential leak in the Swiss investigation were expressed in an interview by a Swiss intelligence officer. From independent sources, we know that the suspected leaker traveled frequently to the United States for meetings with CIA officials and was an admirer of the operation against Khan. He declined to answer questions about the suspected leaks.

16. Mannheim, Germany

PAGE

183   *Sitting at the defense table that morning:* The best account of Lerch's trial was Steve Coll, "The Atomic Emporium," *New Yorker,* August 7 and 14, 2006. A thorough analysis of the legal difficulties surrounding Lerch's trials was presented in a special section of *WMD Insights,* January 2010, written by Philip Johnson of Georgetown University, edited by Leonard "Sandy" Spector of the James L. Martin Center for Nonproliferation Studies of the Monterey Institute of International Studies and sponsored by the U.S. Defense Threat Reduction Agency. Details of the jousting between the German, Malaysian, South African, and Swiss authorities over witnesses and evidence came from interviews with South African and Swiss authorities.

184 *During his months in a German prison:* Interview with Roman Boegli.

185 *"I don't know what I'm allowed to say":* Stephen Graham, "German Seeks to Have Judges Removed," Associated Press, March 17, 2006.

186 *"To produce and supply the goods":* Ian Traynor, "Briton accused of central role in Libya's nuclear bomb plan," *Guardian*, April 27, 2006.

187 *In mid-May, Peter Griffin took the train:* Coll, "The Atomic Emporium."

189 *"As a general rule, we wanted":* Interview with Robert Joseph.

190 *The United States never complained:* Leonard S. Spector, "Punishing A. Q. Khan," *Foreign Policy*, September 10, 2010.

17. WASHINGTON AND BERN

PAGE

192 *The Tinner affair dropped onto Gonzales's desk:* The Swiss parliamentary commission report and related documents provided the dates of the Blocher-Gonzales meeting and some commentary on what was discussed. The substance of the meeting and the "frantic" concerns of the CIA were provided by interviews with an intelligence officer involved in the investigation and with other people with knowledge of the meeting.

196 *At the end of May, the federal police:* The existence of the thirty-nine folders was disclosed in the Swiss press in early 2010. The details surrounding the production of this evidence and its subsequent storage and discovery came from interviews with Swiss officials involved in the investigation.

197 *"They didn't trust each other":* Interview with IAEA investigator.

199 *After several days of scouring the computer files:* Interview with IAEA investigator and confidential documents.

220 *Heinonen studied the folders:* Interviews with Heinonen and Jacques Baute.

18. VIENNA AND BERN

PAGE

202 *Within days of seeing the two weapons designs:* Confidential documents provided the dates of the meetings in Bern and the substance of the discussions.

204 *"Why are you here?":* Interviews with Baute and another person involved in the investigation.

207 *"What is alarming is that we have found":* Heinonen interview.

209   *On November 1, Blocher presented the council:* Swiss parliamentary commission report and related documents.

210   *The Swiss police involved in the investigation:* Interviews with Swiss police and prosecutors involved in the Tinner investigation.

19. WASHINGTON AND BERN

PAGE

212   *In early 2007, Bush said publicly:* David E. Sanger, *The Inheritance: The World Obama Confronts and the Challenges to American Power* (New York: Harmony, 2009), p. xxiv.

213   *The Americans developed a new strategy:* The escalation of U.S. meetings with Swiss officials was chronicled in the Swiss parliamentary commission report and related documents. The report listed meeting dates and participants. The information was augmented by interviews with Senator Janiak, one of his aides, and other Swiss officials.

214   *On the last morning of his trip, Schmid flew:* Schmid's meeting with former president Bush was mentioned in the Swiss parliamentary commission report. The meeting was described in an interview by a Swiss diplomat who had been briefed on the session.

216   *Schmid already agreed with the Americans:* Interview with a member of Swiss Foreign Ministry staff.

218   *On August 9, Rice telephoned Calmy-Rey:* Swiss parliamentary commission report and related documents and interview with Foreign Ministry staff member.

221   *On December 4, three officials from the IAEA:* Confidential documents and interviews with IAEA officials.

222   *"The problem is that we see everything":* Interview with Baute.

223   *Another set of drawings was in the custody of the police:* Confidential documents and interviews with IAEA and Swiss officials.

20. BERN

PAGE

225   *The sheer mass was staggering:* The quantity of material seized from the Tinners was described in inventories that were part of the confidential documents. The documents also contain minutes from the meetings at which the action was debated and finalized and the names of those who

participated. The destruction of the material was described in some of those documents and by an official who was involved.

228 *"I am speaking for myself and not for my colleagues":* Senn's comments were described by someone who attended the meeting and took notes. Senn declined to discuss the episode.

229 *Janiak, a lawyer and member of the liberal:* Interview with Janiak and an aide.

230 *"There are more questions about this":* Helena Bachmann, "Swiss Shredded Nuke Documents," *Time*, June 3, 2008.

231 *A few days after the Swiss president's announcement:* "Pakistani nuclear scientist says evidence of his innocence lost," Kyodo News Service, May 28, 2008.

231 *On August 25, however, David E. Sanger:* William J. Broad and David E. Sanger, "In Nuclear Net's Undoing, a Web of Shadowy Deals," *New York Times*, August 25, 2008.

234 *Mueller's first step was to review the files:* Interviews with Andreas Mueller and confidential documents.

237 *At a press conference, Janiak said cryptically:* "Parliamentary delegation found that Switzerland's government was wrong to destroy documents," Swiss Information, January 26, 2009. The parliamentary commission report was issued that day at the press conference.

237 *In many ways, however, the report's release: The Spy from the Rhine Valley.*

238 *On March 18, Trevor Edwards returned:* Confidential documents.

241 *Leafing through his internal mail:* Interviews with Mueller.

243 *On June 10, the legal director of the IAEA:* E-mail was described in confidential documents.

21. BERN AND WASHINGTON

246 *On the morning of July 9, Mueller gathered:* Interviews with Mueller, his assistant, and a Swiss police official.

247 *The two senior Swiss officials, the chief antagonists:* The confrontation with Edwards was described in confidential documents and in an interview with a participant in the discussions.

249 *Not everyone wished Kinsman a peaceful retirement:* Interview with Swiss police official.

250 *But Kappes had other problems:* The best account of Stephen Kappes's career at the CIA and the factors that figured in his resignation was by Jeff Stein, "Inside Man," *Washingtonian*, March 25, 2010. Additional information about Kappes came from interviews with former colleagues at the CIA.

250 *"It was one of the most deeply disturbing":* R. Jeffrey Smith, Michael D. Shear, and Walter Pincus, "In Obama's Inner Circle, Debate Over Memos' Release Was Intense," *Washington Post*, April 29, 2009.

22. Buchs, Switzerland, Islamabad, and Washington

PAGE

256 *In an extensive interview with an Urdu-language:* "Dr. Abdul Qadeer Khan Discusses Nuclear Program in TV Talk," Aaj News Television, August 31, 2009; transcript available at www.fas.org/nuke/guide/pakistan/aqkhan-083109.pdf.

257 *Bruce Riedel, a former CIA official, said in May 2010:* Bruce O. Riedel, "U.S. Options Limited in Pakistan," Council on Foreign Relations, May 10, 2010, www.cfr.org/publication/22099/us_options_limited_in_pakistan.html.

258 *At various points in recent years, Iranian nuclear officials:* "Iran Moves Uranium Gas from Isfahan to Natanz, Diplomats Say," Agence France-Presse, February 19, 2007. Similar technical difficulties were described in interviews with IAEA officials.

259 *On May 31, the IAEA issued another in its long series:* "Implementation of the NPT Safeguards Agreement and relevant provisions of Security Council resolutions 1737 (2006), 1747 (2007), 1803 (2008) and 1835 (2008) in the Islamic Republic of Iran," International Atomic Energy Agency, May 31, 2010.

259 *In August 2008, Iran stopped answering questions:* Interview with Heinonen.

260 *"Based on an overall analysis undertaken":* "Implementation of the NPT," p. 8.

261 *Still, a former senior U.S. intelligence officer:* Interview with former senior CIA official.

INDEX

ABOUT THE AUTHORS

Catherine Collins has been a reporter for the *Chicago Tribune* and written for the *Los Angeles Times* and *The New York Times*. She has written several books with her husband, Douglas Frantz, including *The Nuclear Jihadist* and *Death on the Black Sea*.

Douglas Frantz is a former managing editor of the *Los Angeles Times* and a former investigative reporter and foreign correspondent at the *New York Times*. He was part of the *New York Times* team that won the Pulitzer Prize for Public Service in 2002 for coverage of the aftermath of 9/11.